5 STEPS TO A 5™

500
AP English Literature Questions
to Know by Test Day

5 STEPS TO A 5™

500
AP English Literature Questions to Know by Test Day

Third Edition

Shveta Verma Miller

New York   Chicago   San Francisco   Athens   London   Madrid
Mexico City   Milan   New Delhi   Singapore   Sydney   Toronto

SHVETA VERMA MILLER taught AP English Literature in New York City Public Schools. She also taught English at the college level in the United States and abroad. As a tutor, she has specialized in helping students manage anxiety around high-stakes testing, teaching them to apply their skills and knowledge in formal, timed, and often stressful situations. Now a teacher-educator, she supports gifted and talented services as an instructional coach at a school district in Oregon. She is working to increase the identification of students from underrepresented populations as gifted and supports teachers with differentiating instruction in heterogeneous class settings. For several years, she was a national consultant, presenting courses on best practices for teaching English Language Arts and coaching teachers in classrooms and online. She continues to present at national and international conferences and consults with education publishers to ensure their curriculum and assessments are unbiased, rigorous, and culturally responsive. She writes regularly for *Edutopia* and *Book Riot*, and her new book, *Hacking Graphic Novels*, helps teachers use comics and graphic narratives to cultivate students' visual analysis skills. Contact her online at ShvetaMiller.com to submit feedback about the questions in this book and find short videos of her and her students discussing the passages.

1 2 3 4 5 6 7 8 9   LCR   26 25 24 23 22 21

ISBN   978-1-260-47473-2
MHID   1-260-47473-9

e-ISBN   978-1-260-47474-9
e-MHID   1-260-47474-7

McGraw Hill products are available at special quantity discounts to use as premiums and sales promotions or for use in corporate training programs. To contact a representative, please visit the Contact Us pages at www.mhprofessional.com.

CONTENTS

PREFACE

The third edition of this book includes significant updates based on recent changes to the AP English Literature and Composition exam. There are 16 new passages, many from twentieth-century/contemporary texts, and more than 250 new questions ranging in style and level of difficulty. The passage questions from previous editions have also been revised to include only those that align closely with those found on recent AP exams. Every question in the third edition directs students to carefully consider the function or effects of symbolism, imagery, and word choice, as well as the function of the narrator or speaker, character, setting, comparisons, plot, and structure. Thus the student will be able to draw conclusions about the passage's overall meaning that are substantiated by the text.

The Purpose of This Book

On the surface, this book appears to be a study guide for just the multiple-choice questions on the AP English Literature and Composition exam. But all high school students can benefit from practicing with the passages and questions in this study guide, not just AP students.

This book is for AP students, pre-AP students, and any high school students looking for reading practice to prepare for high-level coursework or to simply enrich their reading lives. By completing the questions, students don't simply prepare for multiple-choice questions on an exam—they develop close reading skills through critically engaging with questions that promote curiosity about a diverse collection of texts, authors, genres, cultures, and time periods. Each question is designed to prompt students to reread the passage with careful attention to significant words and phrases, shifts, perspectives, and literary devices. The questions encourage students to carefully consider a text's style and structure, effects, and messages. Reading the provided answer explanations also helps students develop their own analytical writing skills.

Although there is one correct answer for each question, the passages and questions are designed to stimulate discussion. If possible, work with others on the passages. Share your responses, discuss and debate the different answer choices, argue with the explanations provided in the book, and even try writing your own questions for aspects of the text that warrant closer analysis.

Teachers: How to Use This Book in Class

Diagnostic Quiz and Practice Exams   Use the 20-question Diagnostic Quiz on pages 5–10 to roughly determine students' multiple-choice question (MCQ) strengths and needs at the start of the course. To create full-length MCQ sections for ongoing practice and progress monitoring, select five passages from this book, totaling approximately 55 questions. Select a balance of prose and poetry and pre-twentieth-century and contemporary texts. As students develop their skills, time them for 60 minutes and provide a 10-minute warning before the end. If you plan to teach a unit or lesson on one of the poems or texts excerpted in this book, you might also assign the questions as practice and formative assessment.

Weekly Timed Practice   Many AP English Literature teachers comment that their students enjoy and benefit from frequent short bursts of MCQ practice throughout the year. Choose one passage for timed practice as a lesson opener once a week. For example, every Friday, students can begin class with a 10-minute passage from a chapter that aligns with the text type they are studying. If they are reading Yaa Gyasi's *Homegoing* in class, you might choose a passage from Chapter 2: 20th-Century/Contemporary Prose.

Have students track their progress from week to week and notice trends or topics in need of review. Do they consistently struggle with questions related to narrative perspective? Do they generally answer questions about tone and mood correctly? Are there time periods or text types they are less familiar with? Do they answer questions correctly but find it difficult to work within the 10-minute time frame? As students complete short bursts of timed practice, their results can help you determine where to provide instructional support.

Discuss and Debate the Answers   The most value from this book comes from discussing the answers to the questions, especially those second-best "distractor" choices that compel students to revisit the passage to locate and weigh text evidence. Provide opportunities for students to write their own short explanations for the answers they choose. In pairs or groups, they can share their choices and reasoning, and decide to change any answers based on what they learn from their peers. Once they check their selections against the answers in the book, invite them to compare their reasoning with the explanations provided. If they disagree with the explanation, encourage them to submit their feedback for consideration: ShvetaMiller.com/contact.

Prepare for Free Response Questions   Though this book does not include any Free Response Questions (FRQ), students can practice the close-reading and analytical skills required for AP and college-level essay writing by completing the MCQ. Students who have completed the passages in this book consistently comment that the questions brought their attention to critical and subtle elements of a passage they had overlooked on their first read. The provided explanations also serve as examples of how to analyze and write about a passage's structure, style, and meaning. Once students complete the questions and review the explanations of a passage, ask them to articulate their more sophisticated understanding of it by writing an essay analyzing the passage. Visit the College Board's AP Central website to access FRQ from recent exams.

Create Questions and Write Answer Explanations Writing the questions in this book gave me profound insight into each passage. Even poems and passages from books that I have taught for years or studied closely in graduate school became more interesting once I had to create 8 to 13 questions and several compelling answer choices for each. I learned to anticipate the multiple misinterpretations that were likely and craft subtle differences between the best choice and a plausible one. Writing the explanations often led me to see more in the text than I initially noticed and forced me to reconsider what I thought was correct. Testing the questions with students and discussing the nuances of each answer choice always led me to deepen my understanding of the text and revise the questions further.

Writing passage-based MCQ is excellent preparation for rigorous, college-level reading. Encourage students to write two new questions for a passage they have completed in this book. Students can familiarize themselves with the AP English Literature MCQ types, then reread passages and look for opportunities to ask additional questions. I could not have asked about every significant feature in a passage—some do not have questions about tone, how a syntactical structure conveys meaning, or the effect of a simile. Students must consider what readers will likely assume if they read carelessly or quickly and incorporate those misinterpretations into plausible but incorrect answer choices. When writing their own explanations for the correct answer, they might see flaws in their own reading, which will prompt them to examine the text even more deeply. Once students have practiced writing a few questions to add to those already written for a passage in this book, they can discuss and answer each other's questions.

Once they start thinking like question-writers, they will notice and note the complexities of everything they read, forming stimulating questions that prompt them to read with greater insight.

Students: How to Use This Book at Home

Even if you are not enrolled in an AP English Literature class, you can use this book to sharpen your reading skills, discover a wide range of literary texts and authors, and prepare for high school and college-level reading.

Start by taking the Diagnostic Quiz on pages 5–10. Which passage was more challenging for you? Which questions asked about unfamiliar text features and concepts? You might choose to begin with passages that are familiar (language, time period, author, etc.) so that you can focus on the deeper close reading of a text you already enjoy. As you gain confidence with the question types, move on to less familiar passages.

After completing a passage and questions, write your own explanations for your answers and then compare them with a partner's. This exercise will force you to think carefully about why you are picking certain answers. It may help you avoid picking certain answers on a whim if you know you will have to justify those choices in writing. Discussing the questions with a partner will help you see aspects of the passage you may have overlooked, prompt you to consider a different connotation of a word in an answer choice, or direct you to lines that challenge your initial interpretation.

As you practice the questions, read the answer explanations of the questions you get wrong *and* the explanations of the questions you get right. You will learn the logic and reasoning for why one answer choice is the best compared with other options that are plausible but not correct.

Keep track of the concepts, terms, and types of questions that are consistently challenging for you. Do you tend to miss questions about narrative perspective or figurative language? Or maybe you don't notice significant shifts. Ask a teacher for more guidance on these topics, or reference the companion study guide to this book: McGraw-Hill's *5 Steps to a 5: AP English Literature 2021 Elite Student Edition.*

Highlight and study any unfamiliar vocabulary, especially from the answer choices. This book has followed the AP exam's example in the level of vocabulary used in the answer choices. The words are reflective of a college-level vocabulary. If you take the time to learn new words as they appear, you will notice that over time you will begin to recognize more of the words in the answer choices. More important, you will develop a nuanced vocabulary to express what is happening in a complex text—one that will also enhance your clarity of thinking, along with your written and oral expression.

There are only 8 to 13 questions per passage, but there are countless additional questions that could be asked for each passage. Try creating additional questions that ask about nuances, effects, stylistic choices, and meaning that have not already been covered, as well as plausible but incorrect answer choices. Use the book's questions as a model. Thinking like a question-writer will train you to read closely and critically, and it will help you recognize what would make a tempting answer ultimately incorrect.

If you are preparing to take the AP exam, use the passages for timed practice: spend 10 minutes per passage or 60 minutes for five passages to simulate the real exam. After reviewing the answers, demonstrate your more sophisticated understanding of the text in writing by completing a practice Free Response Question. Go to the College Board's APStudent website for FRQ from recent exams.

Strategies for Answering the Questions

Use the Questions to Guide Your Rereading of the Passage

It is common for readers to feel confused after their preliminary read through a passage. The questions focus on the most subtle, complex, and relevant portions of a passage, so they will guide you to the areas where a second read, a closer look, will help you gain a deeper understanding of the passage. Approach the passages with the mindset that your understanding will develop over multiple reads of key lines to which the questions direct you. Remain flexible as you move through questions, open to the possibility that your first impression may not have been the most astute.

Notice Keywords in the Questions

- *"paraphrase," "summarizes," "stated as," "means"* These keywords tell you not to infer, interpret, or analyze the given lines. You are being asked about your comprehension of what is directly stated or indicated in the passage. Avoid answer choices that require you to draw conclusions, assume, or analyze.

- *"suggest," "implies," "it can be inferred," "is best interpreted as"* These keywords give you license to analyze the lines or passage. As you analyze, you must rely on textual evidence from the passage. Avoid choosing answers that restate or indicate what is directly or explicitly stated in the passage, and focus only on answers that reflect analysis of the lines.

- *"based on the passage as a whole," "according to"* Even if a line is referenced in the question, consider how that line fits within the passage as a whole. Do not interpret the lines out of context of the passage. If the passage has established a sarcastic tone, the referenced lines might need to be read as satirical or ironic.

- *"primarily," "most," "best"* These can be the most challenging questions since you will likely encounter multiple answer choices that are reasonable, but you are being asked to consider the larger themes, purpose, tone, style, and function of the passage to identify the *best* answer choice. For example, if you are asked how a character is *primarily* characterized, avoid choosing an answer that describes a character's less significant feature that is mentioned only once or is secondary. Look in all the paragraphs to identify a recurring pattern or consistency to the portrayal of the character.

- *"in context"* When asked about a phrase or word "in context," you are being reminded to consider how the phrase is being used in this specific situation. Beware of answer choices that provide common usages of the word or phrase, as the writer may be using the word/phrase in a less common way. You may try crossing out the given word/phrase in the passage, reading the surrounding lines, and then predicting your own word/phrase to replace the current one. In so doing, you will force yourself to consider only the context when deciding what idea should be expressed in that spot. Choose the answer that most closely matches the tone and meaning of your own predicted word.

- *"all of the following except"* Four of the choices do answer the question and one does not. Keep your eyes out for the lone wolf in the group: Which word/phrase does not belong with the other four? This type of question can be more time-consuming than others. Consider whether you should skip it and return to it if time allows.

Process of Elimination

When challenging vocabulary or terms appear in answer choices, do not eliminate them as possible choices, because these answers could be correct. Look closely at the answer choices you *do* understand and consider whether those answers articulate the most appropriate response to the question. If you suspect there is something better out there, eliminate these choices and choose one of the remaining answers, even if you do not know what they mean.

Remember that there can only be one correct answer. If you identify a common theme to three or four of the answer choices, consider that the correct answer is often the one that is different from the others.

For Roman-style MCQ (I, II, III, or IV), you can approach the options one at a time and eliminate answer choices as you go. For example, if you know choice II is incorrect, eliminate any answers (A–E) that include it. You might see that the remaining options include only III, so you may not need to consider I and IV.

When You Disagree with an Answer

Reread the question   Often an answer choice is incorrect because it is not the *best* choice, even though it is plausible. Have you overlooked any key words in the question, like "all of the following *except*" or "based on the passage *as a whole*"? Does your answer interpret the lines when the question asks for a paraphrase ("most nearly means")?

Read the explanation carefully   In most cases, the answer explanations address the flaws with all the incorrect choices, but sometimes only the most probable choices are explained. Read the explanations for all the questions in a passage—even for the questions you answered correctly—to get a better sense of the whole passage's meaning and development.

Revisit the passage to locate evidence for your chosen answer   In testing situations, students sometimes choose answers based on our first instincts and based on overall impressions and memory, especially if they are timed. Go back to make sure you have evidence for your choice. Weigh your reasoning against that of the explanation provided to see why the given answer is better.

Submit feedback   If you are convinced that an answer provided in the book is incorrect and you have evidence and reasoning to justify a different choice, please submit your feedback at ShvetaMiller.com/contact. Feedback received from students and teachers has significantly enhanced the quality of the questions in this book, so please get in touch to share your thinking!

Shveta Verma Miller

ACKNOWLEDGMENTS

Every question in this book has been tested by high school students, including current and graduated AP English Literature students and pre-AP scholars, as well as English teachers, college professors, recent college graduates, and parents working alongside their children during pandemic homeschooling. I am grateful to the following reviewers for their particularly helpful feedback:

Meghana Kandlur (Wesleyan 2018) significantly contributed to this book by carefully reviewing nearly every question and its accompanying answer explanation with her close-reading expertise. Her interpretations helped me craft answer choices that challenge readers to consider subtle and critical elements of each passage.

Stephanie Pollicino's 2019–20 AP English Literature students at Brooklyn Technical High School, in Brooklyn, New York, tested the passages that are new to this edition. Their insightful feedback about the answer choices helped improve the quality of the questions. A special thank-you goes to Janice Lin, Olivia Georgalas, and Carina Ploshchadin for working with me after graduation to closely examine the quality of nearly every question in the book.

Derek Heid's 2019–20 AP English Literature students at Temecula Valley High School, in Temecula, California, tested many of the questions, offering shrewd observations about incorrect answer choices that could potentially be supported by the text. Their comments helped ensure that the correct answer was the best choice.

Naomi Lowinger (Stumptown Test Prep) had stimulating conversations about the passages with me, which inspired the creation of many questions.

The third edition now includes 13 passages from contemporary authors and poets, providing students with significant practice analyzing diverse texts by living writers. This would not have been possible without the generous permissions granted by Sarabande Books. I also want to thank Sherri Marmon at Penguin Random House for her prompt assistance with securing permissions for several excerpts in this book.

Finally, a special thank-you goes to Kaden Nagar Hamilton, a student at Laguna Hills High School, in Laguna Hills, California, who spent his months of pandemic homeschooling completing every single passage in this book, discussing his answers and interpretations with me over e-mail. Through his work on this book, he sharpened his analytical reading skills, but—most exciting to me—he grew to enjoy critical reading.

CREDITS

INTRODUCTION

Congratulations! You've taken a big step toward AP success by purchasing *5 Steps to a 5: 500 AP English Literature Questions to Know by Test Day*. We are here to help you take the next step and score high on your AP exam so you can earn college credits and get into the college or university of your choice!

This book gives you 500 AP-style multiple-choice questions that cover all the most essential course material. Each question has a detailed answer explanation. These questions will give you valuable independent practice to supplement your regular textbook and the groundwork you are already doing in your AP classroom.

This and the other books in this series were written by expert AP teachers who know your exam inside out and can identify the crucial exam information as well as questions that are most likely to appear on the exam.

You might be the kind of student who takes several AP courses and needs to study extra questions a few weeks before the exam for a final review. Or you might be the kind of student who puts off preparing until the last weeks before the exam. No matter what your preparation style, you will surely benefit from reviewing these 500 questions, which closely parallel the content, format, and degree of difficulty of the questions on the actual AP exam. These questions and their answer explanations are the ideal last-minute study tool for those final few weeks before the test.

Remember the old saying "Practice makes perfect." If you practice with all the questions and answers in this book, we are certain you will build the skills and confidence needed to do great on the exam. Good luck!

Editors of McGraw-Hill Education

Diagnostic Quiz

GETTING STARTED: THE DIAGNOSTIC QUIZ

The following passages and questions are like those you will encounter in this book. These questions will help you test your understanding of the concepts presented on the AP exam and give you an idea of where you need to focus your attention as you prepare. Unlike the AP exam, this quiz has only multiple-choice questions.

For each question, simply circle the letter of your choice. Once you have finished the exam, check your work against the given answers, which will suggest similar passages in this book that you can use for additional practice.

Good luck!

DIAGNOSTIC QUIZ QUESTIONS

Passage 1. Elizabeth Barrett Browning, "Sonnet 32"

THE FIRST time that the sun rose on thine oath
To love me, I looked forward to the moon
To slacken all those bonds which seemed too soon
And quickly tied to make a lasting troth.
Quick-loving hearts, I thought, may quickly loathe;   5
And, looking on myself, I seemed not one
For such man's love;—more like an out-of-tune
Worn viol, a good singer would be wroth
To spoil his song with, and which, snatched in haste,
Is laid down at the first ill-sounding note.   10
I did not wrong myself so, but I placed
A wrong on *thee*. For perfect strains may float
'Neath master-hands, from instruments defaced,—
And great souls, at one stroke, may do and dote.

1. In contrast to the sun, the moon is portrayed as
    (A) hindered
    (B) gloomy
    (C) menacing
    (D) loosening
    (E) calculating

2. What is "too soon/ And quickly tied" (line 3–4)?
    I.   "thine oath" (1)
    II. "those bonds" (3)
    III. "a lasting troth" (4)

    (A) I only
    (B) II only
    (C) I and II only
    (D) II and III only
    (E) I, II, and III

3. The words "Quick" and "quickly" in line 5 serve to emphasize
   (A) the fickle nature of attraction
   (B) the partner's manic behavior
   (C) the degree of the speaker's regret
   (D) the musicality of the poem
   (E) the speaker's chastisement of her partner

4. A contrast to the speaker's initial assumption is found in which of the following line(s)?
   (A) line 4
   (B) lines 6–7
   (C) lines 7–10
   (D) line 10
   (E) lines 11–12

5. The speaker uses a simile to emphasize her
   (A) view of her inadequacies
   (B) mistake in loving an unworthy mate
   (C) prudence in entering a romantic relationship
   (D) hope that her mate will deem her worthy of his love
   (E) regret over her hasty betrothal

6. In line 9, "the song" is likely a symbol for
   (A) wasted passion
   (B) estimable love
   (C) the temporality of love
   (D) the mate's musical talent
   (E) the speaker's love

7. The connotation of "ill-sounding note" in line 10 is most in line with the idea expressed in which other phrase in the poem?
   (A) "I seemed not one/ For such man's love" (6–7)
   (B) "I looked forward to the moon" (2)
   (C) "Quick-loving hearts" (5)
   (D) "For perfect strains may float" (12)
   (E) "snatched in haste" (9)

8. The speaker implies that her initial concerns would have been abated if
   (A) her vows were heartfelt
   (B) her mate had been genuine
   (C) she exercised more patience
   (D) she and her mate procrastinated
   (E) their commitment had been made over time

9. In the final four lines of the poem, the speaker reveals

(A) her error in judging herself too harshly
(B) her regret at overestimating her mate's love
(C) her paranoia about her mate's potential infidelity
(D) her underestimation of her mate's potential
(E) her concern that she married too quickly

10. The poem's central idea is developed mainly through

(A) a metaphorical comparison between the sun and moon
(B) a parallel between an ardent lover and a talented musician
(C) repeated assertions that a mistake was made
(D) a consistently regretful tone
(E) a contrast between the speaker's and her mate's devotion

11. Throughout the poem, the speaker experiences

(A) reflection
(B) guilt
(C) fear
(D) foresight
(E) infatuation

Passage 2. Robert Yune, "Life from Plasticville" from *Impossible Children*

You would pity anyone living in my father's town. First, it isn't big. Oval railroad tracks cut the place off from the rest of the world, and trains often pass dangerously close to homes and businesses. There is a post office and a radio station but no grocery stores or restaurants. Families stroll stiffly down Main Street, heading somewhere they'll never reach.   5

When I say it isn't big, I mean the town itself is about forty square feet, on an elevated platform in my father's basement. No one in town has ever seen the sun, only a fluorescent lamp that reflects dully off their faces.

My father was an officer and a veteran. After he retired, he built this little plastic world. And he loved it. Or, I should say, he loved the trains. Lionel   10
O-Gauges. My sons loved them when they were young. In the dark, you could see hundreds of pinpoint red and green signal lights, and the trains lit up. Silhouettes of cheery passengers steamed by. But as I grew older, I worried that my father spent all his time in the basement. I never resented it—every man deserves a hobby—but I didn't understand the hold these trains had over a grown   15
man. I never asked. My father passed away last week, and much was left unsaid between us.

Tonight, I am not the unemployed middle-aged son whose best wasn't enough. Tonight, I'm the son who will catalog each train before returning it to its original box. I will gather the happy little families and place them in plastic baggies. Tonight, after a long day of settling his estate, I will walk upstairs and fold myself into bed. Everything will be perfect, in place, under a round glowing moon, so that my father, hopefully looking down from somewhere, might see us and be pleased.

20

12. The assertion made in the first sentence is supported by all of the following details *except*
    (A) "a fluorescent lamp . . . reflects dully off their faces" (8)
    (B) "the town itself is about forty square feet" (6)
    (C) "he loved it" (10)
    (D) "heading somewhere they'll never reach" (5)
    (E) "Oval railroad tracks cut the place off from the rest of the world" (1–2)

13. In context of the passage as a whole, the phrase "my father's town" (line 1) in the opening sentence functions as
    (A) a literal reference to the narrator's hometown
    (B) a somewhat misleading reference that is never clarified
    (C) a purposely ambiguous reference that gives an impression that is later corrected
    (D) a neutral noun phrase that introduces the passage's topic
    (E) a description of the father's hobby

14. The detail about the father's profession
    (A) further develops the father's character as someone who values order and precision
    (B) adds to the biographical tone of the passage
    (C) implies that his work life was so tasking that he needed a relaxing hobby
    (D) serves as a transition in the passage from a description of the town to a more explicit description of the father
    (E) explains the narrator's later reference to his father's disapproval of his own unemployment

15. The narrator's attitude toward the father's hobby can best be described as
    (A) irritated
    (B) bemused
    (C) incredulous
    (D) intrigued
    (E) neutral

16. Which of the following conveys the effect of the first four sentences in the final paragraph ("Tonight . . . into bed")?

    I. Repetition of the word "tonight" creates a sense of urgency, determination, and resolution.

    II. Parallel structures help contrast the narrator's insecurity with his sense of confidence about what to do for his father.

    III. A list of mundane actions presents the narrator's grieving as mild and perfunctory.

    (A) I only

    (B) III only

    (C) II and III only

    (D) I and II only

    (E) I, II, and III

17. In context of the passage as a whole, the narrator's decision described in the final paragraph is

    (A) shocking because he never approved of his father's train obsession before

    (B) confusing because he worried about his father's hobby when he was alive

    (C) impressive because he handles his father's death with ease

    (D) uplifting because he wants to honor what was important to his father even if he never quite understood its value

    (E) unbelievable because he did not "understand the hold these trains had" (15) on his father

18. The narrator expects his father might "be pleased" (line 24) most likely because

    (A) he had earned his respect

    (B) he has recreated Plasticville in a sense

    (C) he knows his father loved him

    (D) his father lived a satisfying life

    (E) he has tried hard to please him by settling his estate

19. Which of the following best describes the development of the passage?

    (A) A narrator reveals his ambivalence toward his father's death through elaborate sensory imagery.

    (B) A first person narrator indirectly broaches the topic of mourning his father with spare language and an aloof tone.

    (C) A narrator uses his father's cherished hobby to explore his feelings about him and their relationship.

    (D) A central metaphor explicitly compares a father–son relationship to a plastic town.

    (E) Simple sentence structures and common, everyday diction convey the narrator's straightforward feelings about his father's death.

20. Based on the passage, the relationship between the narrator and his father can be described as
(A) estranged
(B) strained
(C) bitter
(D) sympathetic
(E) reserved

After you have completed and scored your Diagnostic Quiz, read the answer explanations for questions you answered incorrectly *and* for those you answered correctly. This will help you identify aspects of the passages you might have misinterpreted and key words in the question stems you may have overlooked.

Once you have reviewed the answers, you will have a better sense of where to begin your study. If you found the poetry passage more challenging, either because of the poetic form or the older language, you might begin with Chapter 3: Pre-20th-Century Poetry and then move on to Chapter 1: Pre-20th-Century Prose. If the second passage was more challenging for you, begin with Chapter 2: 20th-Century/Contemporary Prose.

DIAGNOSTIC QUIZ ANSWERS

Passage 1. Elizabeth Barrett Browning, "Sonnet 32"

1. (D) While the sun is equated with the excitement of their "oath" (1) of love, the speaker mentions the moon only in the context of hoping for its arrival because of its power to "slacken all those bonds which seemed too soon/ And quickly tied to make a lasting troth" (3–4). The moon is not blocked or hindered (A), it is not menacing or threatening (C), and it is not calculating (intending harm, strategizing) (E). A moon is generally associated with brightness, so it cannot be said to be gloomy, especially in this context since the speaker anticipates its arrival (B). The context of the poem reveals that the moon is longed for because of its ability to loosen the bonds/promises that might have been made only in haste and not in truth.

2. (C) If read as prose, the sentence in lines 1–4 says, "The first time that the sun rose on thine oath to love me, I looked forward to the moon to slacken all those bonds which seemed too soon and quickly tied to make a lasting troth." The clause "which seemed too soon and quickly tied" is referring to "those bonds," which themselves refer to "thine oath to love me." The "lasting troth" is not quickly tied; rather, the speaker is indicating that she worries a lasting troth (truth, loyalty) may not be realistic, given how hastily the oath was made.

3. (A) The speaker communicates her initial worry that her mate declared his oath of love so rashly that he would be likely to change his mind. By using the word "quick" (5) in two different contexts, she draws a parallel between being quick to love or to profess love and quick to change one's mind drastically (loathe). Fickle means "inconstant, wavering, vacillating."

4. (E) The speaker's initial assumption is signaled by the phrase, "The first time . . ." (1). She goes on to say that she "thought" (5) that "Quick-loving hearts . . . may quickly loathe" (5) and that "looking on myself, I seemed not one/ For such man's love" (6–7). The speaker's initial fear is that her mate will realize she is not worthy of his love and that he may "Quickly loathe" (5) her. Line 11 reveals a contrast to this initial thought. She realizes that she "placed a wrong on" (11–12) her mate, that she underestimated his potential to love someone less masterful than himself.

5. (A) The speaker's **simile** is in lines 6–10: "And looking on myself, I seemed not one/ For such man's love;—more *like* an out-of-tune/ Worn viol, a good singer would be wroth/ To spoil his song with, and which, snatched in haste,/ Is laid down at the first ill-sounding note." She compares herself ("myself," "I") to an out-of-tune instrument to illustrate her own insecurity about being worthy of her mate's love and attention. She worries that her mate, compared in the simile to "a good singer" (8), would lay down the out-of-tune instrument (herself) that was "snatched in haste" (9) (he professed his love too quickly, without careful consideration) at the "first ill-sounding note" (10) (evidence of her inadequacies).

6. (B) In the **simile** discussed in question 5, the "good singer" (8) is the speaker's mate, who snatches (quickly grabs) an out-of-tune instrument (the speaker). She worries he will put her down once she "spoils his song" (9). In this comparison, the good singer's song would then be symbolic of what she fears she is not worthy of: his estimable love.

7. (A) In the **simile** discussed in questions 5 and 6, the "ill-sounding note" (10) is symbolic of the speaker's insecurity about being worthy of her impressive mate's love. This idea is clearly expressed in lines 6–7: "I seemed not one/ For such man's love!"

8. (E) The speaker never explicitly charges her mate with being disingenuous in his oath to love her (B); rather, she merely articulates her worry that his love may quickly change to "loathe" (5). Choice C is incorrect because the speaker does not ascribe any blame solely to herself for rushing into an oath. Choice D is incorrect because the **tone** of the word "procrastinate" implies delaying due to indifference or apathy. She does not wish they delayed their oath out of disinterest. Choice A is incorrect because the speaker implies that her own vows were genuine, as she views her mate as a "good singer" (8) whom she may not be worthy of. The speaker does explicitly express the wish for the oath and bonds that were "too soon/ And quickly tied" (3–4) to be "slackened" (3) by the moon so that the "Quick-loving hearts" (5) would not "quickly loathe" (5) and that the good singer's song would not be spoiled by an ill-sounding instrument that was grabbed in haste. Her worry about the effects of their rash commitment would have been assuaged if their commitment had been made over time.

9. (D) In these lines, the speaker explains that her initial concerns about her and her mate's "quickly tied" (4) bonds were misguided because she "placed a wrong on *thee* [her mate]" (11–12), meaning she wrongly assumed he, like the "good singer" (8) in the **simile**, would quickly put down the inadequate instrument (herself) once he realized it was not as it seemed. She goes on to explain her reasoning for why she was initially wrong: "For perfect strains (a good song, true love) may float/ 'Neath master-hands (like her mate's), from instruments defaced—(the speaker)/ And great souls (her mate), at one stroke (a quickly tied bond), may do and dote (give genuine love)" (12–14). When she says she placed a wrong on her addressee, she is saying she underestimated his potential for being genuine and loyal, despite his speedy oath. She now realizes that "master-hands" (13) like his have the ability to make perfect music (true love) even with inadequate instruments (herself). Choice A is incorrect because she states that she was not wrong about her views of herself: "I did not wrong myself so, but I placed/ A wrong on *thee*" (11–12).

10. (B) The poem's central idea is that the speaker's mate turns out to be steadfast in his love, despite the speaker's initial worry that his passion would quickly fade. The discovery that she was wrong is made clear by the comparison between her mate and a masterful musician. The poem opens with a **metaphorical** comparison between the sun and moon to describe the speaker's initial worry, but her worry is not the central idea (A). The speaker worries that her mate may regret (D) his quickly tied bond, but the poem ends with appreciation of his true love. The speaker does not discuss her own devotion; rather, she mentions her perceived inadequacies (E).

11. (A) The speaker does refer to her initial worries and fear (C), but this fear is later revealed to be misplaced and "wrong" (11). The question asks us to identify what the speaker experiences *throughout* the poem, and reflection (A) is the speaker's state of mind for all 14 lines. In lines 1–10, she thinks back to "The first time" their oath was made and reflects on her reactions and emotions at that time. She moves on in line 11 to reflect on her misguided assumption.

Passage 2. Robert Yune, "Life from Plasticville" from *Impossible Children*

12. (C) The narrator asserts that we would "pity anyone living in" (1) his father's town. The subsequent details of that town support this claim, such as the fact that "[o]val railroad tracks cut the place off from the rest of the world" (1–2) (E), "[f]amilies stroll stiffly down Main Street, heading somewhere they'll never reach" (4–5) (D), "the town itself is about forty square feet" (6) (B), and "[n]o one in town has ever seen the sun, only a fluorescent lamp that reflects dully off their faces" (7–8) (A). The father's love for the town he built does not support the assertion that we would pity everyone living there, making choice C correct.

13. (C) The narrator tells us in the first sentence that we would pity anyone living in his father's town. He does not explicitly say that the town is a plastic construction his father made. Instead, he obliquely shares details that could potentially describe both a fake toy town and a real town. He only clarifies that the town is, in fact, "about forty square feet, on an elevated platform in [his] father's basement" (6–7) in the second paragraph.

14. (A) The additional detail about the father having been an officer and a veteran adds to the portrayal of the father who is obsessed with his fake town and toy trains. An officer and veteran can be assumed to have some regard for order, planning, and precision, which coincides with the father's love for organizing and overseeing a fake little world. The passage is more of an exploration of the narrator's feelings toward his father than a biography of his father, making B incorrect. While the working life of an officer might be tasking, the father was retired when he had the hobby, making C incorrect. The third paragraph continues to discuss the town in detail, making D incorrect. Knowing the father had a long career as an officer and veteran does shed some light on his disapproval of his son's unemployment, but it does not *explain* his disapproval, making E incorrect.

15. (B) The narrator says he didn't resent his father's hobby, but he "didn't understand the hold these trains had over a grown man" (15–16), and he never figured it out because he "never asked" (16). The narrator is perplexed and bemused by the hobby, but not intrigued enough to have actually asked his father about it, making D incorrect. He is not incredulous (C) or irritated (A), because he admits that "every man deserves a hobby" (14–15). His worries about his father's hobby mean that he does not feel indifferent or neutral about it (E).

16. (D) In the first two sentences, the same construction (Tonight, I am/I'm) is repeated to state what the narrator is and is *not*. Tonight, he *is not* the "unemployed middle-aged son whose best wasn't enough" (18–19). He *is* "the son who will . . ." (19). Even though he was confused by his father's obsession with his trains—a hobby he never understood and will never get the chance to ask his father about—he appears determined to honor his father, and possibly redeem himself in his father's eyes, by doing something the father would approve of: respectfully packing up his cherished trains and plastic town. The **parallel construction** and **repetition** (Tonight, I will . . .) convey the narrator's resolve and confidence that he is doing something his father would appreciate, suggesting that his grief is far from perfunctory (routine, without effort or reflection), making choice III incorrect.

17. (D) Even though the narrator was confused by his father's obsession with his trains—a hobby he never understood and will never get the chance to ask his father about—he appears determined to honor his father by respectfully packing up his cherished trains and plastic town. It is uplifting to see that, even though "much was left unsaid" (16) between them, the narrator is resolved to overlook his own feelings about his father's hobby and create a scene that is so "perfect, in place" (22) that his father would be pleased. Such a reaction is not shocking (A) or unbelievable (E). It makes sense that the narrator would want to attempt to please his father, given that he mentions packing up his trains and creating a perfect scene for the father to look down upon would mean he is "not the unemployed middle-aged son whose best wasn't enough" (18–19).

18. (B) The narrator mentions that tonight he is no longer "the unemployed middle-aged son whose best wasn't enough" (18–19) because he will earn his father's approval by creating a sort of "Plasticville" that he can look down upon and "be pleased" (24). By cataloging "each train before returning it to its original box" (19–20) and gathering "the happy little families" (20) and placing them "in plastic baggies" (20–21), he is practicing the same attention to detail his father enjoyed when spending time with his plastic town in the basement. He will "walk upstairs and fold [himself] into bed" (21–22), completing a "perfect" (22) scene with everything "in place" (22), just like his father liked to do with his town. Choice E is incorrect because settling the father's estate involves more than recreating a perfect scene and carefully packing up the trains and town, making B the best choice.

19. (C) A **first person narrator** describes his deceased father's plastic town and toy trains as a hobby that he didn't understand himself (and caused him to worry) but that his father loved. In describing the hobby, the narrator reflects on their relationship: "I never resented it . . . I didn't understand the hold these trains had . . . much was left unsaid between us" (14–17). As a way to cope with his loss, with the sense that his best "wasn't enough" (18–19) to please his father, the narrator attempts to create a "perfect, in place" (22) scene that his father could observe and enjoy "from somewhere" (23). The narrator's feelings toward his father's death are complex, not straightforward (E). While the narrator does use simple, direct, and spare language, the **tone** is not aloof and the topic of mourning his father is not broached indirectly, making B incorrect. The narrator admits to feeling worried about his father's hobby and feeling like he "wasn't enough" (18–19). The great care he takes to please his father in the final paragraph does not suggest he is removed from his death. His feelings are complex but not ambivalent (A), since it is clear that he feels his father's loss. While the plastic town could serve as a **metaphor**, the comparison is not made explicit (D), making choice C the best answer.

20. (B) In lines 13–17, the narrator reveals that he "worried that [his] father spent all his time in the basement" (13–14), that he "never resented it" (14) but "didn't understand the hold these trains had over a grown man" (15–16) and "never asked" (16). He goes on to say that "much was left unsaid" (16) between them. His attempt to finally please his father by creating a scene that is "perfect, in place" (22) speaks to all that was not communicated directly between them when the father was alive. Although they did not communicate much, the relationship is more strained than reserved (E) because the narrator felt like his "best wasn't enough" (18–19), indicating that their lack of communication is about more than being shy or quiet.

For practice with passages similar to Passage 1, see Chapter 3: Pre-20th-Century poetry. For more practice with poetic form, structure, devices, and analysis, also see Chapter 4: 20th-Century/Contemporary Poetry.

For practice with passages similar to Passage 2, see Chapter 2: 20th-Century/Contemporary Prose. For more practice with prose fiction, also see Chapter 1: Pre-20th-Century Prose.

CHAPTER 1

Pre-20th-Century Prose

Passage 1. Louisa May Alcott, "An Old-fashioned Girl"

"It's time to go to the station, Tom."

"Come on, then."

"Oh, I'm not going; it's too wet. Shouldn't have a crimp left if I went out such a day as this; and I want to look nice when Polly comes."

"You don't expect me to go and bring home a strange girl alone, do you?" 5
And Tom looked as much alarmed as if his sister had proposed to him to escort the wild woman of Australia.

"Of course I do. It's your place to go and get her; and if you wasn't a bear, you'd like it."

"Well, I call that mean! I supposed I'd got to go; but you said you'd go, too. 10
Catch me bothering about your friends another time! No, *sir!* " And Tom rose from the sofa with an air of indignant resolution, the impressive effect of which was somewhat damaged by a tousled head, and the hunched appearance of his garments generally.

"Now, don't be cross; and I'll get mamma to let you have that horrid Ned 15
Miller, that you are so fond of, come and make you a visit after Polly's gone," said Fanny, hoping to soothe his ruffled feelings.

"How long is she going to stay?" demanded Tom, making his toilet by a promiscuous shake.

"A month or two, maybe. She's ever so nice; and I shall keep her as long as 20
she's happy."

"She won't stay long then, if I can help it," muttered Tom, who regarded girls as a very unnecessary portion of creation. Boys of fourteen are apt to think so, and perhaps it is a wise arrangement; for, being fond of turning somersaults, they have an opportunity of indulging in a good one, metaphorically speaking, when, three or four years later, they become the abject slaves of "those bothering girls." 25

"Look here! how am I going to know the creature? I never saw her, and she never saw me. You'll have to come too, Fan," he added, pausing on his way to the door, arrested by the awful idea that he might have to address several strange girls before he got the right one. 30

"You'll find her easy enough; she'll probably be standing round looking for us. I dare say she'll know *you*, though I'm not there, because I've described you to her."

"Guess she won't, then;" and Tom gave a hasty smooth to his curly pate and a glance at the mirror, feeling sure that his sister hadn't done him justice. Sisters 35 never do, as "we fellows" know too well.

"Do go along, or you'll be too late; and then, what *will* Polly think of me?" cried Fanny, with the impatient poke which is peculiarly aggravating to masculine dignity.

"She'll think you cared more about your frizzles than your friends, and she'll 40 be about right, too."

Feeling that he said rather a neat and cutting thing, Tom sauntered leisurely away, perfectly conscious that it *was* late, but bent on not being hurried while in sight, though he ran himself off his legs to make up for it afterward.

"If I was the President, I'd make a law to shut up all boys till they were 45 grown; for they certainly are the most provoking toads in the world," said Fanny, as she watched the slouchy figure of her brother strolling down the street. She might have changed her mind, however, if she had followed him, for as soon as he turned the corner, his whole aspect altered; his hands came out of his pockets, he stopped whistling, buttoned his jacket, gave his cap a pull, and went off at a 50 great pace.

The train was just in when he reached the station, panting like a race-horse, and as red as a lobster with the wind and the run.

"Suppose she'll wear a top-knot and a thingumbob, like everyone else; and however shall I know her? Too bad of Fan to make me come alone!" thought Tom, as he stood watching the crowd stream through the depot, and feeling rather daunted at the array of young ladies who passed. As none of them seemed looking for any one, he did not accost them, but eyed each new batch with the air of a martyr. "That's her," he said to himself, as he presently caught sight of a girl in gorgeous array, standing with her hands folded, and a very small hat perched on the top of a very large "chig-non," as Tom pronounced it. "I suppose I've got to speak to her, so here goes;" and, nerving himself to the task, Tom slowly approached the damsel, who looked as if the wind had blown her clothes into rags, such a flapping of sashes, scallops, ruffles, curls, and feathers was there.

"I say, if you please, is your name Polly Milton?" meekly asked Tom, pausing before the breezy stranger.

"No, it isn't," answered the young lady, with a cool stare that utterly quenched him.

1. The humor in lines 11–14 ("And Tom rose . . . generally") is primarily created by
   (A) the indignant resolution
   (B) Tom's antipathy toward Fanny
   (C) Tom's biting comments about Fanny's friends
   (D) the dissonance between what Tom does and how he appears
   (E) Tom's tousled head

2. Which of the following lines indicates the narrator has access to the characters' points of view?
   I. "hoping to soothe his ruffled feelings" (17)
   II. "And Tom rose from the sofa . . . generally" (11–14)
   III. "who regarded girls as a very unnecessary portion of creation" (22–23)
   IV. "Boys of fourteen are apt to think so" (23)
   (A) I and III only
   (B) I, II, and III only
   (C) II and IV only
   (D) III and IV only
   (E) I, II, III, and IV

3. The author uses the word "somersaults" (line 24) in this context
   - (A) literally and figuratively
   - (B) arrogantly
   - (C) sarcastically
   - (D) regretfully
   - (E) didactically

4. The phrases "we fellows" (line 36) and "those bothering girls" (line 26) are in quotation marks to indicate
   - (A) sarcasm
   - (B) dialogue
   - (C) the views of an expert
   - (D) specialized terms
   - (E) a distinct voice

5. Tom's "hasty smooth" and "glance at the mirror" (lines 34–35) are actions that are meant to
   - (A) confirm Fanny's opinion
   - (B) belie Fanny's opinion
   - (C) reveal Tom's superficiality
   - (D) suggest Tom's arrogance
   - (E) indicate Tom's wariness

6. Fanny appears to be primarily concerned with
   - (A) her brother's willfulness
   - (B) vexing her brother
   - (C) looking better than Polly
   - (D) pleasing Polly
   - (E) her hair

7. The narration in lines 42–44 reveals that Tom communicates with his sister with
   - (A) hesitation
   - (B) anger
   - (C) posturing
   - (D) frankness
   - (E) refusal

8. The details provided in lines 49–51 ("his hands . . . at a great pace")
   provide a contrast to the details provided in which of the following lines?
   (A) "he ran himself off his legs to make up for it afterward" (44)
   (B) "Tom gave a hasty smooth to his curly pate" (34)
   (C) "Tom sauntered leisurely away" (42–43)
   (D) "hoping to soothe his ruffled feathers" (17)
   (E) "feeling sure that his sister hadn't done him justice" (35)

9. The reference to "chig-non" (line 61) is a detail that is intended to develop
   (A) Tom's unfamiliarity and awkwardness around girls
   (B) Tom's laughable naiveté and ignorance
   (C) Tom's uncultured background
   (D) Tom's unique form of expression
   (E) the colloquial pronunciation and vocabulary of the time period

10. The function of the figurative language in lines 52–53 ("The train . . . run")
    is best described by which of the following?
    (A) Personification dramatizes the forbidding obstacle Tom faces.
    (B) Visual imagery reveals Tom's posturing.
    (C) A metaphor compares Tom's behavior to Fanny's expectations of him.
    (D) Two similes dramatize Tom's actual intention as opposed to his
        feigned intention.
    (E) Two similes highlight Tom's behaviors as animalistic.

11. The passage implies that Tom is most apprehensive about
    (A) following orders
    (B) interacting with girls
    (C) antagonizing Fanny
    (D) appearing to be a gentleman
    (E) pleasing girls

12. In context, the phrase "utterly quenched him" (lines 67–68) is meant to
    emphasize
    (A) the anxiety Tom feels when approaching females
    (B) how unwarranted and misplaced Tom's reaction is
    (C) the cruel and powerful influence young ladies have on young men
    (D) Tom's relief that the young lady is not Polly
    (E) Tom's frustration that the young lady is not Polly

Passage 2. Frances Burney, *Evelina*

We are to go this evening to a private ball, given by Mrs. Stanley, a very fashionable lady of Mrs. Mirvan's acquaintance.

We have been a-shopping as Mrs. Mirvan calls it, all this morning, to buy silks, caps, gauzes, and so forth.

The shops are really very entertaining, especially the mercers; there seem to be   5
six or seven men belonging to each shop; and every one took care by bowing and smirking, to be noticed. We were conducted from one to another, and carried from room to room with so much ceremony, that I was almost afraid to go on.

I thought I should never have chosen a silk: for they produced so many, I knew not which to fix upon; and they recommended them all so strongly, that I   10
fancy they thought I only wanted persuasion to buy every thing they showed me. And, indeed, they took so much trouble, that I was almost ashamed I could not.

At the milliners, the ladies we met were so much dressed, that I should rather have imagined they were making visits than purchases. But what most diverted me was, that we were more frequently served by men than by women; and such   15
men! so finical, so affected! they seemed to understand every part of a woman's dress better than we do ourselves; and they recommended caps and ribbands with an air of so much importance, that I wished to ask them how long they had left off wearing them.

The dispatch with which they work in these great shops is amazing, for they   20
have promised me a complete suit of linen against the evening.

I have just had my hair dressed. You can't think how oddly my head feels; full of powder and black pins, and a great cushion on the top of it. I believe you would hardly know me, for my face looks quite different to what it did before my hair was dressed. When I shall be able to make use of a comb for myself I cannot tell; for my   25
hair is so much entangled, frizzled they call it, that I fear it will be very difficult.

I am half afraid of this ball to-night; for, you know, I have never danced but at school: however, Miss Mirvan says there is nothing in it. Yet, I wish it was over.

Adieu, my dear Sir, pray excuse the wretched stuff I write; perhaps I may improve by being in this town, and then my letters will be less unworthy your   30
reading. Meantime, I am, Your dutiful and affectionate, though unpolished,
EVELINA

13. The mercers (line 5) are primarily characterized as
    (A) solicitous
    (B) excessive
    (C) redundant
    (D) generous
    (E) conscientious

14. The speaker's tone in the phrase "and such men!" (lines 15–16) can best be described as

(A) perturbed
(B) frightened
(C) bewildered
(D) disappointed
(E) disturbed

15. The word "affected" in line 16 indicates the speaker views the men as

(A) unnatural
(B) influential
(C) ridiculous
(D) offensive
(E) helpful

16. Lines 20–21 reveal that the speaker is impressed by the shops'

(A) dresses
(B) communication
(C) efficiency
(D) respect
(E) accommodation

17. Regarding her "dressed" (line 22) hair, the speaker feels

(A) disillusioned
(B) relieved
(C) dissatisfied
(D) proud
(E) disoriented

18. Based on the passage as a whole, it can be interpreted that the speaker is "half afraid" (line 27) mostly due to

(A) her fear of the unpredictable
(B) her new hairstyle and clothing
(C) the "affected" (16) workers at the milliners
(D) her insecurity and apprehension
(E) her poor dance skills

19. The reader can infer that the speaker is here primarily
    - (A) to ingratiate herself
    - (B) to become refined
    - (C) to please her "dear Sir" (29)
    - (D) to meet a husband
    - (E) to study

20. The repetition of the word "almost" (lines 8, 12) suggests
    - (A) the speaker is unsure how to describe events
    - (B) the speaker misremembers her experience
    - (C) the speaker exercises caution when narrating to her "dear Sir" (29)
    - (D) the speaker's hesitancy during the unfamiliar experience of shopping
    - (E) the speaker's desire to have new clothes is stronger than her fear

21. The qualification in the final line of the passage serves to
    - (A) characterize Evelina as obtuse
    - (B) underscore Evelina's self-image
    - (C) berate Evelina
    - (D) contrast Evelina with her addressee
    - (E) undermine Evelina's authority

22. The purpose of the passage as a whole is
    - (A) to criticize the values of a particular society
    - (B) to characterize the speaker as guileless and uncouth
    - (C) to present a culture as odd
    - (D) to reveal the speaker's perception of her experiences
    - (E) to characterize the speaker as tenacious and wise

Passage 3. Miguel de Cervantes, *Don Quixote*

These preliminaries settled, he did not care to put off any longer the execution of his design, urged on to it by the thought of all the world was losing by his delay, seeing what wrongs he intended to right, grievances to redress, injustices to repair, abuses to remove, and duties to discharge. So, without giving notice of his intention to anyone, and without anybody seeing him, one morning before   5
the dawning of the day (which was one of the hottest of the month of July) he donned his suit of armour, mounted Rocinante with his patched-up helmet on, braced his buckler, took his lance, and by the back door of the yard sallied forth upon the plain in the highest contentment and satisfaction at seeing with what ease he had made a beginning with his grand purpose. But scarcely did he find   10

himself upon the open plain, when a terrible thought struck him, one all but enough to make him abandon the enterprise at the very outset. It occurred to him that he had not been dubbed a knight, and that according to the law of chivalry he neither could nor ought to bear arms against any knight; and that even if he had been, still he ought, as a novice knight, to wear white armour, without a device upon the shield until by his prowess he had earned one. These reflections made him waver in his purpose, but his craze being stronger than any reasoning, he made up his mind to have himself dubbed a knight by the first one he came across, following the example of others in the same case, as he had read in the books that brought him to this pass. As for white armor, he resolved, on the first opportunity, to scour his until it was whiter than an ermine; and so comforting himself he pursued his way, taking that which his horse chose, for in this he believed lay the essence of adventures.

Thus setting out, our new-fledged adventurer paced along, talking to himself and saying, "Who knows but that in time to come, when the veracious history of my famous deeds is made known, the sage who writes it, when he has to set forth my first sally in the early morning, will do it after this fashion? 'Scarce had the rubicund Apollo spread o'er the face of the broad spacious earth the golden threads of his bright hair, scarce had the little birds of painted plumage attuned their notes to hail with dulcet and mellifluous harmony the coming of the rosy Dawn, that, deserting the soft couch of her jealous spouse, was appearing to mortals at the gates and balconies of the Manchegan horizon, when the renowned knight Don Quixote of La Mancha, quitting the lazy down, mounted his celebrated steed Rocinante and began to traverse the ancient and famous Campo de Montiel;'" which in fact was actually traversing. "Happy the age, happy the time," he continued, "in which shall be made known my deeds of fame, worthy to be molded in brass, carved in marble, limned in pictures, for a memorial for ever. And thou, O sage magician, whoever thou art, to whom it shall fall to be the chronicler of this wondrous history, forget not, I entreat thee, my good Rocinante, the constant companion of my ways and wanderings." Presently he broke out again, as if he were love-stricken in earnest, "O Princess Dulcinea, lady of this captive heart, a grievous wrong hast thou done me to drive me forth with scorn, and with inexorable obduracy banish me from the presence of thy beauty. O lady, deign to hold in remembrance this heart, thy vassal, that thus in anguish pines for love of thee."

23. The "terrible thought" (line 11) that Don Quixote had refers to
- (A) his leaving home without telling anyone
- (B) his not knowing where he was going
- (C) the wrongs that his lady had done him
- (D) his status not being quite legitimate
- (E) his ambitions being too great

24. According to the narrator, Don Quixote was able to overcome his initial hesitation because

(A) he was unable to reason coherently
(B) his fantasizing was resourceful
(C) he had a tenuous grasp on reality
(D) he had faith in his good fortune
(E) he was unwilling to return home

25. Don Quixote's use of the expression "veracious history" in line 25 can best be described as

(A) skeptical
(B) hilarious
(C) ironic
(D) disingenuous
(E) emphatic

26. The tone of the sentence in lines 27–35, "'Scarce had the rubicund Apollo . . . Campo de Montiel,'" can best be described as

(A) ridiculous
(B) sarcastic
(C) sophisticated
(D) grandiloquent
(E) neutral

27. It can be interpreted that the addressee in the sentence in lines 38–40 ("And thou, O sage magician . . . and wanderings") is likely a reference to

(A) Don Quixote himself
(B) Dulcinea
(C) someone imaginary
(D) the narrator
(E) a historian Don Quixote admires

28. According to Don Quixote's chivalric code, a knight is meant to do all of the following *except*

(A) travel without a clear sense of direction
(B) speak loftily
(C) express humility
(D) seek romance
(E) adhere to precise rules

29. The passage's tone is primarily established through
    (A) the protagonist's unwarranted and exaggerated hubris
    (B) the imminent failure of the protagonist's adventure
    (C) the sincerity of the protagonist's hallucinatory experiences
    (D) the lowly status of the aspirational protagonist
    (E) the repeated references to a sage

30. The narrator's attitude toward the protagonist can best be described as
    (A) magnanimous
    (B) belittling
    (C) spiteful
    (D) sympathetic
    (E) dispassionate

Passage 4. Kate Chopin, "The Kiss"

It was still quite light out of doors, but inside with the curtains drawn and the smouldering fire sending out a dim, uncertain glow, the room was full of deep shadows.

Brantain sat in one of these shadows; it had overtaken him and he did not mind. The obscurity lent him courage to keep his eyes fastened as ardently as he   5
liked upon the girl who sat in the firelight.

She was very handsome, with a certain fine, rich coloring that belongs to the healthy brune type. She was quite composed, as she idly stroked the satiny coat of the cat that lay curled in her lap, and she occasionally sent a slow glance into the shadow where her companion sat. They were talking low, of indifferent   10
things which plainly were not the things that occupied their thoughts. She knew that he loved her—a frank, blustering fellow without guile enough to conceal his feelings, and no desire to do so. For two weeks past he had sought her society eagerly and persistently. She was confidently waiting for him to declare himself and she meant to accept him. The rather insignificant and unattractive Brantain   15
was enormously rich; and she liked and required the entourage which wealth could give her.

During one of the pauses between their talk of the last tea and the next reception the door opened and a young man entered whom Brantain knew quite well. The girl turned her face toward him. A stride or two brought him to her side,   20
and bending over her chair—before she could suspect his intention, for she did not realize that he had not seen her visitor—he pressed an ardent, lingering kiss upon her lips.

Brantain slowly arose; so did the girl arise, but quickly, and the newcomer stood between them, a little amusement and some defiance struggling with the   25
confusion in his face.

"I believe," stammered Brantain, "I see that I have stayed too long. I—I had no idea—that is, I must wish you good-by." He was clutching his hat with both hands, and probably did not perceive that she was extending her hand to him, her presence of mind had not completely deserted her; but she could not have trusted herself to speak.

"Hang me if I saw him sitting there, Nattie! I know it's deuced awkward for you. But I hope you'll forgive me this once—this very first break. Why, what's the matter?"

"Don't touch me; don't come near me," she returned angrily. "What do you mean by entering the house without ringing?"

"I came in with your brother, as I often do," he answered coldly, in self-justification. "We came in the side way. He went upstairs and I came in here hoping to find you. The explanation is simple enough and ought to satisfy you that the misadventure was unavoidable. But do say that you forgive me, Nathalie," he entreated, softening.

"Forgive you! You don't know what you are talking about. Let me pass. It depends upon—a good deal whether I ever forgive you."

At that next reception which she and Brantain had been talking about she approached the young man with a delicious frankness of manner when she saw him there.

"Will you let me speak to you a moment or two, Mr. Brantain?" she asked with an engaging but perturbed smile. He seemed extremely unhappy; but when she took his arm and walked away with him, seeking a retired corner, a ray of hope mingled with the almost comical misery of his expression. She was apparently very outspoken.

"Perhaps I should not have sought this interview, Mr. Brantain; but—but, oh, I have been very uncomfortable, almost miserable since that little encounter the other afternoon. When I thought how you might have misinterpreted it, and believed things"—hope was plainly gaining the ascendancy over misery in Brantain's round, guileless face—"Of course, I know it is nothing to you, but for my own sake I do want you to understand that Mr. Harvy is an intimate friend of long standing. Why, we have always been like cousins—like brother and sister, I may say. He is my brother's most intimate associate and often fancies that he is entitled to the same privileges as the family. Oh, I know it is absurd, uncalled for, to tell you this; undignified even," she was almost weeping, "but it makes so much difference to me what you think of—of me." Her voice had grown very low and agitated. The misery had all disappeared from Brantain's face.

"Then you do really care what I think, Miss Nathalie? May I call you Miss Nathalie?" They turned into a long, dim corridor that was lined on either side with tall, graceful plants. They walked slowly to the very end of it. When they turned to retrace their steps Brantain's face was radiant and hers was triumphant.

Harvy was among the guests at the wedding; and he sought her out in a rare moment when she stood alone.

"Your husband," he said, smiling, "has sent me over to kiss you." 70

A quick blush suffused her face and round polished throat. "I suppose it's natural for a man to feel and act generously on an occasion of this kind. He tells me he doesn't want his marriage to interrupt wholly that pleasant intimacy which has existed between you and me. I don't know what you've been telling him," with an insolent smile, "but he has sent me here to kiss you." 75

She felt like a chess player who, by the clever handling of his pieces, sees the game taking the course intended. Her eyes were bright and tender with a smile as they glanced up into his; and her lips looked hungry for the kiss which they invited.

"But, you know," he went on quietly, "I didn't tell him so, it would have 80 seemed ungrateful, but I can tell you. I've stopped kissing women; it's dangerous." Well, she had Brantain and his million left. A person can't have everything in this world; and it was a little unreasonable of her to expect it.

31. The imagery in the opening paragraph creates what type of atmosphere?

(A) matrimonial
(B) tender
(C) morose
(D) solemn
(E) surreptitious

32. Brantain, as opposed to Harvy, is

(A) affectionate
(B) bold
(C) lustful
(D) meek
(E) forthright

33. Lines 15–17 reveal Nathalie's

(A) indifference
(B) ardor
(C) frankness
(D) opportunism
(E) venality

34. Characters are developed in part through
    I. descriptions of physical gestures that provide insight on their
       intentions and motivations
    II. idiosyncrasies in the dialogue between characters
    III. descriptions of light that hint at the character's intentions

    (A) I only
    (B) II only
    (C) II and III only
    (D) III only
    (E) I, II, and III

35. In context, Nathalie's "delicious frankness" of manner (line 45) implies

    (A) she is extremely frank
    (B) she is amorous toward Brantain
    (C) she is ambivalent about Braintain
    (D) she is genuinely remorseful
    (E) she is more wily than frank

36. The "privileges" mentioned in line 60 are meant to refer to

    (A) friendship
    (B) sharing secrets
    (C) familial intimacy
    (D) material comforts
    (E) marriage

37. Nathalie's speech to Brantain is notable for its use of all of the following
    except

    (A) a logical explanation
    (B) an admittance of her own wrongdoing
    (C) a tactful evasion to prevent Brantain's embarrassment
    (D) a display of intense emotion
    (E) an appeal to Brantain's ego

38. In context, the word "triumphant" (line 67) contributes most to

    (A) the passage's imagery
    (B) the characterization of Nathalie
    (C) the passage's tone
    (D) the characterization of Brantain
    (E) the passage's mood

39. The phrase "Her eyes were bright and tender with a smile . . . " (line 77) suggests that Nathalie

(A) is still thinking about Brantain
(B) is torn between her love for Brantain and for Harvy
(C) is interested primarily in Harvy's riches
(D) is guileful in her interactions with all men
(E) may have a genuinely romantic interest in Harvy

40. The simile in lines 76–77 coincides most with which other phrase?

(A) "Brantain's face was radiant and hers was triumphant" (67)
(B) "She was very handsome" (7)
(C) "'Don't touch me; don't come near me'" (35)
(D) "'but it makes so much difference to me what you think of—of me'" (61–62)
(E) "Her voice had grown very low and agitated" (62–63)

41. In the phrase "A person can't have everything in this world" (lines 82–83), the word "everything" refers to

(A) unrequited affection
(B) having every man's attention
(C) kissing Harvy
(D) having her emotional and financial needs met
(E) "Brantain and his million"

42. The narrative perspective in lines 82–83 is best described as that of

(A) an objective narrator
(B) a removed narrator
(C) most women of the time
(D) an omniscient narrator
(E) Nathalie

Passage 5. William Congreve, *The Way of the World: A Comedy* (1895)

Fainall, in love with Mrs. Marwood, married to Mrs. Fainall, daughter to Lady
Wishfort
Mirabell, in love with Mrs. Millamant
Witwoud, follower of Mrs. Millamant
Mrs. Millamant, a fine lady, niece to Lady Wishfort, and loves Mirabell   5
Sir Wilfull Witwoud, half-brother to Witwoud, and nephew to Lady Wishfort

MIRA.	What, is the chief of that noble family in town, Sir Wilfull Witwoud?
FAIN.	He is expected to-day. Do you know him?
MIRA.	I have seen him; he promises to be an extraordinary person. I think you have the honour to be related to him. 10
FAIN.	Yes; he is half-brother to this Witwoud by a former wife, who was sister to my Lady Wishfort, my wife's mother. If you marry Millamant, you must call cousins too.
MIRA.	I had rather be his relation than his acquaintance.
FAIN.	He comes to town in order to equip himself for travel. 15
MIRA.	For travel! Why the man that I mean is above forty.
FAIN.	No matter for that; 'tis for the honour of England that all Europe should know we have blockheads of all ages.
MIRA.	I wonder there is not an act of parliament to save the credit of the nation and prohibit the exportation of fools. 20
FAIN.	By no means, 'tis better as 'tis; 'tis better to trade with a little loss, than to be quite eaten up with being overstocked.
MIRA.	Pray, are the follies of this knight-errant and those of the squire, his brother, anything related?
FAIN.	Not at all: Witwoud grows by the knight like a medlar grafted on 25 a crab. One will melt in your mouth and t'other set your teeth on edge; one is all pulp and the other all core.
MIRA.	So one will be rotten before he be ripe, and the other will be rotten without ever being ripe at all.
FAIN.	Sir Wilfull is an odd mixture of bashfulness and obstinacy. But 30 when he's drunk, he's as loving as the monster in The Tempest, and much after the same manner. To give bother his due, he has something of good-nature, and does not always want wit.

MIRA.   Not always: but as often as his memory fails him and his commonplace of comparisons. He is a fool with a good memory and some   35
few scraps of other folks' wit. He is one whose conversation can
never be approved, yet it is now and then to be endured. He has
indeed one good quality: he is not exceptious, for he so passionately affects the reputation of understanding raillery that he will
construe an affront into a jest, and call downright rudeness and ill   40
language satire and fire.

FAIN.   If you have a mind to finish his picture, you have an opportunity
to do it at full length. Behold the original.

43.   Fainall's comment in lines 17–18 (" 'tis for the honour of England . . . all
ages") is best interpreted as

(A)   a euphemism for his antipathy toward Sir Wilfull Witwoud
(B)   a genuine comment on the benefits of travel outside of England
(C)   a guileful way of criticizing his nation's policies
(D)   a sardonic comment that reveals his low opinion of a distant relative
(E)   symbolic of his complicated feelings toward an acquaintance

44.   The words "credit" (line 19), "exportation" (line 20), "trade" (line 21),
"loss" (line 21), and "overstocked"(line 22) are used in the passage to

(A)   lend credibility to the characters' opinions about their nation's affairs
(B)   provide background information about Sir Wilfull Witwoud
(C)   symbolically hint at the political and economic views of Fainall and
Mirabell
(D)   suggest that Sir Wilfull Witwoud is not deserving of his nobility
(E)   develop a metaphor that humorously conveys how two characters
view another

45.   Which best conveys the effect of the sentences in lines 25–27 ("Witwoud
grows by the knight . . . the other all core")?

(A)   A comparison between two unlike things emphasizes the differences
between two brothers' flaws.
(B)   A simile comparing Witwoud to a knight underscores Fainall's high
impression of him.
(C)   Figurative language illustrates the similarities between two brothers
who each have uniquely admirable qualities.
(D)   A metaphor implies that one brother is far superior to the other.
(E)   Fainall employs imagery and allusions to soften the tone of his critical
response to Mirabell's question.

46. Sir Wilfull Witwoud is portrayed as all of the following *except*

(A) irritating
(B) connected in useful or important ways
(C) clever
(D) redeemable
(E) tolerable

47. Regarding Sir Wilfull Witwoud's "wit" (lines 33, 36), Fainall and Mirabell

(A) completely agree that his sense of humor is lacking
(B) slightly disagree; Fainall believes he can be witty, but Mirabell believes he never is
(C) somewhat agree that he has some sense of wit, but Mirabell believes he barely comprehends raillery
(D) completely disagree; Fainall defends his relative's generous sense of humor while Mirabell thoroughly criticizes it
(E) agree that he can be hilarious in the right circumstances

48. The opportunity to "finish his picture . . . at full length" (lines 42–43) most nearly means

(A) Sir Wilfull Witwoud is approaching now, so Mirabell can confirm and develop his impressions even further
(B) Mirabell will get a different picture of Sir Wilfull Witwoud when he meets him in person
(C) Fainall believes Mirabell's negative impressions of his esteemed relative will be corrected upon Sir Wilfull Witwoud's imminent arrival
(D) Fainall warns Mirabell not to judge Sir Wilfull Witwoud before he meets him
(E) the honorable man himself is here for Mirabell to praise in person

49. In context of the passage as a whole, the tone of the phrases "chief of that noble family" (line 7), "extraordinary person" (line 9), and "honour to be related" (line 10), can best be described as

(A) playful but envious
(B) somewhat sarcastic
(C) genuine admiration
(D) belittling
(E) fully sardonic

50. The passage can best be described as

    (A) a social critique of noble families

    (B) a conversation between friends that quickly turns oppositional

    (C) two friends exchanging witty banter about a shared acquaintance

    (D) an indirect but thorough introduction to an important figure

    (E) a disagreement about the merits and flaws of a shared acquaintance

Passage 6. Hannah Cowley, "The Belle's Strategem"

Enter Courtall *singing.*

SAVILLE.   Ha, Courtall!—Bid him keep the horses in motion, and then enquire at all the chambers round.

                                                           [Exit servant.]

    What the devil brings you to this part of the town?—Have any of   5
the Long Robes, handsome wives, sisters or chambermaids?

COURTALL.   Perhaps they have;—but I came on a different errand; and, had thy good fortune brought thee here half an hour sooner, I'd have given thee such a treat, ha! ha! ha!

SAV.   I'm sorry I miss'd it: what was it?   10

COURT.   I was informed a few days since, that my cousins Fallow were come to town, and desired earnestly to see me at their lodgings in Warwick-Court, Holborn. Away drove I, painting them all the way as so many Hebes. They came from the farthest part of Northumberland, had never been in town, and in course were made up of   15
rusticity, innocence, and beauty.

SAV.   Well!

COURT.   After waiting thirty minutes, during which there was a violent bustle, in bounced five fallow damsels, four of them maypoles;—the fifth, Nature, by way of variety, had bent in the Æsop style.—   20
But they all opened at once, like hounds on a fresh scent:—"Oh, cousin Courtall!—How do you do, cousin Courtall! Lord, cousin, I am glad you are come! We want you to go with us to the Park, and the Plays, and the Opera, and Almack's, and all the fine places!"——The devil, thought I, my dears, may attend you, for I   25
am sure I won't.—However, I heroically stayed an hour with them, and discovered, the virgins were all come to town with the hopes of leaving it—Wives:—their heads full of Knight-Baronights, Fops, and adventures.

SAV.   Well, how did you get off?   30

COURT.   Oh, pleaded a million engagements.——However, conscience twitched me; so I breakfasted with them this morning, and afterwards 'squired them to the gardens here, as the most private place in town; and then took a sorrowful leave, complaining of my hard, hard fortune, that obliged me to set off immediately for   35 Dorsetshire, ha! ha! ha!

SAV.   I congratulate your escape!—Courtall at Almack's, with five aukward country cousins! ha! ha! ha!—Why, your existence, as a Man of Gallantry, could never have survived it.

COURT.   Death, and fire! had they come to town, like the rustics of the   40 last age, to see Paul's, the Lions, and the Wax-work—at their service;—but the cousins of our days come up Ladies—and, with the knowledge they glean from magazines and pocket-books, Fine Ladies; laugh at the bashfulness of their grandmothers, and boldly demand their *entrées* in the first circles.   45

51.   In context, Courtall's phrase "painting them" (line 13) is best paraphrased as

(A)   disparaging them
(B)   imagining them
(C)   designing them
(D)   creating them
(E)   avoiding them

52.   In context, Courtall's use of the term "Hebes" (line 14) is meant

(A)   positively
(B)   malevolently
(C)   ignorantly
(D)   lovingly
(E)   derisively

53. Which of the following lines provides a significant contrast to Courtall's initial expectations of his cousins in lines 14–16 ("They came from . . . beauty")?

    I. "boldly demand their *entrées* in the first circles" (44–45)
   II. "I breakfasted with them this morning, and afterwards 'squired them to the gardens here" (32–33)
  III. "five fallow damsels, four of them maypoles" (19)

    (A) I only
    (B) I and II only
    (C) III only
    (D) II and III only
    (E) I and III only

54. In context of the passage as a whole, Courtall's use of the word "fallow" (line 11) in reference to his cousins can be interpreted to mean both

    (A) virginal and moral
    (B) lustful and uncouth
    (C) spirited and disciplined
    (D) unmarried and rustic
    (E) unrefined and dirty

55. In the passage as a whole, Courtall's cousins are characterized as all of the following *except*

    (A) opportunistic
    (B) country dwellers
    (C) demure
    (D) aspirational
    (E) audacious

56. It can be interpreted that "Almack's" (lines 24, 37) must be

    (A) a casual gathering space for everyone in town
    (B) a secluded place in the country
    (C) a city place perfect for visitors from the country
    (D) an exclusive and refined place
    (E) a tourist trap

57. Which of the following phrases suggests insincerity?
    I. "Man of Gallantry" (39)
    II. "my hard, hard fortune" (35)
    III. "Fine Ladies" (43–44)

    (A) I only
    (B) II only
    (C) I and II only
    (D) III only
    (E) I, II, and III

58. In contrast to the places mentioned in line 24 ("the Park, and the Plays, and the Opera, and Almack's"), the places mentioned in lines 41 ("Paul's . . .") are most likely preferred by Courtall because

    (A) they are easy to get to
    (B) they have free admission
    (C) they are better suited to rustic visitors
    (D) they are public places
    (E) they are tourist traps

59. An example of Courtall's sincerity is found in which of the following phrases?

    (A) "I'd have given thee such a treat" (8–9)
    (B) "I heroically stayed an hour" (26)
    (C) "took a sorrowful leave" (34)
    (D) "pleaded a million engagements" (31)
    (E) "conscience twitched me" (31–32)

60. Courtall most likely chooses "the most private place in town" (lines 33–34) because

    (A) he prefers privacy
    (B) he knows his cousins will prefer an isolated setting
    (C) he does not want his cousins to meet men in the city
    (D) he is concerned for his reputation
    (E) he is concerned about safety

61. Based on Courtall's comparison (lines 40–45) between "cousins of our day" and "rustics of the last age," Courtall has a clear preference for

    (A) social mobility
    (B) "Fine Ladies" (43–44)
    (C) cosmopolitanism
    (D) sightseeing
    (E) timidity

62. Which of the following best articulates the primary source of humor in the scene?

    (A) Courtall and Saville's joint distaste for rustic girls
    (B) Courtall's commentary on "rustics of the last age" (40–41)
    (C) Courtall's depictions of his gauche cousins
    (D) the cousins' country background
    (E) Courtall's successful escape

63. Saville's role in the conversation is most similar to that of

    (A) a concerned friend
    (B) a commiserating acquaintance
    (C) an intimidating peer
    (D) a toadying admirer
    (E) a pitying relative

Passage 7. Fyodor Dostoyevsky, *Crime and Punishment*

On an exceptionally hot evening early in July a young man came out of the garret in which he lodged in S. Place and walked slowly, as though in hesitation, towards K. bridge.

He had successfully avoided meeting his landlady on the staircase. His garret was under the roof of a high, five-storied house and was more like a cupboard   5
than a room. The landlady who provided him with garret, dinners, and attendance, lived on the floor below, and every time he went out he was obliged to pass her kitchen, the door of which invariably stood open. And each time he passed, the young man had a sick, frightened feeling, which made him scowl and feel ashamed. He was hopelessly in debt to his landlady, and was afraid of   10
meeting her.

This was not because he was cowardly and abject, quite the contrary; but for some time past he had been in an overstrained irritable condition, verging on hypochondria. He had become so completely absorbed in himself, and isolated from his fellows that he dreaded meeting, not only his landlady, but anyone at   15
all. He was crushed by poverty, but the anxieties of his position had of late ceased to weigh upon him. He had given up attending to matters of practical importance; he had lost all desire to do so. Nothing that any landlady could do had a real terror for him. But to be stopped on the stairs, to be forced to listen to her trivial, irrelevant gossip, to pestering demands for payment, threats and com-   20
plaints, and to rack his brains for excuses, to prevaricate, to lie—no, rather than that, he would creep down the stairs like a cat and slip out unseen.

This evening, however, on coming out into the street, he became acutely aware of his fears.

"I want to attempt a thing like that and am frightened by these trifles," he   25
thought, with an odd smile. "Hm . . . yes, all is in a man's hands and he lets it all
slip from cowardice, that's an axiom. It would be interesting to know what it is
men are most afraid of. Taking a new step, uttering a new word is what they fear
most . . . . But I am talking too much. It's because I chatter that I do nothing.
Or perhaps it is that I chatter because I do nothing. I've learned to chatter this   30
last month, lying for days together in my den thinking . . . of Jack the Giant-
killer. Why am I going there now? Am I capable of that? Is that serious? It is not
serious at all. It's simply a fantasy to amuse myself; a plaything! Yes, maybe it is a
plaything."

The heat in the street was terrible: and the airlessness, the bustle and the   35
plaster, scaffolding, bricks, and dust all about him, and that special Petersburg
stench, so familiar to all who are unable to get out of town in summer—all
worked painfully upon the young man's already overwrought nerves. The
insufferable stench from the pot-houses, which are particularly numerous in that
part of the town, and the drunken men whom he met continually, although it   40
was a working day, completed the revolting misery of the picture. An expression
of the profoundest disgust gleamed for a moment in the young man's refined
face. He was, by the way, exceptionally handsome, above the average in height,
slim, well-built, with beautiful dark eyes and dark brown hair. Soon he sank into
deep thought, or more accurately speaking into a complete blankness of mind;   45
he walked along not observing what was about him and not caring to observe
it. From time to time, he would mutter something, from the habit of talking to
himself, to which he had just confessed. At these moments he would become
conscious that his ideas were sometimes in a tangle and that he was very weak;
for two days he had scarcely tasted food.   50

64. The primary function of the sentence in lines 10–11 ("He was hopelessly . . .
    meeting her") is
    (A) to repeat key information
    (B) to speculate
    (C) to pose a theory
    (D) to provide context
    (E) to characterize the landlady

65. The third paragraph differs from the second in that
    (A) the third paragraph refutes the analysis introduced in the second
        paragraph
    (B) the third paragraph responds to a question raised in the second
        paragraph
    (C) the third paragraph focuses on characterizing the protagonist's
        emotional state
    (D) the third paragraph mentions a character that the second does not
    (E) the third paragraph's tone is melancholy

66. The protagonist's avoidance of his landlady is eventually attributed (in the third paragraph) to
    (A) his abject poverty
    (B) the terror the landlady inspires
    (C) a sense of shame
    (D) his self-absorption
    (E) his crippling fear

67. What is the "axiom" the protagonist refers to in line 27?
    (A) that men lose their minds because of their cowardice
    (B) that a man's cowardice causes him to squander opportunities
    (C) careful consideration of consequences leads to intelligent action
    (D) his conjecture that doing nothing causes him to chatter
    (E) his conjecture that chatter prevents him from doing things

68. The two sentences in lines 29–30 ("It's because I chatter that I do nothing. Or perhaps it is that I chatter because I do nothing") are
    (A) chiastic and reveal the protagonist's self-doubt
    (B) axiomatic and reveal an eternal truth
    (C) veracious and provide commentary on the times
    (D) hyperbolic and suggest the tone is satirical
    (E) delusional and characterize the protagonist as absurd

69. The words "there," "that," and "It" in line 32 do all of the following *except*
    (A) provoke curiosity
    (B) characterize the protagonist's reluctance and fear
    (C) elucidate the protagonist's desires
    (D) create a sense of mystery
    (E) hide the protagonist's actual fantasy from the reader

70. The description of the setting serves to
    I. provide justification for the protagonist's feelings
    II. develop the overall tone of misery
    III. critique the government of "Petersburg"
    (A) I only
    (B) I and II only
    (C) II and III only
    (D) I and III
    (E) III only

71. In the final paragraph, a contrast is established between

    (A) beauty and ugliness
    (B) rich and poor
    (C) cleanliness and filth
    (D) good and evil
    (E) hunger and satiation

72. The protagonist is described as all of the following *except*

    (A) emotionally detached
    (B) distinctive
    (C) unwell
    (D) destitute
    (E) bold

73. The narrator's tone can best be described as

    (A) observant
    (B) gently disapproving
    (C) aloof
    (D) pitying
    (E) empathetic

74. The passage provides answers to all of the following questions *except*

    (A) Why does the protagonist avoid his landlady?
    (B) Why is the protagonist physically weak?
    (C) What precisely is the protagonist fearful of doing?
    (D) How does the protagonist feel about his environment?
    (E) How does the protagonist look?

Passage 8. Euripides, *Medea*

MEDEA. From the house I have come forth, Corinthian ladies, for fear lest
you be blaming me; for well I know that amongst men many by
showing pride have gotten them an ill name and a reputation for
indifference, both those who shun men's gaze and those who move
amid the stranger crowd, and likewise they who choose a quiet   5
walk in life. For there is no just discernment in the eyes of men, for
they, or ever they have surely learnt their neighbour's heart, loathe
him at first sight, though never wronged by him; and so a stranger
most of all should adopt a city's views; nor do I commend that
citizen, who, in the stubbornness of his heart, from churlishness   10
resents the city's will.

But on me hath fallen this unforeseen disaster, and sapped my life; ruined I am, and long to resign the boon of existence, kind friends, and die. For he who was all the world to me, as well thou knowest, hath turned out the worst of men, my own husband. Of all things 15
that have life and sense we women are the most hapless creatures; first must we buy a husband at a great price, and o'er ourselves a tyrant set which is an evil worse than the first; and herein lies the most important issue, whether our choice be good or bad. For divorce is not honourable to women, nor can we disown our lords. 20
Next must the wife, coming as she does to ways and customs new, since she hath not learnt the lesson in her home, have a diviner's eye to see how best to treat the partner of her life. If haply we perform these tasks with thoroughness and tact, and the husband live with us, without resenting the yoke, our life is a happy one; if 25
not, 'twere best to die. But when a man is vexed with what he finds indoors, he goeth forth and rids his soul of its disgust, betaking him to some friend or comrade of like age; whilst we must needs regard his single self.

And yet they say we live secure at home, while they are at the 30
wars, with their sorry reasoning, for I would gladly take my stand in battle array three times o'er, than once give birth. But enough! this language suits not thee as it does me; thou hast a city here, a father's house, some joy in life, and friends to share thy thoughts, but I am destitute, without a city, and therefore scorned by my 35
husband, a captive I from a foreign shore, with no mother, brother, or kinsman in whom to find a new haven of refuge from this calamity. Wherefore this one boon and only this I wish to win from thee, thy silence, if haply I can some way or means devise to avenge me on my husband for this cruel treatment, and on the 40
man who gave to him his daughter, and on her who is his wife. For though woman be timorous enough in all else, and as regards courage, a coward at the mere sight of steel, yet in the moment she finds her honour wronged, no heart is filled with deadlier thoughts than hers. 45

75. According to the first paragraph, Medea has come out of her house

(A) because she is fearless
(B) to criticize the lack of justice among men
(C) to show her pride
(D) to mitigate the people's judgment of her
(E) because she fears the town's wrath

76. According to Medea, why is there "no just discernment in the eyes of men" (line 6)?

     I. because people hold grudges against those who have wronged them
     II. because people resent the city's will
     III. because people form immutable opinions of people they may not even know

    (A) I only
    (B) II only
    (C) III only
    (D) I and III only
    (E) I, II, and III

77. How does the second paragraph differ from the first?

    (A) The first is addressed to women and the second to men.
    (B) The first introduces the topic that the second develops.
    (C) The first poses a question that the second attempts to answer.
    (D) The first is general, and the second is specific.
    (E) The first is a diatribe, and the second is a justification.

78. Which of the following best describes the structure of Medea's commentary on womens' lives?

    (A) a list of complaints in no logical order
    (B) a side-by-side comparison of the experiences of men and women
    (C) a thesis statement, followed by reasons, examples, a counter-argument, and a rebuttal
    (D) hyperbolic descriptions of hardship tempered by optimism
    (E) a catalogue of misfortunes listed in order of importance

79. According to lines 15–29, Media believes marital bliss would initially depend mostly on

    (A) a woman's skill in pleasing her finicky husband
    (B) the support of friends and family
    (C) societal approval of divorce
    (D) fate
    (E) true love

80. What does Medea suggest are the differences between the lives of men and women?

    I. Men have easy access to camaraderie but women do not
    II. Men do not have to suffer as much physical pain as women
    III. Men have authority while women are expected to be servile

    (A) I only
    (B) I and III only
    (C) II only
    (D) II and III only
    (E) I, II, and III

81. Medea cites all of the following as examples of women being "hapless" (line 16) *except*

    (A) their forced isolation from "some friend or comrade of like age" (28)
    (B) the fact that they have to "buy a husband" (17)
    (C) the fact that they have to raise children
    (D) their submission to their husbands
    (E) the fact that they cannot be unfettered

82. Which of the following best describes the function of the phrase "And yet" (line 30)?

    (A) It anticipates a counter-argument that will be addressed.
    (B) It indicates a digression.
    (C) It signals a rebuttal.
    (D) It foreshadows a qualifier for the previous argument.
    (E) It disrupts the flow of the otherwise coherent argument.

83. The phrase "But enough!" (line 32) can best be paraphrased as

    (A) Sorry to have wasted your time!
    (B) Do not disagree!
    (C) Let me get to my main point!
    (D) But I digress!
    (E) Stop distracting me!

84. Medea distinguishes herself from the other women by

    (A) describing their families
    (B) comparing their husbands
    (C) insisting on their silence
    (D) assuming they have all that she lacks
    (E) listing what she has that they lack

85. According to Medea, when a woman "finds her honour wronged" (line 44), she
    (A) relinquishes her honor
    (B) is overcome with resilience
    (C) fears the sight of steel
    (D) questions her values
    (E) is consumed by thoughts of revenge

86. The passage closes on a note of
    (A) hopelessness
    (B) optimism
    (C) cruelty
    (D) moralism
    (E) indecision

87. Based on the passage, all of the following describe how Medea views herself
    except
    (A) not responsible for her current predicament
    (B) innately courageous
    (C) worthy of sympathy
    (D) victimized
    (E) alienated

Passage 9. Gustave Flaubert, *Madame Bovary*

We were in class when the head-master came in, followed by a "new fellow,"
not wearing the school uniform, and a school servant carrying a large desk. Those
who had been asleep woke up, and every one rose as if just surprised at his work.

The head-master made a sign to us to sit down. Then, turning to the class-
master, he said to him in a low voice: 5

"Monsieur Roger, here is a pupil whom I recommend to your care; he'll be
in the second. If his work and conduct are satisfactory, he will go into one of the
upper classes, as becomes his age."

The "new fellow," standing in the corner behind the door so that he could
hardly be seen, was a country lad of about fifteen, and taller than any of us. His   10
hair was cut square on his forehead like a village chorister's; he looked reliable,
but very ill at ease. Although he was not broad-shouldered, his short school jacket
of green cloth with black buttons must have been tight about the armholes, and
showed at the opening of the cuffs red wrists accustomed to being bare. His
legs, in blue stockings, looked out from beneath yellow trousers, drawn tight by   15
braces. He wore stout, ill-cleaned, hobnailed boots.

We began repeating the lesson. He listened with all his ears, as attentive as if
at a sermon, not daring even to cross his legs or lean on his elbow; and when at

two o'clock the bell rang, the master was obliged to tell him to fall into line with
the rest of us.   20

When we came back to work, we were in the habit of throwing our caps on
the floor so as to have our hands more free; we used from the door to toss them
under the form, so that they hit against the wall and made a lot of dust: it was
"the thing."

But, whether he had not noticed the trick, or did not dare to attempt it, the   25
"new fellow" was still holding his cap on his knees even after prayers were over.
It was one of those head-gears of composite order, in which we can find traces of
the bearskin, shako, billycock hat, sealskin cap, and cotton nightcap; one of those
poor things, in fine, whose dumb ugliness has depths of expression, like an imbe-
cile's face. Oval, stiffened with whalebone, it began with three round knobs; then   30
came in succession lozenges of velvet and rabbit-skin separated by a red band;
after that a sort of bag that ended in a cardboard polygon covered with complicated braiding, from which hung, at the end of a long, thin cord, small twisted
gold threads in the manner of a tassel. The cap was new; its peak shone.

88. The passage implies that the narrator and his peers view their time at
    school as
    (A) wasteful
    (B) essential
    (C) a privilege
    (D) an exclusive right
    (E) habitual

89. The narrator most likely describes the new fellow's attire (lines 12–16) to
    emphasize
    (A) that he does not want to be there
    (B) how he does not fit in
    (C) how varied the available school uniforms are
    (D) how apprehensive the new fellow is
    (E) that he appears to have academic potential

90. Lines 17–20 ("We began . . . rest of us") imply
    (A) the new fellow is misbehaving
    (B) the new fellow is difficult
    (C) the new fellow is conscientious
    (D) the new fellow is an outcast
    (E) the narrator is belittling the new fellow

91. The phrase "'the thing'" (line 24) is in quotation marks because
    (A) it is part of a dialogue
    (B) it is an idiomatic expression
    (C) it is sarcastic
    (D) it is ironic
    (E) it is being mocked

92. The detailed description of the new fellow's cap (lines 25–34)
    (A) highlights similarities between the new fellow and others
    (B) suggests it is symbolic of the new fellow himself
    (C) emphasizes the new fellow's piety
    (D) is intended purely to ridicule the new fellow
    (E) highlights a motif of the passage

93. Which of the following best conveys the effect created in the final sentence?
    (A) A concise, direct, compound sentence draws attention to the cap's significance.
    (B) A paradox casts doubt on earlier descriptions.
    (C) A contradiction provokes curiosity about the new fellow.
    (D) The redundant description of the cap belabors a point.
    (E) Florid language summarizes the precise details provided in the previous sentence.

94. Which of the following describes the primary purpose of the passage?
      I. to portray the culture of a specific school
     II. to provide insight into class differences
    III. to portray a character through others' observations
    (A) I and III only
    (B) II and III only
    (C) III only
    (D) I and II only
    (E) I, II, and III

95. The narrator of the passage is best described as
    (A) an unreliable witness
    (B) a charming raconteur
    (C) a sanctimonious moralizer
    (D) an unfair biographer
    (E) a subjective onlooker

96. In the passage, the new fellow differs from the narrator in all of the following ways *except*

(A) his attire
(B) his height
(C) his deportment
(D) his environment
(E) his interests

Passage 10. Nathaniel Hawthorne, *The Scarlet Letter*

It may seem marvellous that, with the world before her—kept by no restrictive clause of her condemnation within the limits of the Puritan settlement, so remote and so obscure—free to return to her birth-place, or to any other European land, and there hide her character and identity under a new exterior, as completely as if emerging into another state of being—and having also the passes   5
of the dark, inscrutable forest open to her, where the wildness of her nature might assimilate itself with a people whose customs and life were alien from the law that had condemned her—it may seem marvellous that this woman should still call that place her home, where, and where only, she must needs be the type of shame. But there is a fatality, a feeling so irresistible and inevitable that it has   10
the force of doom, which almost invariably compels human beings to linger around and haunt, ghost-like, the spot where some great and marked event has given the colour to their lifetime; and, still the more irresistibly, the darker the tinge that saddens it. Her sin, her ignominy, were the roots which she had struck into the soil. It was as if a new birth, with stronger assimilations than the   15
first, had converted the forest-land, still so uncongenial to every other pilgrim and wanderer, into Hester Prynne's wild and dreary, but life-long home. All other scenes of earth—even that village of rural England, where happy infancy and stainless maidenhood seemed yet to be in her mother's keeping, like garments put off long ago—were foreign to her, in comparison. The chain that bound her here   20
was of iron links, and galling to her inmost soul, but could never be broken.

It might be, too—doubtless it was so, although she hid the secret from herself, and grew pale whenever it struggled out of her heart, like a serpent from its hole—it might be that another feeling kept her within the scene and pathway that had been so fatal. There dwelt, there trode, the feet of one with whom she   25
deemed herself connected in a union that, unrecognised on earth, would bring them together before the bar of final judgment, and make that their marriage-altar, for a joint futurity of endless retribution. Over and over again, the tempter of souls had thrust this idea upon Hester's contemplation, and laughed at the passionate and desperate joy with which she seized, and then strove to cast it   30
from her. She barely looked the idea in the face, and hastened to bar it in its dungeon. What she compelled herself to believe—what, finally, she reasoned upon as her motive for continuing a resident of New England—was half a truth, and half

a self-delusion. Here, she said to herself had been the scene of her guilt, and here
should be the scene of her earthly punishment; and so, perchance, the torture   35
of her daily shame would at length purge her soul, and work out another purity
than that which she had lost: more saint-like, because the result of martyrdom.

97. In context, "marvellous" (line 1) means

    (A) grand
    (B) hyperbolic
    (C) splendid
    (D) appropriate
    (E) baffling

98. The clauses set apart in dashes in lines 1–10 serve primarily to

    (A) distract the reader from the subject of the sentence
    (B) present a character as unstable
    (C) cast doubt upon the reliability of the narrator
    (D) elucidate the alternative possibilities to a problem
    (E) explain the reasons for a character's choice

99. The speaker immediately follows up on the idea expressed in lines 1–10
with

    (A) skepticism
    (B) a personal anecdote
    (C) a generality about human nature
    (D) irrefutable counter-evidence
    (E) increased uncertainty

100. For Hester, the "marked event" mentioned in line 12 is later suggested to be

    (A) the sighting of a ghost
    (B) a transgression committed with someone else
    (C) "a new birth" (15)
    (D) her "secret" (22)
    (E) being bound by chains

101. Which of the following describes an effect of the figurative language in lines 14–21 ("Her sin . . . broken")?
  I. Metaphors help develop a theory of why Hester has chosen to stay in "that place" (9).
  II. Similes help portray "that place" (9) as more suitable than Hester's childhood home.
  III. Symbolic comparisons prove the narrator's theories about Hester's decision.

(A) I and II only
(B) I and III only
(C) II and III only
(D) III only
(E) I, II, and III

102. The second paragraph differs from the first in that it introduces Hester's

(A) fatality
(B) sin
(C) predicament
(D) chosen setting
(E) private justifications

103. In the phrase "the feet of one" in line 25, "one" refers to

(A) Hester's child
(B) Hester's mother
(C) the tempter of souls
(D) Hester's husband
(E) Hester's accomplice

104. The second paragraph suggests that Hester Prynne stays in New England because

(A) she has been exiled from her home
(B) she is ambivalent
(C) it is better than her birth-place
(D) she longs for eventual absolution
(E) it has been the most important place in her life

105. The laughable secret described in the second paragraph is best summarized
as

(A) Hester's sincere atonement for her crime
(B) Hester's twisted attempt at a kind of marriage with her accomplice
(C) Hester's expectation that she will be forgiven if she remains at the site
of her crime
(D) Hester's sense that her punishment is unwarranted
(E) Hester's hope that she can escape and return to her birth-place

106. The phrase "marriage-altar" (line 27) is used

(A) incorrectly; Hester is not getting married
(B) appropriately; Hester dreams of marrying despite her sin
(C) cruelly; Hester's chances of marrying are doomed
(D) symbolically; it represents the life she could have had
(E) metaphorically; it refers to an unconventional but meaningful union

107. The narrator's attitude toward Hester can best be described as

(A) condescending
(B) critical
(C) doting
(D) intrigued
(E) aloof

Passage 11. Mary Shelley, *Frankenstein*

There was a considerable difference between the ages of my parents, but
this circumstance seemed to unite them only closer in bonds of devoted affection. There was a sense of justice in my father's upright mind which rendered it
necessary that he should approve highly to love strongly. Perhaps during former
years he had suffered from the late-discovered unworthiness of one beloved   5
and so was disposed to set a greater value on tried worth. There was a show of
gratitude and worship in his attachment to my mother, differing wholly from
the doting fondness of age, for it was inspired by reverence for her virtues and
a desire to be the means of, in some degree, recompensing her for the sorrows
she had endured, but which gave inexpressible grace to his behaviour to her.   10
Everything was made to yield to her wishes and her convenience. He strove to
shelter her, as a fair exotic is sheltered by the gardener, from every rougher wind
and to surround her with all that could tend to excite pleasurable emotion in her
soft and benevolent mind. Her health, and even the tranquillity of her hitherto
constant spirit, had been shaken by what she had gone through. During the two   15
years that had elapsed previous to their marriage my father had gradually relin-
quished all his public functions; and immediately after their union they sought
the pleasant climate of Italy, and the change of scene and interest attendant on a
tour through that land of wonders, as a restorative for her weakened frame.

From Italy they visited Germany and France. I, their eldest child, was born at   20
Naples, and as an infant accompanied them in their rambles. I remained for several years their only child. Much as they were attached to each other, they seemed
to draw inexhaustible stores of affection from a very mine of love to bestow
them upon me. My mother's tender caresses and my father's smile of benevolent
pleasure while regarding me are my first recollections. I was their plaything and   25
their idol, and something better—their child, the innocent and helpless creature
bestowed on them by heaven, whom to bring up to good, and whose future lot
it was in their hands to direct to happiness or misery, according as they fulfilled
their duties towards me. With this deep consciousness of what they owed towards
the being to which they had given life, added to the active spirit of tenderness that   30
animated both, it may be imagined that while during every hour of my infant life
I received a lesson of patience, of charity, and of self-control, I was so guided by
a silken cord that all seemed but one train of enjoyment to me. For a long time
I was their only care. My mother had much desired to have a daughter, but I
continued their single offspring. When I was about five years old, while making   35
an excursion beyond the frontiers of Italy, they passed a week on the shores of the
Lake of Como. Their benevolent disposition often made them enter the cottages
of the poor. This, to my mother, was more than a duty; it was a necessity, a passion —remembering what she had suffered, and how she had been relieved—for
her to act in her turn the guardian angel to the afflicted. During one of their   40
walks a poor cot in the foldings of a vale attracted their notice as being singularly
disconsolate, while the number of half-clothed children gathered about it spoke
of penury in its worst shape. One day, when my father had gone by himself to
Milan, my mother, accompanied by me, visited this abode. She found a peas-
ant and his wife, hard working, bent down by care and labour, distributing a   45
scanty meal to five hungry babes. Among these there was one which attracted my
mother far above all the rest. She appeared of a different stock. The four others
were dark-eyed, hardy little vagrants; this child was thin and very fair. Her hair
was the brightest living gold, and despite the poverty of her clothing, seemed
to set a crown of distinction on her head. Her brow was clear and ample, her   50
blue eyes cloudless, and her lips and the moulding of her face so expressive of
sensibility and sweetness that none could behold her without looking on her as
of a distinct species, a being heaven-sent, and bearing a celestial stamp in all her
features.

108. The passage implies that the father's behavior and attitude toward the
mother is due to all of the following *except*

(A) the desire to be useful
(B) the mother's reverential virtues
(C) the considerable difference between their ages
(D) the mother's frailty
(E) his habit of loving unconditionally

109. The mother is primarily presented as

(A) demanding of her husband's complete devotion
(B) captivating because of her youth and virtue
(C) dependent on children for happiness
(D) benevolent despite her hardships
(E) partial to beauty

110. The simile in line 12 characterizes

(A) the mother as needy
(B) the mother as distinguished
(C) the father as nurturing
(D) the mother as a child
(E) the father as officious

111. What is the relationship between the first and second paragraphs?

(A) The first asks questions that the second answers.
(B) The first poses theories that the second explores.
(C) The second belies assumptions made in the first.
(D) The first provides background for comprehension of the second.
(E) The first sparks curiosity that the second satisfies.

112. The metaphor in lines 22–24 ("Much as they were . . . upon me") gives particular emphasis to

(A) the parents' infinite capacity to love
(B) the parents' industriousness
(C) the parents' economic class
(D) the speaker's importance in the family
(E) the hierarchy within the family

113. The word "idol" in line 26 implies that

(A) the parents saw religious power in their child
(B) the child is like a prophet
(C) the parents admire their child
(D) the speaker is arrogant
(E) the parents worship their child

114. The effect of the sentence in lines 29–33 ("With this deep . . . to me") can best be described by which of the following?

   (A) An allegory draws parallels between the parents' devotion and a train.
   (B) It is a delusional statement about the parents' affection.
   (C) A developed anecdote illustrates a specific example of the narrator's privileged childhood.
   (D) A series of dependent clauses highlights the numerous factors contributing to the narrator's "train of enjoyment" (33).
   (E) A metaphor suggests the parents exercised excessive influence on the narrator.

115. The memory of visiting the abode (lines 44–54) is most likely included to

   (A) contrast the narrator's family with those less fortunate
   (B) complicate the otherwise generous portrayal of the narrator's mother
   (C) imply that the narrator is resentful of his mother's relationship with the girl in the abode
   (D) highlight yet another example of the mother's virtue
   (E) explain the origins of how the family encounters someone who may play a pivotal role in their lives

116. The girl described in lines 46–54 is characterized as

   I. conspicuous
   II. otherworldly
   III. evocative

   (A) I only
   (B) I and II only
   (C) II only
   (D) I and III only
   (E) I, II, and III

117. The narrator's tone can be described as

   (A) grave
   (B) factual
   (C) earnest
   (D) resentful
   (E) objective

118. The passage can best be described as

(A) an adult reminiscing about fond childhood memories

(B) a psychological consideration of one's childhood trauma

(C) a subjective portrayal of a typical middle-class family during a certain time period

(D) a reflection on one's family origins and relationships

(E) an example of an obsessive and somewhat suffocating approach to parenting

Passage 12. Jonathan Swift, *Gulliver's Travels*

One morning, about a fortnight after I had obtained my liberty, Reldresal, principal secretary (as they style him) for private affairs, came to my house, attended only by one servant. He ordered his coach to wait at a distance, and desired I would give him an hour's audience; which I readily consented to, on account of his quality and personal merits, as well as of the many good offices he had done me during my solicitations at court. I offered to lie down, that he might the more conveniently reach my ear; but he chose rather to let me hold him in my hand during our conversation.

He began with compliments on my liberty; said he might pretend to some merit in it. But however, added, that if it had not been for the present situation of things at court, perhaps I might not have obtained it so soon. For, said he, as flourishing a condition as we may appear to be in to foreigners, we labor under two mighty evils: a violent faction at home, and the danger of an invasion, by a most potent enemy, from abroad. As to the first, you are to understand, that, for above seventy moons past, there have been two struggling parties in this empire, under the names of *Tramecksan* and *Slamecksan*, from the high and low heels of their shoes, by which they distinguish themselves. It is alleged, indeed, that the high heels are most agreeable to our ancient constitution; but, however this may be, his majesty hath determined to make use only of low heels in the administration of the government, and all offices in the gift of the crown, as you cannot but observe: and particularly, that his majesty's imperial heels are lower, at least by a *drurr*, than any of his court (*drurr* is a measure about the fourteenth part of an inch). The animosities between these two parties run so high, that they will neither eat nor drink nor talk with each other. We compute the *Tramecksan*, or high heels, to exceed us in number; but the power is wholly on our side. We apprehend his imperial highness, the heir to the crown, to have some tendency towards the high heels; at least, we can plainly discover that one of his heels is higher than the other, which gives him a hobble in his gait. Now, in the midst of these intestine disquiets, we are threatened with an invasion from the island of Blefuscu, which is the other great empire of the universe, almost as large and powerful as this of his majesty. For, as to what we have heard you affirm, that there are other kingdoms and states in the world, inhabited by human creatures as large as yourself, our philosophers are in much doubt, and would rather conjecture that you dropped from the moon or one of the stars, because it is certain,

that an hundred mortals of your bulk would, in a short time, destroy all the   35
fruits and cattle of his majesty's dominions. Besides, our histories of six thousand
moons make no mention of any other regions than the two great empires of
Lilliput and Blefuscu. Which two mighty powers have, as I was going to tell you,
been engaged in a most obstinate war for six-and-thirty moons past. It began
upon the following occasion: It is allowed on all hands, that the primitive way   40
of breaking eggs, before we eat them, was upon the larger end; but his present
majesty's grandfather, while he was a boy, going to eat an egg, and breaking it
according to the ancient practice, happened to cut one of his fingers. Whereupon
the emperor, his father, published an edict, commanding all his subjects, upon
great penalties, to break the smaller end of their eggs. The people so highly   45
resented this law, that our histories tell us, there have been six rebellions raised
on that account, wherein one emperor lost his life, and another his crown. These
civil commotions were constantly fomented by the monarchs of Blefuscu; and
when they were quelled, the exiles always fled for refuge to that empire. It is com-
puted, that eleven thousand persons have, at several times, suffered death, rather   50
than submit to break their eggs at the smaller end. Many hundred large volumes
have been published upon this controversy, but the books of the Big-endians have
been long forbidden, and the whole party rendered incapable, by law, of holding
employments. During the course of these troubles, the Emperors of Blefuscu did
frequently expostulate, by their ambassadors, accusing us of making a schism   55
in religion, by offending against a fundamental doctrine of our great prophet
Lustrog, in the fifty-fourth chapter of the *Blundecral* (which is their *Alcoran*).
This, however, is thought to be a mere strain upon the text; for the words are
these: *That all true believers break their eggs at the convenient end*. And which
is the convenient end, seems, in my humble opinion, to be left to every man's   60
conscience, or, at least, in the power of the chief magistrate to determine. Now,
the Big-endian exiles have found so much credit in the emperor of Blefuscu's
court, and so much private assistance and encouragement from their party here
at home, that a bloody war hath been carried on between the two empires for
six-and-thirty moons, with various success; during which time we have lost forty   65
capital ships, and a much greater number of smaller vessels, together with thirty
thousand of our best seamen and soldiers; and the damage received by the enemy
is reckoned to be somewhat greater than ours. However, they have now equipped
a numerous fleet, and are just preparing to make a descent upon us; and his
imperial majesty, placing great confidence in your valor and strength, hath   70
commanded me to lay this account of his affairs before you.

119. The first paragraph implies that the speaker is all of the following *except*

    (A) grateful
    (B) recently emancipated
    (C) obedient
    (D) gracious
    (E) large

120. The phrase "pretend to some merit in it" (lines 9–10) indicates that
    (A) Reldresal's compliments are deceptive
    (B) Reldresal is demonstrating guile
    (C) the speaker's freedom was hard won
    (D) the speaker's freedom was unwarranted
    (E) Reldresal believes there were weightier factors involved

121. The speaker who begins speaking at line 12 ("we labor under . . .") is a member of
     I. the high heels
    II. *Tramecksan*
   III. *Slamecksan*
    (A) I only
    (B) II only
    (C) III only
    (D) I and III only
    (E) I, II, and III

122. The heir's "hobble" (line 28) is worrying because
    (A) he is in need of convalescence
    (B) it suggests his potential defection to the *Tramecksan* party
    (C) it is unsightly
    (D) it suggests he is partial to the *Slamecksan* party
    (E) it suggests he and his father are estranged

123. In line 29, the phrase "intestine disquiets" most likely means
    (A) physical illness
    (B) municipal elections
    (C) political treason
    (D) domestic strife
    (E) the speaker's inner turmoil

124. Based on lines 31–38, it can be interpreted that the addressee's claims are viewed as fallible due to
    (A) the philosophers' logical reasoning
    (B) the philosophers' research-based claims
    (C) the existence of fruit and cattle
    (D) overwhelming evidence
    (E) the philosophers' convenient denial

125. The word "fomented" in line 48 most nearly means

(A) goaded
(B) quelled
(C) dispelled
(D) formed
(E) derided

126. The *Blundecral* is mentioned to emphasize

(A) its inferiority to the *Alcoran*
(B) the Big-endians' sacrilege
(C) the source of "the most obstinate war" (39)
(D) Blefuscu's role in inciting conflict
(E) Lilliput's misinterpretation of a religious edict

127. The argument between Blefuscu and Lilliput described in lines 53–60 is most similar to

(A) physical sparring
(B) familial spats
(C) altercations about facts
(D) conflicting interpretations
(E) ad hominem attacks

128. In the passage, the words "*Slamecksan*," "*Tramecksan*," "*drurr*," "*Alcoran*," and "*Blundecral*" are all written in italics to indicate

(A) that they are the names of renowned people and places
(B) that they are important
(C) that they are words from this world's language
(D) a lack of respect
(E) emphasis

129. The passage suggests that the imperial majesty expects the speaker of the first paragraph

   I. to use his valor and strength to assist with the invasion
  II. to use the liberty he has been granted to conquer Blefuscu
 III. to protect his kingdom from the *Slamecksan* party

(A) I only
(B) II only
(C) I and II only
(D) II and III only
(E) I, II, and III

130. The speaker of lines 11–71, as opposed to the passage as a whole, carries a tone of

(A) gravity
(B) irony
(C) absurdity
(D) amicability
(E) neutrality

Passage 13. Sophocles, *Oedipus the King*

OEDIPUS.   My children, fruit of Cadmus' ancient tree
New springing, wherefore thus with bended knee
Press ye upon us, laden all with wreaths
And suppliant branches? And the city breathes
Heavy with incense, heavy with dim prayer   5
And shrieks to affright the Slayer.—Children, care
For this so moves me, I have scorned withal
Message or writing: seeing 'tis I ye call,
'Tis I am come, world-honoured Oedipus.

Old Man, do thou declare—the rest have thus   10
Their champion—in what mood stand ye so still,
In dread or sure hope? Know ye not, my will
Is yours for aid 'gainst all? Stern were indeed
The heart that felt not for so dire a need.

PRIEST.   O Oedipus, who holdest in thy hand   15
My city, thou canst see what ages stand
At these thine altars; some whose little wing
Scarce flieth yet, and some with long living
O'erburdened; priests, as I of Zeus am priest,
And chosen youths: and wailing hath not ceased   20
Of thousands in the market-place, and by
Athena's two-fold temples and the dry
Ash of Ismênus' portent-breathing shore.

For all our ship, thou see'st, is weak and sore
Shaken with storms, and no more lighteneth   25
Her head above the waves whose trough is death.
She wasteth in the fruitless buds of earth,
In parchèd herds and travail without birth
Of dying women: yea, and midst of it
A burning and a loathly god hath lit   30
Sudden, and sweeps our land, this Plague of power;

Till Cadmus' house grows empty, hour by hour,
And Hell's house rich with steam of tears and blood.

O King, not God indeed nor peer to God
We deem thee, that we kneel before thine hearth,   35
Children and old men, praying; but of earth
A thing consummate by thy star confessed
Thou walkest and by converse with the blest;
Who came to Thebes so swift, and swept away
The Sphinx's song, the tribute of dismay,   40
That all were bowed beneath, and made us free.
A stranger, thou, naught knowing more than we,
Nor taught of any man, but by God's breath
Filled, thou didst raise our life. So the world saith;
So we say.   45

Therefore now, O Lord and Chief,
We come to thee again; we lay our grief
On thy head, if thou find us not some aid.

131. The passage begins with

(A) a command
(B) a rhetorical question
(C) an invocation
(D) an inquiry
(E) an aside

132. In lines 4–6, personification is used to present the city as

(A) macabre
(B) diabolical
(C) desperate
(D) alive
(E) pious

133. In lines 7–9 and lines 12–14, Oedipus characterizes himself as

   I. venerable
  II. concerned primarily for his citizens
III. preoccupied

(A) I only
(B) II only
(C) I and II only
(D) I and III only
(E) I, II, and III

134. Oedipus implies that he has decided to appear in person because

    (A) it is his obligation as king

    (B) it is the custom of the time

    (C) he was summoned

    (D) he is deeply concerned for his people

    (E) he is concerned for his image

135. According to line 7, what moves Oedipus?

    (A) signs indicating the city's desperate plight

    (B) his responsibility to his people

    (C) the Slayer

    (D) the city

    (E) the suffering of children

136. The people appeal to Oedipus for help primarily because

    (A) he is filled with God's breath

    (B) he has rescued them previously

    (C) he is a peer to God

    (D) he knows more than they know

    (E) rumors of his accomplishments have reached them

137. According to the priest, the city has been harmed by

    (A) a shipwreck

    (B) a disease

    (C) dying women

    (D) deadly waves

    (E) a ruthless scourge

138. The metaphor in lines 24–26

    (A) compares a ship to the city and the sea to death

    (B) emphasizes the futility of fighting back

    (C) highlights the people's resilience

    (D) contrasts life and death

    (E) compares a ship to the priest; the sea to the gods

139. The word "house" in lines 32 and 33 functions primarily as

    (A) a metaphor that compares people to furniture

    (B) a literal description of where the people are located

    (C) part of an internal rhyme that contributes to the mournful tone

    (D) a figurative way to show the vulnerability of the "fruit of Cadmus' ancient tree" (1)

    (E) a symbol of both heaven and hell

140. Which of the following provides the best summary of the priest's final lines (46–48)?

(A) We have faith in your ability to bring us aid.

(B) Please liberate us as you have done before.

(C) You will be responsible if our turmoil does not end.

(D) Your help is invaluable to us.

(E) We will be utterly disappointed in you if you do not provide aid.

141. The priest's tone differs from Oedipus's in that it is

(A) grave as opposed to compassionate

(B) bitter as opposed to reverent

(C) pitiful as opposed to patriotic

(D) elegiac as opposed to remorseful

(E) laudatory as opposed to loving

142. We can infer from the passage that Cadmus (lines 1, 32) is

(A) the founder of Thebes

(B) the current king

(C) their God

(D) the city's name

(E) an ancient tree

Passage 14. Oscar Wilde, *The Picture of Dorian Gray*

The studio was filled with the rich odour of roses, and when the light summer wind stirred amidst the trees of the garden, there came through the open door the heavy scent of the lilac, or the more delicate perfume of the pink-flowering thorn.

From the corner of the divan of Persian saddle-bags on which he was lying,   5
smoking, as was his custom, innumerable cigarettes, Lord Henry Wotton could just catch the gleam of the honey-sweet and honey-coloured blossoms of a laburnum, whose tremulous branches seemed hardly able to bear the burden of a beauty so flamelike as theirs; and now and then the fantastic shadows of birds in flight flitted across the long tussore-silk curtains that were stretched in front of   10
the huge window, producing a kind of momentary Japanese effect, and making him think of those pallid, jade-faced painters of Tokyo who, through the medium of an art that is necessarily immobile, seek to convey the sense of swiftness and motion. The sullen murmur of the bees shouldering their way through the long unmown grass, or circling with monotonous insistence round the dusty gilt horns   15
of the straggling woodbine, seemed to make the stillness more oppressive. The dim roar of London was like the bourdon note of a distant organ. In the centre of the room, clamped to an upright easel, stood the full-length portrait of a young

man of extraordinary personal beauty, and in front of it, some little distance
away, was sitting the artist himself, Basil Hallward, whose sudden disappearance   20
some years ago caused, at the time, such public excitement and gave rise to so
many strange conjectures.

As the painter looked at the gracious and comely form he had so skillfully
mirrored in his art, a smile of pleasure passed across his face, and seemed about
to linger there. But he suddenly started up, and closing his eyes, placed his fingers   25
upon the lids, as though he sought to imprison within his brain some curious
dream from which he feared he might awake. "It is your best work, Basil, the best
thing you have ever done," said Lord Henry languidly. "You must certainly send
it next year to the Grosvenor. The Academy is too large and too vulgar. Whenever I have gone there, there have been either so many people that I have not   30
been able to see the pictures, which was dreadful, or so many pictures that I have
not been able to see the people, which was worse. The Grosvenor is really the
only place."

"I don't think I shall send it anywhere," he answered, tossing his head back
in that odd way that used to make his friends laugh at him at Oxford. "No, I   35
won't send it anywhere." Lord Henry elevated his eyebrows and looked at him
in amazement through the thin blue wreaths of smoke that curled up in such
fanciful whorls from his heavy, opium-tainted cigarette. "Not send it anywhere?
My dear fellow, why? Have you any reason? What odd chaps you painters are!
You do anything in the world to gain a reputation. As soon as you have one,   40
you seem to want to throw it away. It is silly of you, for there is only one thing
in the world worse than being talked about, and that is not being talked about.
A portrait like this would set you far above all the young men in England, and
make the old men quite jealous, if old men are ever capable of any emotion."

143. The "momentary Japanese effect" in line 11 functions as
    (A) a parallel between London and Tokyo
    (B) a contrast between movement and stillness
    (C) an indication that Lord Henry prefers Japanese art
    (D) a detail that emphasizes the pleasure offered by the setting
    (E) an attack on Japanese painters

144. The description of the setting in the first and second paragraphs makes
    particular use of
    (A) common adjectives and simple sentences to describe an ordinary
        scene
    (B) sensory imagery and figurative comparisons to convey a lavish
        environment
    (C) surprising similes that present the beautiful scenery as oppressive
    (D) botanical facts that add an intellectual tone to the story
    (E) objective narration that establishes a hedonistic mood

145. Lord Henry's reaction to Basil is developed primarily through

(A) his facial expressions and exclamatory tone
(B) his cool indifference and languid tone
(C) the "fanciful whorls from his heavy, opium-tainted cigarette" (38)
(D) his sincerely offered advice about becoming a successful artist
(E) his sarcastic questions

146. Lord Henry's statements indicate that he values

(A) artistic integrity
(B) public reputation
(C) Basil's talent
(D) his social relationships
(E) monetary accolades

147. A notable shift in the passage occurs

(A) in line 5; the focus shifts from outside the studio to inside
(B) in line 9; the description transitions from plants to animals
(C) in line 20; the focus shifts from describing the setting to introducing a character
(D) in the third paragraph; the tone shifts from laudatory to accusatory
(E) in line 39; the mood shifts from apathy to anger

148. Lord Henry's speech is notable for its use of all of the following *except*

(A) wit
(B) incredulity
(C) flattery
(D) humility
(E) exhortation

149. Which of the following best conveys the effect of lines 25–27 ("But he suddenly . . . might awake")?

(A) A straightforward gesture belies the previous description of Basil's impression of his painting.
(B) A mysterious gesture casts doubt on Basil's pleased reaction to his own painting.
(C) Lord Henry uses a simile to add to the characterization of Basil as strange.
(D) An odd reaction adds credence to Lord Henry's assertion that artists are "'odd chaps'"(39).
(E) A description of Basil's physical reaction to his painting reveals that he is certainly unstable.

150. The dialogue in the passage serves primarily to
    (A) contrast Lord Henry with his environment
    (B) demonstrate the characters' level of education
    (C) develop Lord Henry's viewpoint
    (D) draw a correlation between wealth and intellect
    (E) criticize the art industry

151. A question that remains unanswered by the passage is
    (A) Why is there a stillness in the room?
    (B) Why is Basil determined not to send his painting anywhere?
    (C) Why is Lord Henry amazed?
    (D) What is Basil's painting of?
    (E) How does Lord Henry view artists?

152. The passage as a whole serves primarily to
    (A) present Basil Hallward as a talented artist
    (B) show the friendship between Lord Henry and Basil Hallward
    (C) critique London's high society
    (D) introduce characters and the central motif of art
    (E) demonstrate highly ornate descriptions of a natural setting

20th-Century/Contemporary Prose

Passage 15. Maya Angelou, *I Know Why the Caged Bird Sings*

Weighing the half-pounds of flour, excluding the scoop, and depositing them dust-free into the thin paper sacks held a simple kind of adventure for me. I developed an eye for measuring how full a silver-looking ladle of flour, mash, meal, sugar or corn had to be to push the scale indicator over to eight ounces or one pound. When I was absolutely accurate our appreciative customers used to admire: "Sister Henderson sure got some smart grandchildrens." If I was off in the Store's favor, the eagle-eyed women would say, "Put some more in that sack child. Don't you try to make your profit offa me."

Then I would quietly but persistently punish myself. For every bad judgment, the fine was no silver-wrapped Kisses, the sweet chocolate drops that I loved more than anything in the world, except Bailey. And maybe canned pineapples. My obsession with pineapples nearly drove me mad. I dreamt of the days when I would be grown and able to buy a whole carton for myself alone.

Although the syrupy golden rings sat in their exotic cans on our shelves year round, we only tasted them during Christmas. Momma used the juice to make almost-black fruit cakes. Then she lined heavy soot-encrusted iron skillets with the pineapple rings for rich, upside-down cakes. Bailey and I received one slice each, and I carried mine around for hours, shredding off the fruit until nothing was left except the perfume on my fingers. I'd like to think that my desire for pineapples was so sacred that I wouldn't allow myself to steal a can (which was possible) and eat it alone out in the garden, but I'm certain that I must have weighed the possibility of the scent exposing me and didn't have the nerve to attempt it.

Until I was thirteen and left Arkansas for good, the Store was my favorite place to be. Alone and empty in the mornings, it looked like an unopened present from a stranger. Opening the front doors was pulling the ribbon off the unexpected gift. The light would come in softly (we faced north), easing itself over the shelves of mackerel, salmon, tobacco, thread. It fell flat on the big vat of

5

10

15

20

25

lard and by noontime during the summer the grease had softened to a thick soup. Whenever I walked into the Store in the afternoon, I sensed that it was tired. 30 I alone could hear the slow pulse of its job half done. But just before bedtime, after numerous people had walked in and out, had argued over their bills, or joked about their neighbors, or just dropped in "to give Sister Henderson a 'Hi y'all,'" the promise of magic mornings returned to the Store and spread itself over the family in washed life waves. 35

153. The verbs "Weighing," "excluding," "depositing," and "measuring" (line 1) are intended to

    (A) create a sense of verity by accurately describing the narrator's actions

    (B) objectively portray the narrator's job as demanding

    (C) underscore the care and attention the narrator puts into her work

    (D) belie the description of the narrator's job as an "adventure" (2)

    (E) convey the monotony of the routine tasks the narrator must do in the Store

154. The passage implies that the "adventure" mentioned in the first paragraph (line 2) is created mostly by

    (A) the thrill of getting to earn money

    (B) the empowering sense of independence the narrator experiences

    (C) the process of learning how to accurately measure goods

    (D) enduring self-inflicted punishments

    (E) the tension the narrator creates for herself between earning praise and deserving punishment

155. The fines the narrator imposes on herself are presented as

    (A) thoughtfully chosen

    (B) pathetic

    (C) laughable

    (D) overly severe

    (E) appropriate to the time period

156. The third paragraph's relationship to the rest of the passage can best be described by which of the following?

(A) It is an unnecessary digression that showcases the author's figurative style.

(B) It explains that the Store's "exotic" (14) goods are the reason why the narrator says "the Store was [her] favorite place to be" (24–25) in the fourth paragraph.

(C) It conveys the intensity of the self-inflicted punishments mentioned in the second paragraph by elaborating on the narrator's complex relationship with a desire.

(D) It adds validity to the depiction of the narrator as having "bad judgment" (9) by explaining her urge to steal.

(E) It lends credence to the portrayal of the narrator as honest by mentioning that she "wouldn't allow" (20) herself to steal.

157. In the passage, pineapples function primarily as

(A) a reminder that the narrator's deprivation defines her life

(B) a vivid symbol of the sustenance the Store provides for the town

(C) a reward for the narrator's honesty and accuracy as an employee of the store

(D) an indulgence that brings the family together in hard times

(E) a rare luxury that incites complicated feelings and behaviors

158. In context, the certainty mentioned in lines 21–23 ("but I'm certain . . . attempt it") primarily suggests which of the following about the narrator?

(A) She is dishonest.

(B) She is self-aware.

(C) She would do anything for pineapples.

(D) She is motivated only by a fear of shame.

(E) Her desires are tempered by her sense of loyalty.

159. The description of the Store relies on all of the following *except*

(A) quotations from regular customers

(B) a balance of positive and negative diction

(C) auditory imagery

(D) figurative comparison

(E) personification

160. The list in lines 31–33 ("after numerous people . . . 'Hi y'all'") functions primarily to
    (A) describe a particularly hectic day in the Store
    (B) illustrate the Store as the narrator sees it first thing in the morning
    (C) contrast the image provided earlier of how the Store feels first thing in the morning
    (D) add historical credence to a depiction of a fictional store
    (E) portray the Store's customers as demanding and particular

161. The context reveals that Sister Henderson must be
    (A) another employee of the Store
    (B) the narrator
    (C) the narrator's boss
    (D) the narrator's family
    (E) a patron of the Store

162. For the narrator, the phrase "I alone" (line 31) implies the Store is
    (A) a secret hiding place
    (B) a refuge
    (C) her best friend
    (D) most appreciated by her
    (E) her legacy

163. The narrator's assertion that "the Store was my favorite place to be" (lines 24–25) is
    (A) dubious; she considers stealing from it
    (B) an exaggeration; she simply means that she likes the Store
    (C) an expression; it isn't literally her favorite place
    (D) believable; she notices its unique and subtle qualities
    (E) honest; she doesn't experience adventure anywhere else

Passage 16. Joseph Conrad, *Heart of Darkness*

The Nellie, a cruising yawl, swung to her anchor without a flutter of the sails, and was at rest. The flood had made, the wind was nearly calm, and being bound down the river, the only thing for it was to come to and wait for the turn of the tide.

The sea-reach of the Thames stretched before us like the beginning of an interminable waterway. In the offing the sea and the sky were welded together without a joint, and in the luminous space the tanned sails of the barges drifting up with the tide seemed to stand still in red clusters of canvas sharply peaked, with gleams of varnished sprits. A haze rested on the low shores that ran out to sea in vanishing flatness. The air was dark above Gravesend, and farther back still seemed condensed into a mournful gloom, brooding motionless over the biggest, and the greatest, town on earth.

The Director of Companies was our captain and our host. We four affectionately watched his back as he stood in the bows looking to seaward. On the whole river there was nothing that looked half so nautical. He resembled a pilot, which to a seaman is trustworthiness personified. It was difficult to realize his work was not out there in the luminous estuary, but behind him, within the brooding gloom.

Between us there was, as I have already said somewhere, the bond of the sea. Besides holding our hearts together through long periods of separation, it had the effect of making us tolerant of each other's yarns—and even convictions. The Lawyer—the best of old fellows—had, because of his many years and many virtues, the only cushion on deck, and was lying on the only rug. The Accountant had brought out already a box of dominoes, and was toying architecturally with the bones. Marlow sat cross-legged right aft, leaning against the mizzen mast. He had sunken cheeks, a yellow complexion, a straight back, an ascetic aspect, and, with his arms dropped, the palms of hands outwards, resembled an idol. The director, satisfied the anchor had good hold, made his way aft and sat down amongst us. We exchanged a few words lazily. Afterwards there was silence on board the yacht. For some reason or other we did not begin that game of dominoes. We felt meditative, and fit for nothing but placid staring. The day was ending in a serenity of still and exquisite brilliance. The water shone pacifically; the sky, without a speck, was a benign immensity of unstained light; the very mist on the Essex marsh was like a gauzy and radiant fabric, hung from the wooded rises inland, and draping the low shores in diaphanous folds. Only the gloom to the west, brooding over the upper reaches, became more sombre every minute, as if angered by the approach of the sun.

And at last, in its curved and imperceptible fall, the sun sank low, and from glowing white changed to a dull red without rays and without heat, as if about to go out suddenly, stricken to death by the touch of that gloom brooding over a crowd of men.

164. The mood established in the opening paragraph is

    (A) unclear due to contradictory words such as "cruising" (1) and "calm" (2)

    (B) a mix between peaceful and anticipatory

    (C) eerie due to a ship without any "flutter of the sails" (1)

    (D) a combination of calmness and threat due to the reference to a "flood" (2) and "wind" (2)

    (E) surprising because a ship is associated with movement and adventure, not stillness

165. The sentence in lines 10–12 ("The air was dark . . . earth") marks a shift in the paragraph from

    (A) a focus on the sea to the air

    (B) a mystically calm mood to a dark and gloomy mood

    (C) vivid to vague descriptions

    (D) a sense of fear to anticipation

    (E) a threatening tone to a mystical tone

166. Lines 16–17 ("It was difficult . . . brooding gloom") suggest which of the following about the Director's "work"?

    (A) It is nautical.

    (B) It takes place in foreign lands.

    (C) It is adventurous.

    (D) It is meaningful.

    (E) It is municipal.

167. The descriptions of the setting throughout the passage primarily serve to

    (A) establish mood and symbolically represent a potential theme

    (B) contrast the descriptions of the characters

    (C) highlight that the world is magical and beautiful

    (D) reveal the narrator's appreciation of his environment

    (E) establish a poetic and peaceful tone

168. According to the narrator, the Director of Companies is

    (A) affectionate and authoritative

    (B) demonstrative and trustworthy

    (C) naval and venerable

    (D) principled and brooding

    (E) sociable and esteemed

169. The narrator introduces his companions

    (A) with objective descriptions
    (B) by comparing them to each other
    (C) with a hint of envy and pity
    (D) with a poetic and generous perspective
    (E) as tolerant of each other due to the circumstances

170. The context of the passage suggests that a potential reason the crew "did not begin that game of dominoes" (lines 29–30) is that

    (A) the setting induces stillness
    (B) they are growing slightly intolerant of each other's yarns and convictions
    (C) they have just come out of a period of long separation
    (D) each crew member is occupied with another task
    (E) "the Accountant" (22) does not intend to share his dominoes

171. Lines 30–36, "The day was ending . . . approach of the sun," contrast

    (A) the opening paragraph
    (B) day and night
    (C) the crew and their environment
    (D) light and dark
    (E) the west and the south

172. The passage's final sentence creates what type of mood?

    (A) morbid
    (B) ominous
    (C) sanguine
    (D) sorrowful
    (E) regretful

173. The passage as a whole serves primarily to

    I. foreshadow later events
    II. establish a symbolic setting
    III. develop the main character

    (A) I only
    (B) III only
    (C) I and II only
    (D) I and III only
    (E) I, II, and III

Passage 17. Ralph Ellison, *Invisible Man*

It goes a long way back, some twenty years. All my life I had been looking
for something, and everywhere I turned someone tried to tell me what it was.
I accepted their answers too, though they were often in contradiction and even
self-contradictory. I was naive. I was looking for myself and asking everyone
except myself questions which I, and only I, could answer. It took me a long   5
time and much painful boomeranging of my expectations to achieve a realization
everyone else appears to have been born with: That I am nobody but myself. But
first I had to discover that I am an invisible man!

And yet I am no freak of nature, nor of history. I was in the cards, other
things having been equal (or unequal) eighty-five years ago. I am not ashamed of   10
my grandparents for having been slaves. I am only ashamed of myself for having
at one time been ashamed. About eighty-five years ago they were told that they
were free, united with others of our country in everything pertaining to the common good, and, in everything social, separate like the fingers of the hand. And
they believed it. They exulted in it. They stayed in their place, worked hard, and 15
brought up my father to do the same. But my grandfather is the one. He was
an odd old guy, my grandfather, and I am told I take after him. It was he who
caused the trouble. On his deathbed he called my father to him and said, "Son,
after I'm gone I want you to keep up the good fight. I never told you, but our life
is a war and I have been a traitor all my born days, a spy in the enemy's country   20
ever since I give up my gun back in the Reconstruction. Live with your head in
the lion's mouth. I want you to overcome 'em with yeses, undermine 'em with
grins, agree 'em to death and destruction, let 'em swoller you till they vomit or
bust wide open." They thought the old man had gone out of his mind. He had
been the meekest of men. The younger children were rushed from the room,   25
the shades drawn and the flame of the lamp turned so low that it sputtered on
the wick like the old man's breathing. "Learn it to the younguns," he whispered
fiercely; then he died.

174. The narrator considers his former self "naive" (line 4) because

    (A) he was confident about his destiny
    (B) he thought he knew who he was
    (C) he was ashamed of slavery
    (D) he sought answers from others
    (E) he trusted his grandfather

175. The "answers" (line 3) the narrator receives from others can be described as

    (A) conflicting and perplexing
    (B) believable but naive
    (C) painful but sincere
    (D) hard to understand but well-meaning
    (E) duplicitous and misguided

176. By "I was in the cards" (line 9), the narrator most probably means

(A) his fate has doomed his existence
(B) his parents planned his birth
(C) slavery was inevitable
(D) his existence has been ordinary considering the context
(E) his "invisibility" (8) could not have been predicted

177. The comparison to "the fingers of the hand" (line 14) serves to emphasize

(A) how blacks were united now that slavery ended
(B) the separate but equal conditions for blacks after slavery ended
(C) that blacks were still slaves
(D) that racial tensions were worsening
(E) "everything pertaining to the common good" (13–14)

178. Based on the passage as a whole, it can be interpreted that the narrator sees his grandfather as

(A) a hypocrite
(B) a meek yes-man
(C) a traitor
(D) disconcerting
(E) delirious

179. In the passage, the grandfather's dying message is treated by the family with

(A) indifference
(B) sympathy
(C) contempt
(D) ambivalence
(E) bewilderment

180. In context of the grandfather's message, the "lion's mouth" (line 22) refers to

(A) war
(B) slavery
(C) whites
(D) violence
(E) corruption

181. Based on the passage, the grandfather's message is surprising mostly because

(A) it is revisionist
(B) it is ahead of its time
(C) it belies the grandfather's earlier behavior
(D) it underscores the grandfather's hypocrisy
(E) it was an unconventional perspective for the time

182. The magnitude of the grandfather's message is communicated through

(A) a detailed anecdote about a racist experience
(B) a litany of complaints against whites
(C) an excoriation of servile blacks
(D) exhortations laced with metaphors
(E) biblical allusions and threats

183. Which of the following actions coincides with the directives the grandfather gives the narrator's father?

(A) protesting unequal treatment of blacks
(B) resisting orders from whites
(C) officiously obliging with white society's expectations
(D) fighting oppression with violence
(E) treating whites as allies

184. In contrast to twenty years ago, the narrator is now

(A) no longer seeking answers
(B) seeking answers
(C) naive
(D) a contradiction
(E) an invisible man

Passage 18. Susan Glaspell, "Suppressed Desires"

Scene I *A studio apartment in an upper story, Washington Square South. Through an immense north window in the back wall appear tree tops and the upper part of the Washington Arch. Beyond it you look up Fifth Avenue. Near the window is a big table, loaded at one end with serious-looking books and austere scientific periodicals. At the other end are architect's drawings, blue prints, dividing compasses, square, ruler, etc. At the left is a door leading to the rest of the apartment; at the right the outer door. A breakfast table is set for three, but only two are seated at it—Henrietta and Stephen Brewster. As the curtains withdraw Steve pushes back his coffee cup and sits dejected.*

HENRIETTA: It isn't the coffee, Steve dear. There's nothing the matter with the   10
coffee. There's something the matter with *you*.

STEVE: [*Doggedly.*] There may be something the matter with my stomach.

HENRIETTA: [*Scornfully.*] Your stomach! The trouble is not with your stomach
but in your subconscious mind.

STEVE: Subconscious piffle! [*Takes morning paper and tries to read.*]   15

HENRIETTA: Steve, you never used to be so disagreeable. You certainly have got
some sort of a complex. You're all inhibited. You're no longer open
to new ideas. You won't listen to a word about psychoanalysis.

STEVE: A word! I've listened to volumes!

HENRIETTA: You've ceased to be creative in architecture—your work isn't going   20
well. You're not sleeping well—

STEVE: How can I sleep, Henrietta, when you're always waking me up to
find out what I'm dreaming?

HENRIETTA: But dreams are so important, Steve. If you'd tell yours to
Dr. Russell he'd find out exactly what's wrong with you.   25

STEVE: There's nothing wrong with me.

HENRIETTA: You don't even talk as well as you used to.

STEVE: Talk? I can't say a thing without you looking at me in that dark
fashion you have when you're on the trail of a complex.

HENRIETTA: This very irritability indicates that you're suffering from some sup-   30
pressed desire.

STEVE: I'm suffering from a suppressed desire for a little peace.

HENRIETTA: Dr. Russell is doing simply wonderful things with nervous cases.
Won't you go to him, Steve?

STEVE: [*Slamming down his newspaper.*] No, Henrietta, I won't!   35

HENRIETTA: But, Stephen—!

STEVE: Tst! I hear Mabel coming. Let's not be at each other's throats the
first day of her visit.

[*He takes out cigarettes.* Mabel *comes in from door left, the side opposite* Steve, *so
that he is facing her. She is wearing a rather fussy negligee in contrast to* Henrietta,   40
who wears "radical" clothes. Mabel *is what is called plump.*]

MABEL: Good morning.

HENRIETTA: Oh, here you are, little sister.

STEVE: Good morning, Mabel.

[Mabel *nods to him and turns, her face lighting up, to* Henrietta.] 45

HENRIETTA: [*Giving* Mabel *a hug as she leans against her.*] It's so good to have you here. I was going to let you sleep, thinking you'd be tired after the long trip. Sit down. There'll be fresh toast in a minute and [*Rising*] will you have—

MABEL: Oh, I ought to have told you, Henrietta. Don't get anything for 50 me. I'm not eating breakfast.

HENRIETTA: [*At first in mere surprise.*] Not eating breakfast?

[*She sits down, then leans toward* Mabel *who is seated now, and scrutinizes her.*]

STEVE: [*Half to himself.*] The psychoanalytical look!

HENRIETTA: Mabel, why are you not eating breakfast? 55

MABEL: [*A little startled.*] Why, no particular reason. I just don't care much for breakfast, and they say it keeps down—[*A hand on her hip—the gesture of one who is "reducing"*] that is, it's a good thing to go without it.

HENRIETTA: Don't you sleep well? Did you sleep well last night? 60

MABEL: Oh, yes, I slept all right. Yes, I slept fine last night, only [*Laughing.*] I did have the funniest dream!

STEVE: S-h! S-t!

HENRIETTA: [*Moving closer.*] And what did you dream, Mabel?

STEVE: Look-a-here, Mabel, I feel it's my duty to put you on. Don't tell 65 Henrietta your dreams. If you do she'll find out that you have an underground desire to kill your father and marry your mother—

HENRIETTA: Don't be absurd, Stephen Brewster. [*Sweetly to* Mabel.] What was your dream, dear?

MABEL: [*Laughing.*] Well, I dreamed I was a hen. 70

HENRIETTA: A hen?

MABEL: Yes; and I was pushing along through a crowd as fast as I could, but being a hen I couldn't walk very fast—it was like having a tight skirt, you know; and there was some sort of creature in a blue cap—you know how mixed up dreams are—and it kept shouting 75 after me, "Step, Hen! Step, Hen!" until I got all excited and just couldn't move at all.

HENRIETTA: [*Resting chin in palm and peering.*] You say you became much excited?

MABEL: [*Laughing.*] Oh, yes; I was in a terrible state.   80

HENRIETTA: [*Leaning back, murmurs.*] This is significant.

STEVE: She dreams she's a hen. She is told to step lively. She becomes violently agitated. What can it mean?

HENRIETTA: [*Turning impatiently from him.*] Mabel, do you know anything about psychoanalysis?   85

MABEL: [*Feebly.*] Oh—not much. No—I—[*Brightening.*] It's something about the war, isn't it?

STEVE: Not that kind of war.

MABEL: [*Abashed.*] I thought it might be the name of a new explosive.

STEVE: It *is*.   90

---

185. In context, Henrietta's comment in lines 10–11 ("It isn't the coffee . . . matter with *you"*) reveals that she

    I. interprets Steve's body language as a sign of a deeper problem
    II. is hurt by Steve's lack of self-awareness
    III. is wholeheartedly concerned with helping Steve

    (A) I only
    (B) I and II only
    (C) II and III only
    (D) III only
    (E) I, II, and III

186. Henrietta's tone in lines 16–36 ("Steve, you never used to be so disagreeable . . . But, Stephen—!") is best described as

    (A) relentless insistence
    (B) cool detachment
    (C) scholarly curiosity
    (D) mild skepticism
    (E) ruthless

187. Steve's use of the phrase "suppressed desire" (line 32) can best be described as

(A) a humbling concession to Henrietta's proposition
(B) a candid acknowledgment of his inner state
(C) a sardonic twist on Henrietta's words
(D) a logical counterargument in a balanced discussion
(E) a subtle interrogation of psychoanalytic theory

188. Steve's comment to Mabel in lines 65–67 ("Look-a-here . . . mother—") is developed through all of the following *except*

(A) a literary allusion
(B) drollery
(C) dramatic exaggeration
(D) feigned interest
(E) a resentful tone

189. Henrietta's conversations with Mabel and Steve suggest her relationships with them are

I. similar; she embodies the role of nurturing caretaker to both
II. somewhat different; she loses patience with Steve's resistance but remains calm with Mabel
III. self-serving; her questions and comments suggest she is motivated more by her interest in psychoanalysis than in helping her relatives

(A) I only
(B) I and II only
(C) II only
(D) III only
(E) II and III only

190. Henrietta's intentions with Mabel are conveyed through all of the following *except*

(A) stage directions
(B) rhetorical questions
(C) genuine inquiries
(D) tone of voice
(E) repetition

191. The tone of lines 82–83 ("She dreams she's a hen . . . mean") can best be described as

(A) glib; Steve is indifferent toward Henrietta's interest in Mabel's dreams
(B) mocking; the meaning of Mabel's dream is somewhat obvious
(C) confident; Steve has figured out the meaning behind Mabel's dream
(D) pedantic; Steve believes he knows more about interpreting dreams than Mabel
(E) sanctimonious; Steve has all the answers

192. The emphasis on the word "*is*" in the passage's last line emphasizes

(A) the groundbreaking nature of psychoanalytic theory
(B) Mabel's naivety about psychoanalysis
(C) Steve's view that Henrietta's obsession with dreams is combative
(D) that Henrietta's interest in dreams is warranted
(F) the potential applications of psychoanalysis

Passage 19. Zora Neale Hurston and Langston Hughes, "Mule Bone: A Comedy of Negro Life"

(The noise of cane-chewing is heard again. Enter JOE LINDSAY left with a gun over his shoulder and the large leg bone of a mule in the other hand. He approaches the step wearily.)

HAMBO: Well, did you git any partridges, Joe?

JOE: (Resting his gun and seating himself) Nope, but I made de feathers   5
fly.

HAMBO: I don't see no birds.

JOE: Oh, the feathers flew off on de birds.

LIGE: I don't see nothin but dat bone. Look lak you done kilt a cow and
et 'im raw out in de woods.   10

JOE: Don't y'all know dat hock-bone?

WALTER: How you reckon we gointer know every hock-bone in Orange
County sight unseen?

JOE: (Standing the bone up on the floor of the porch) Dis is a hock-
bone of Brazzle's ole yaller mule. (General pleased interest.   15
Everybody wants to touch it.)

BRAZZLE: (Coming forward) Well, sir! (Takes bone in both hands and looks up and down the length of it) If 'tain't my ole mule! This sho was one hell of a mule, too. He'd fight every inch in front of de plow. . . . he'd turn over de mowing machine . . . run away wid de wagon . . . 20 and you better not look like you wanter ride 'im!

LINDSAY: (Laughing) Yeah, I 'member seein' you comin' down de road just so . . . (He limps wid one hand on his buttocks) one day.

BRAZZLE: Dis mule was so evil he used to try to bite and kick when I'd go in de stable to feed 'im.   25

WALTER: He was too mean to git fat. He was so skinny you could do a week's washing on his ribs for a washboard and hang 'em up on his hip-bones to dry.

LIGE: I member one day, Brazzle, you sent yo' boy to Winter Park after some groceries wid a basket. So here he went down de road ridin 30 dis mule wid dis basket on his arm. . . . Whut you reckon dat ole contrary male done when he got to dat crooked place in de road going round Park Lake? He turnt right round and went through de handle of dat basket . . . wid de boy still up on his back. (General laughter)   35

BRAZZLE: Yeah, he up and died one Sat'day just for spite . . . but he was too contrary to lay down on his side like a mule orter and die decent. Naw, he made out to lay down on his narrer contracted back and die wid his feets sticking straight up in de air just so. (He gets down on his back and illustrates.) We drug him out to de swamp 40 wid 'im dat way, didn't we, Hambo?

JOE CLARK: I God, Brazzle, we all seen it. Didn't we all go to de draggin' out? More folks went to yo' mule's draggin' out than went to last school closing . . . Bet there ain't been a thing right in mule-hell for four years.   45

HAMBO: Been dat long since he been dead?

CLARK: I God, yes, He died de week after I started to cuttin' dat new ground. (The bone is passing from hand to hand. At last a boy about twelve takes it. He has just walked up and is proudly handling the bone when a woman's voice is heard off stage right.)   50

193. Based on the passage as a whole, Joe most likely expects the others to recognize the bone because

(A) they have extensive experience with hunting

(B) of the mule's infamy

(C) it is a particularly impressive bone

(D) it is a "hock-bone" (11, 12, 14–15)

(E) they have all seen the bone before

194. Brazzle's response to seeing the bone is developed through

    I. exclamation

   II. equivocation

  III. reflection

  IV. physicality

(A) I and II only

(B) I, III, and IV only

(C) III and IV only

(D) I, II, and III only

(E) I, II, III, and IV

195. It can be inferred that the limping alluded to in line 23 is intended as

(A) an example of Lindsay's biting humor

(B) a visual of Brazzle's inadequate strength

(C) evidence of the mule's aversion to carrying a rider

(D) a reference to Joe's valor in successfully hunting the stubborn mule

(E) comic relief in the scene

196. Brazzle uses the word "evil" (line 24) in which of the following ways?

(A) regretfully

(B) lightheartedly

(C) literally

(D) metaphorically

(E) symbolically

197. Lige's anecdote (lines 29–35) is notable for all of the following reasons *except*

(A) its visual imagery

(B) the reaction it incites

(C) its shock value

(D) its ability to captivate

(E) its fallibility

198. Joe Clark's assertion in lines 44–45 ("Bet there ain't . . . four years") is best summarized as

(A) no other mules have died since Brazzle's mule died
(B) Brazzle's mule has been sorely missed since he died
(C) Brazzle's mule is probably causing strife in his after-life
(D) things have not been quite right since Brazzle's mule died
(E) Brazzle's mule is where he belongs now

199. Based on the passage as a whole, which of the following is the mule's most defining attribute?

(A) its size and weight
(B) its sense of humor
(C) its cruelty
(D) its intractability
(E) its mode of dying

200. The overall tone of the passage is best described as

(A) historical
(B) comical
(C) dirgelike
(D) ironic
(E) biting

201. Which of the following is most indicative of the characters' fellowship?

(A) "dat hock-bone" (11)
(B) "Brazzle's ole yaller mule" (15)
(C) Brazzle and Hambo's friendship
(D) "de draggin out" (42)
(E) Lige's anecdote (29–35)

202. The diction and language in the passage can be described as all of the following *except*

(A) vernacular
(B) colloquial
(C) minimalist
(D) figurative
(E) culturally specific

203. Which of the following describes the way the characters comment on Brazzle's mule?

    I. They develop the discussion by adding to each other's observations.

    II. They draw on compelling anecdotes to support their claims about the mule.

    III. They try to one-up each other's observations with increasingly dramatic tales.

    (A) I only

    (B) II only

    (C) III only

    (D) I and II only

    (E) I, II, and III

204. In the passage, the mule is treated as

    (A) a martyr—it was sacrificed for the betterment of the town

    (B) a symbol of the town's struggle

    (C) a metaphor for the futility of work

    (D) a relic that inspires comradery

    (E) an omen of tough times to come

Passage 20. Henry James, *The Turn of the Screw*

I remember the whole beginning as a succession of flights and drops, a little seesaw of the right throbs and the wrong. After rising, in town, to meet his appeal, I had at all events a couple of very bad days—found myself doubtful again, felt indeed sure I had made a mistake. In this state of mind I spent the long hours of bumping, swinging coach that carried me to the stopping place at which I was to be met by a vehicle from the house. This convenience, I was told, had been ordered, and I found, toward the close of the June afternoon, a commodious fly in waiting for me. Driving at that hour, on a lovely day, through a country to which the summer sweetness seemed to offer me a friendly welcome, my fortitude mounted afresh and, as we turned into the avenue, encountered a reprieve that was probably but a proof of the point to which it had sunk. I suppose I had expected, or had dreaded, something so melancholy that what greeted me was a good surprise. I remember as a most pleasant impression the broad, clear front, its open windows and fresh curtains and the pair of maids looking out; I remember the lawn and the bright flowers and the crunch of my wheels on the gravel and the clustered treetops over which the rooks circled and cawed in the golden sky. The scene had a greatness that made it a different affair from my own scant home, and there immediately appeared at the door, with a little girl in her hand, a civil person who dropped me as decent a curtsy as if I had been the mistress or a distinguished visitor. I had received in Harley Street a narrower notion of the place, and that, as I recalled it, made me think the proprietor still more of a gentleman, suggested that what I was to enjoy might be something beyond his promise.

    I had no drop again till the next day, for I was carried triumphantly through the following hours by my introduction to the younger of my pupils. The little   25 girl who accompanied Mrs. Grose appeared to me on the spot a creature so charming as to make it a great fortune to have to do with her. She was the most beautiful child I had ever seen, and I afterward wondered that my employer had not told me more of her. I slept little that night—I was too much excited; and this astonished me, too, I recollect, remained with me, adding to my sense of the   30 liberality with which I was treated. The large, impressive room, one of the best in the house, the great state bed, as I almost felt it, the full, figured draperies, the long glasses in which, for the first time, I could see myself from head to foot, all struck me—like the extraordinary charm of my small charge—as so many things thrown in. It was thrown in as well, from the first moment, that I should   35 get on with Mrs. Grose in a relation over which, on my way, in the coach, I fear I had rather brooded. The only thing indeed that in this early outlook might have made me shrink again was the clear circumstance of her being so glad to see me. I perceived within half an hour that she was so glad—stout, simple, plain, clean, wholesome woman—as to be positively on her guard against showing it   40 too much. I wondered even then a little why she should wish not to show it, and that, with reflection, with suspicion, might of course have made me uneasy.

205. Which of the following best conveys the effect of lines 1–13 ("I remember . . . a good surprise")?

    (A) An opening metaphor provides context for the descriptions that follow.
    (B) The simple sentence structure summarizes a simple memory.
    (C) A series of fond recollections carry new meaning for the narrator.
    (D) Contradictory descriptions cast doubt on the narrator's reliability.
    (E) Sensory descriptions create a pleasant image.

206. The "state of mind" mentioned in line 4 can best be described as

    (A) delusional
    (B) volatile
    (C) curious
    (D) anticipatory
    (E) regretful

207. Which of the following best describes the way the passage is narrated?

    (A) An omniscient narrator objectively describes a significant event.

    (B) The point of view shifts from one character to another.

    (C) An anxious narrator tries to make sense of her troubling past.

    (D) An excited narrator describes a series of events with superlatives.

    (E) A narrator recounts the conflicting impressions she had during and after a day's events.

208. The narrator's reaction upon arriving at the residence is attributed to all of the following *except*

    (A) a surprisingly reverential reception

    (B) the stateliness of the residence

    (C) low expectations

    (D) the temperate climate

    (E) Mrs. Grose's forthrightness

209. Which of the following enhances the narrator's excitement in lines 13–17 ("I remember . . . golden sky")?

    I. repetition of the phrase "I remember"

    II. sensory imagery

    III. polysyndeton

    (A) I only

    (B) I and II only

    (C) II only

    (D) II and III only

    (E) I, II, and III

210. From the first paragraph, we can infer that the speaker is

    (A) a precocious girl

    (B) not upper class

    (C) a distinguished visitor

    (D) the overseer

    (E) the proprietor

211. The "drop" in line 24 refers to

    (A) the rain

    (B) a physical fall

    (C) doubts

    (D) sustenance

    (E) excitement

212. What "remained" with the narrator in line 30?

(A) her employer's reticence
(B) the beautiful child
(C) her excitement
(D) the generosity of her hosts
(E) Mrs. Grose

213. The second paragraph differs from the first in its

(A) mention of the narrator's multiple emotions
(B) focus on the narrator's conflicting impressions of other characters
(C) superlative descriptions
(D) illustrative details
(E) narrative point of view

214. Overall, the narrator feels she has been treated

(A) affably
(B) servilely
(C) irreverently
(D) generously
(E) suspiciously

215. Upon meeting Mrs. Grose, the narrator feels both

(A) indifferent and wronged
(B) prejudicial and delusional
(C) relieved and hesitant
(D) ecstatic and relieved
(E) anxious and afraid

Passage 21. James Joyce, "The Dead"

Lily, the caretaker's daughter, was literally run off her feet. Hardly had she brought one gentleman into the little pantry behind the office on the ground floor and helped him off with his overcoat than the wheezy hall-door bell clanged again and she had to scamper along the bare hallway to let in another guest. It was well for her she had not to attend to the ladies also. But Miss Kate and Miss Julia had thought of that and had converted the bathroom upstairs into a ladies' dressing-room. Miss Kate and Miss Julia were there, gossiping and laughing and fussing, walking after each other to the head of the stairs, peering down over the banisters and calling down to Lily to ask her who had come.

It was always a great affair, the Misses Morkan's annual dance. Everybody who knew them came to it, members of the family, old friends of the family, the members of Julia's choir, any of Kate's pupils that were grown up enough, and even some of Mary Jane's pupils too. Never once had it fallen flat. For years and years it had gone off in splendid style, as long as anyone could remember; ever since Kate and Julia, after the death of their brother Pat, had left the house in 15 Stoney Batter and taken Mary Jane, their only niece, to live with them in the dark, gaunt house on Usher's Island, the upper part of which they had rented from Mr. Fulham, the corn-factor on the ground floor. That was a good thirty years ago if it was a day. Mary Jane, who was then a little girl in short clothes, was now the main prop of the household, for she had the organ in Haddington Road. 20 She had been through the Academy and gave a pupils' concert every year in the upper room of the Ancient Concert Rooms. Many of her pupils belonged to the better-class families on the Kingstown and Dalkey line. Old as they were, her aunts also did their share. Julia, though she was quite grey, was still the leading soprano in Adam and Eve's, and Kate, being too feeble to go about much, gave 25 music lessons to beginners on the old square piano in the back room. Lily, the caretaker's daughter, did housemaid's work for them. Though their life was modest, they believed in eating well; the best of everything: diamond-bone sirloins, three-shilling tea and the best bottled stout. But Lily seldom made a mistake in the orders, so that she got on well with her three mistresses. They were fussy, that 30 was all. But the only thing they would not stand was back answers.

Of course, they had good reason to be fussy on such a night. And then it was long after ten o'clock and yet there was no sign of Gabriel and his wife. Besides they were dreadfully afraid that Freddy Malins might turn up screwed. They would not wish for worlds that any of Mary Jane's pupils should see him under 35 the influence; and when he was like that it was sometimes very hard to manage him. Freddy Malins always came late, but they wondered what could be keeping Gabriel: and that was what brought them every two minutes to the banisters to ask Lily had Gabriel or Freddy come.

216. The structure of the second sentence of the passage

    (A) obfuscates meaning

    (B) juxtaposes conflicting ideas

    (C) complements the harried state it describes

    (D) contrasts Lily's emotional state

    (E) corresponds to that of the first sentence of the paragraph

217. The imagery of the first paragraph provides

    (A) spacial and auditory details

    (B) metaphoric and ironic descriptions

    (C) exaggerated and comic details

    (D) a sympathetic and regretful tone

    (E) a partiality toward one character

218. In the context of the second paragraph, the sentence in line 13 ("Never once had it fallen flat") is distinct in which of the following ways?

(A) Its simplicity and proximity to compound sentences allow it to emphasize an essential point.

(B) It repeats information from previous and upcoming sentences, which creates a sense of monotony.

(C) It is markedly short to create anxiety.

(D) It is redundant and serves no ultimate purpose.

(E) It is passive in order to highlight the agency of the characters.

219. The mood in the house is predominantly

(A) pacific

(B) patient

(C) indulgent

(D) anxious

(E) fearful

220. The phrase "main prop" (line 20) reveals that

(A) the two aunts view Mary Jane as servile

(B) Mary Jane is the sole supporter of the household

(C) the two aunts use Mary Jane for their financial survival

(D) Mary Jane is the main provider in the family

(E) Mary Jane is objectified

221. The phrases "run off her feet" (line 1), "if it was a day" (line 19), "They were fussy . . . back answers" (lines 30–31), "turn up screwed" (line 34), and "wish for worlds" (line 35) have what in common?

 I. They are examples of the characters' vernacular.

 II. They help establish a formal tone.

 III. They are intended to emphasize the characters' lack of education.

(A) I only

(B) I and II only

(C) I and III only

(D) II and III only

(E) I, II, and III

222. From the passage as a whole, we can infer that the three women (Julia, Kate, and Mary Jane) are all of the following *except*

(A) discerning

(B) musically inclined

(C) not upper class

(D) oppressive

(E) finicky

223. The first and second paragraphs differ in that
   (A) the second contains Lily's perspective
   (B) the first sets up a problem that the second solves
   (C) the first sets the scene, and the second provides background
   (D) the second provides evidence for opinions expressed in the first
   (E) the first mentions characters that the second does not

224. The passage's closing sentence intends to provide
   (A) the aunts' preference for specific guests
   (B) a resolution that eases the anxiety of the scene
   (C) a weak justification of a character's behavior
   (D) a clarification of the aunts' preoccupation
   (E) a rapport between Freddy and Gabriel

225. The passage provides answers to all of the following questions about the two aunts *except*
   (A) What are some of their interests?
   (B) Why are they eager for Gabriel's arrival?
   (C) How do they know Lily and Mary Jane?
   (D) What are their vocations?
   (E) How did they come to live in this house?

Passage 22. Franz Kafka, "Metamorphosis"

One morning, when Gregor Samsa woke from troubled dreams, he found himself transformed in his bed into a horrible vermin.[1] He lay on his armor-like back, and if he lifted his head a little he could see his brown belly, slightly domed and divided by arches into stiff sections. The bedding was hardly able to cover it and seemed ready to slide off any moment. His many legs, pitifully thin com-   5
pared with the size of the rest of him, waved about helplessly as he looked.

"What's happened to me?" he thought. It wasn't a dream. His room, a proper human room although a little too small, lay peacefully between its four familiar walls. A collection of textile samples lay spread out on the table— Samsa was a travelling salesman—and above it there hung a picture that he had   10
recently cut out of an illustrated magazine and housed in a nice, gilded frame. It showed a lady fitted out with a fur hat and fur boa who sat upright, raising a heavy fur muff that covered the whole of her lower arm towards the viewer.

Gregor then turned to look out the window at the dull weather. Drops of rain could be heard hitting the pane, which made him feel quite sad. "How about if   15
I sleep a little bit longer and forget all this nonsense," he thought, but that was something he was unable to do because he was used to sleeping on his right, and

---

1. Modern translations indicate that the transformation is into a bug or insect, very likely a cockroach.

in his present state couldn't get into that position. However hard he threw himself onto his right, he always rolled back to where he was. He must have tried it a hundred times, shut his eyes so that he wouldn't have to look at the floundering   20
legs, and only stopped when he began to feel a mild, dull pain there that he had never felt before.

"Oh, God," he thought, "what a strenuous career it is that I've chosen! Travelling day in and day out. Doing business like this takes much more effort than doing your own business at home, and on top of that there's the curse   25
of travelling, worries about making train connections, bad and irregular food, contact with different people all the time so that you can never get to know anyone or become friendly with them. It can all go to Hell!" He felt a slight itch up on his belly; pushed himself slowly up on his back towards the headboard so that he could lift his head better; found where the itch was, and saw that it was   30
covered with lots of little white spots which he didn't know what to make of; and when he tried to feel the place with one of his legs he drew it quickly back because as soon as he touched it he was overcome by a cold shudder.

He slid back into his former position. "Getting up early all the time," he thought, "it makes you stupid. You've got to get enough sleep. Other travelling   35
salesmen live a life of luxury. For instance, whenever I go back to the guest house during the morning to copy out the contract, these gentlemen are always still sitting there eating their breakfasts. I ought to just try that with my boss; I'd get kicked out on the spot. But who knows, maybe that would be the best thing for me. If I didn't have my parents to think about I'd have given in my notice a long   40
time ago, I'd have gone up to the boss and told him just what I think, tell him everything I would, let him know just what I feel. He'd fall right off his desk! And it's a funny sort of business to be sitting up there at your desk, talking down at your subordinates from up there, especially when you have to go right up close because the boss is hard of hearing. Well, there's still some hope; once I've got the   45
money together to pay off my parents' debt to him—another five or six years I suppose—that's definitely what I'll do. That's when I'll make the big change. First of all though, I've got to get up, my train leaves at five."

226. In context of the passage as a whole, the first paragraph functions to

    (A) raise suspicion about the narrator's credibility
    (B) upset the reader
    (C) pique interest by setting up a problem
    (D) introduce the setting
    (E) convince the reader of something impossible

227. The descriptions of the setting in the second and third paragraphs serve to

(A) exaggerate the problem Gregor is facing
(B) contrast with Gregor's mood
(C) confirm that Gregor has imagined this transformation
(D) reveal that the story is meant to be fantastical
(E) develop Gregor's character

228. In the context of the passage as a whole, Gregor's failure to get comfortable (lines 15–22) is likely suggestive of

(A) the futility of his daily efforts in the workplace
(B) the severity of a vermin's life
(C) his overall lackadaisical attitude
(D) the ease with which he gives up on problems
(E) the hopelessness that characterizes the society of the time

229. Gregor's exclamation in line 23 is notable for which of the following reasons?

I. It provides a glimpse into Gregor's daily circumstances.
II. It hints at the metaphorical significance of Gregor's transformation.
III. It reveals that Gregor's physical change is less worrying to him than his onerous job.

(A) I only
(B) II only
(C) III only
(D) I and III only
(E) I, II, and III

230. The inclusion of Gregor's thoughts in lines 23–28 primarily serves to

(A) belittle Gregor's choice of career
(B) suggest Gregor's human life is vermin-like
(C) reveal Gregor's concern for keeping his job
(D) emphasize Gregor's frustration with his transformation into a vermin
(E) distract from his physical transformation

231. In context, the word "'stupid'" (line 35) most likely means

(A) disabled
(B) ignorant
(C) pointless
(D) stuporous
(E) without luxury

232. Which of the following best conveys the purpose of including Gregor's thoughts about his job (lines 34–48)?
    (A) They display Gregor's unique vernacular.
    (B) They incite distaste for the main character.
    (C) They critique the modern working world.
    (D) They introduce Gregor's problem.
    (E) They further develop the symbolic meaning of Gregor's metamorphosis.

233. In the last sentence of the passage the author seeks to interest us in the subject by
    (A) confounding us with Gregor's priority
    (B) impressing us with Gregor's fastidiousness
    (C) shocking us with Gregor's denial
    (D) infuriating us with Gregor's tenacity
    (E) distancing us from Gregor's situation

234. Gregor's tone contrasts with the narrator's because it is
    (A) frustrated instead of reportorial
    (B) didactic instead of empathetic
    (C) astonished instead of scientific
    (D) compassionate instead of cryptic
    (E) straightforward instead of sentimental

235. The passage portrays Gregor as all of the following *except*
    (A) spiteful toward his employer
    (B) resentful toward his predicament
    (C) sincerely motivated by his fealty to his parents
    (D) crippled by a lack of agency
    (E) oblivious to his condition

236. The physical metamorphosis into a vermin provides insight on
    (A) the similarities and differences between the human body and that of a vermin
    (B) the way all humans actually behave like scurrying cowards
    (C) the negative impact a dehumanizing job can have on one's sense of self
    (D) how oblivious people are to their own bodily changes
    (E) life's unpredictability

Passage 23. Sinclair Lewis, *Babbitt*

He was busy, from March to June. He kept himself from the bewilderment
of thinking. His wife and the neighbors were generous. Every evening he played
bridge or attended the movies, and the days were blank of face and silent.

In June, Mrs. Babbitt and Tinka went East, to stay with relatives, and Babbitt
was free to do—he was not quite sure what.   5

All day long after their departure he thought of the emancipated house in
which he could, if he desired, go mad and curse the gods without having to keep
up a husbandly front. He considered, "I could have a reg'lar party to-night; stay
out till two and not do any explaining afterwards. Cheers!" He telephoned to
Vergil Gunch, to Eddie Swanson. Both of them were engaged for the evening,   10
and suddenly he was bored by having to take so much trouble to be riotous.

He was silent at dinner, unusually kindly to Ted and Verona, hesitating but
not disapproving when Verona stated her opinion of Kenneth Escott's opinion
of Dr. John Jennison Drew's opinion of the opinions of the evolutionists. Ted
was working in a garage through the summer vacation, and he related his daily   15
triumphs: how he had found a cracked ball-race, what he had said to the Old
Grouch, what he had said to the foreman about the future of wireless telephony.

Ted and Verona went to a dance after dinner. Even the maid was out. Rarely
had Babbitt been alone in the house for an entire evening. He was restless. He
vaguely wanted something more diverting than the newspaper comic strips   20
to read. He ambled up to Verona's room, sat on her maidenly blue and white
bed, humming and grunting in a solid-citizen manner as he examined her
books: Conrad's "Rescue," a volume strangely named "Figures of Earth," poetry
(quite irregular poetry, Babbitt thought) by Vachel Lindsay, and essays by
H. L. Mencken—highly improper essays, making fun of the church and all the   25
decencies. He liked none of the books. In them he felt a spirit of rebellion against
niceness and solid-citizenship. These authors—and he supposed they were
famous ones, too—did not seem to care about telling a good story which would
enable a fellow to forget his troubles. He sighed. He noted a book, "The Three
Black Pennies," by Joseph Hergesheimer. Ah, that was something like it! It would 30
be an adventure story, maybe about counterfeiting—detectives sneaking up on
the old house at night. He tucked the book under his arm, he clumped down-
stairs and solemnly began to read, under the piano-lamp . . .

237. The first paragraph implies that Babbitt's life from March to June is

    (A) intellectually stimulating

    (B) routine

    (C) reclusive

    (D) onerous

    (E) pensive

238. The primary function of the second paragraph (lines 4–5) is to

 (A) highlight a key characteristic of Babbitt that will be developed throughout the passage
 (B) characterize Babbitt's relationship with his wife
 (C) stress the importance of the new characters mentioned
 (D) present Babbitt as independent
 (E) contrast Babbitt with others

239. In context, the word "emancipated" (line 6) suggests that

 (A) Mrs. Babbitt is unrelenting
 (B) Babbitt's home life is constrained
 (C) Babbitt is dying to be with his friends
 (D) Babbitt is lost without his routine
 (E) Babbitt is suffering from ennui

240. The tone of lines 12–14 ("He was silent . . . evolutionists") is best described as

 (A) intentionally mocking
 (B) offended
 (C) somewhat condescending
 (D) scornful
 (E) sympathetic

241. The word "vaguely" in line 20 implies that Babbitt

 (A) abhors comics
 (B) is tenacious
 (C) is frenetic
 (D) is ambivalent
 (E) is apathetic

242. Based on Babbitt's thoughts about the books, we can infer all of the following *except* that
 (A) he is discomfited by their spirit
 (B) he wants them to offer him an escape
 (C) he is quick to judge them
 (D) he dislikes their antisocial themes
 (E) his interests are congruous with Verona's

243. It can be inferred that Babbitt ordinarily responds to Verona's opinions
with
(A) kindness
(B) concordance
(C) antagonism
(D) openness
(E) dismissal

244. Which of the following indicates that the narrator has access to Babbitt's
thoughts?
(A) "Ah, that was something like it!" (30)
(B) "He was busy, from March to June" (1)
(C) "He telephoned to Vergil Gunch, to Eddie Swanson" (9–10)
(D) "Rarely had Babbitt been alone in the house for an entire evening"
(19–20)
(E) "He sighed" (29)

245. The final paragraph primarily characterizes Babbitt as
(A) desperately seeking escape
(B) reveling in solitude
(C) admiringly conservative
(D) perpetually unsatisfied
(E) seeking a mild diversion

Passage 24. Naguib Mahfouz, *Midaq Alley*

Many things combine to show that Midaq Alley is one of the gems of times
gone by and that it once shone forth like a flashing star in the history of Cairo.
Which Cairo do I mean? That of the Fatimads, the Mamlukes, or the Sultans?
Only God and the archaeologists know the answer to that, but in any case, the
alley is certainly an ancient relic and a precious one. How could it be otherwise   5
with its stone-paved surface leading directly to the historic Sanadiqiya Street.
And then there is its café known as Kirsha's. Its walls decorated with multicolored
arabesques, now crumbling, give off strong odors from the medicines of olden
times, smells which have now become the spices and folk cures of today and
tomorrow . . .   10
Although Midaq Alley lives in almost complete isolation from all surrounding
activity, it clamors with a distinctive and personal life of its own. Fundamentally
and basically, its roots connect with life as a whole, and yet, at the same time, it
retains a number of the secrets of a world now past.
The sun began to set and Midaq Alley was veiled in the brown hues of the   15
glow. The darkness was all the greater because it was enclosed like a trap between
three walls. It rose unevenly from Sanadiqiya Street. One of its sides consisted

of a shop, a cafe, and a bakery, the other of another shop and an office. It ends abruptly, just as its ancient glory did, with two adjoining houses, each of three stories.   20

The noises of daytime life had quieted now and those of the evening began to be heard, a whisper here and a whisper there: "Good evening everyone." "Come on in; it's time for the evening get-together." "Wake up, Uncle Kamil, and close your shop!" "Change the water in the hookah, Sanker!" "Put out the oven, Jaada!" "The hashish hurts my chest." "If we've been suffering terrors of blackouts   25 and air raids for five years it's only due to our own wickedness!"

246. Lines 1–5 ("Many things . . . a precious one") present Midaq Alley as

    I. no longer appreciated as it once was
   II. representative of the complete history of Cairo
  III. worthy of appreciation and attention

  (A) I only
  (B) II only
  (C) II and III only
  (D) I and III only
  (E) I, II, and III

247. In the first paragraph, a contrast is established between Midaq Alley's former prominence and its current state by means of

  (A) a reference to its proximity to the "historic Sanadiqiya Street" (6)
  (B) a description of odors that now serve a different purpose
  (C) a rhetorical question inquiring about its relevance to contemporary Cairo
  (D) a suggestion that only "God and the archaeologists" (4) know of its value
  (E) an image of "its stone-paved surface" (6)

248. From the narrator's perspective, Midaq Alley is particularly special because

  (A) it invokes the history of Cairo's leaders
  (B) it is a relic of Cairo's most impressive past
  (C) its isolated setting allows it to retain the charms of Cairo's past and avoid the corrupting influence of present-day values
  (D) it both serves as a valuable reminder of the past and is a firm connection to current life in Cairo
  (E) it is a secret that only Cairo's most devoted denizens can appreciate

249. The third paragraph, in relation to the rest of the passage, offers

    (A) a more elaborate comparison of Midaq Alley's past and its present state

    (B) a personal connection to Midaq Alley's history

    (C) a precise yet symbolic description of Midaq Alley's features

    (D) a lively portrayal of Midaq Alley's residents

    (E) an objective list of Midaq Alley's most important elements

250. The "complete isolation" (line 11) is most enhanced by which of the following phrases?

    (A) "enclosed like a trap" (16)

    (B) "The sun began to set" (15)

    (C) "veiled in the brown hues of the glow" (15–16)

    (D) "It rose unevenly" (17)

    (E) "It ends abruptly" (18–19)

251. The phrase "It ends abruptly" (lines 18–19) is used

    (A) both literally and figuratively

    (B) negatively

    (C) critically

    (D) apologetically

    (E) regretfully

252. The narrator's perspective might best be described as that of

    (A) a former resident recalling memorable moments in Midaq Alley

    (B) a pedantic historian asserting the preeminence of a particular place

    (C) a passionate advocate for restoring the former grandeur of Midaq Alley

    (D) an interested observer who wants to highlight the complex value of a place

    (E) an objective chronicler of a historic period

253. The quoted statements in the final paragraph function mainly as all of the following *except*

    (A) details that support the earlier claim that Midaq Alley "clamors with a distinctive and personal life of its own" (12)

    (B) representations of the variety of voices and perspectives heard on Midaq Alley

    (C) illustrations of the alley coming to life in the evening

    (D) an indication of the shift from Midaq Alley's "daytime life" (21)

    (E) an indication that there is discord among the residents of Midaq Alley

Passage 25. Rohinton Mistry, *A Fine Balance*

The savings were sufficient to pay for bus fares. Dina went to parks, wandered in museums and markets, visited cinemas (just from the outside, to look at posters), and ventured timidly into public libraries. The heads bent over books made her feel out of place; everyone in there seemed so learned, and she hadn't even matriculated.

This impression was dispelled when she realized that the reading materials in the hands of these grave individuals could range from something unpronounceable like *Areopagitica* by John Milton to *The Illustrated Weekly of India*. Eventually, the enormous old reading rooms, with their high ceilings, creaky floorboards and dark panelling, became her favourite sanctuary. The stately ceiling fans that hung from long poles swept the air with a comforting *whoosh*, and the deep leather chairs, musty smells, and rustle of turning pages were soothing. Best of all, people spoke in whispers. The only time Dina heard a shout was when the doorman scolded a beggar trying to sneak inside. Hours passed as she flipped through encyclopedias, gazed into art books, and curiously opened dusty medical tomes, rounding off the visit by sitting for a few minutes with eyes closed in a dark corner of the old building, where time could stand still if one wanted it to.

The more modern libraries were equipped with music rooms. They also had fluorescent lights, Formica tables, air-conditioning, and brightly painted walls, and were always crowded. She found them cold and inhospitable, going there only if she wanted to listen to records. She knew very little about music—a few names like Brahms, Mozart, Schumann, and Bach, which her ears had picked up in childhood when her father would turn on the radio or put something on the gramophone, take her in his lap and say, "It makes you forget the troubles of this world, doesn't it?" and Dina would nod her head seriously.

In the library, she selected records at random, trying to memorize the names of the ones she enjoyed so she could play them again another day. It was tricky, because the symphonies and concertos and sonatas were distinguished only by numbers that were preceded by letters like Op. and K. and BWV, and she did not know what any of it meant. If she was lucky she found something with a name that resonated richly in her memory; and when the familiar music filled her head, the past was conquered for a brief while, and she felt herself ache with the ecstasy of completion, as though a missing limb had been recovered.

254. Lines 1–8 ("Dina went to parks . . . *India*") convey a shift in Dina's assumptions about

   (A) libraries; instead of being intimidating, they are humble
   (B) public places; instead of being expensive, they are accessible
   (C) all library patrons; instead of being gravely scholarly, their interests are diverse
   (D) exploring the city; instead of feeling eager, she feels timid
   (E) books; instead of being impenetrable, they are entertaining

255. Based on the context provided in lines 6–8 ("This impression . . . *India*"),
which of the following would Dina consider most similar to *The Illustrated
Weekly of India*?

(A) a historical account of India's independence
(B) a holy screed
(C) a classic European novel
(D) an art history textbook
(E) a comic strip

256. In the second paragraph, the narrator develops the characterization of the
library through the use of

I.   sensory imagery that describes the sounds, smells, textures, and
     objects in the library
II. a figurative comparison to a sanctuary
III. hyperbole

(A) I only
(B) I and II only
(C) II and III only
(D) I and III only
(E) I, II, and III

257. In the context of the passage as a whole, the third paragraph's various
functions include all of the following *except*

(A) it presents modern libraries as especially intimidating because of the
    harsh setting and sophisticated music
(B) it conveys Dina as particularly motivated to listen to music by
    describing the modern libraries as "cold and inhospitable" (20)
(C) it introduces a memory of Dina's father that helps contextualize her
    interest in music
(D) it further develops Dina's character by discussing an interest of hers
(E) it reveals details about Dina's childhood that help establish her
    motivation

258. The passage presents Dina's attitude as changing from

(A) self-pitying to disillusioned
(B) timid to indifferent
(C) curious to anxious
(D) realistic to idealistic
(E) hesitant to self-confident

259. It can be inferred that the phrase "the past was conquered" (line 32) most nearly means

(A) the familiar music that fills Dina's head helps her forget the troubles of her past

(B) Dina's humiliation upon entering the library is mitigated by the pleasant music

(C) the memory of her father's absence will no longer upset Dina

(D) learning about classical composers helps Dina come to terms with her troubling childhood

(E) Dina is able to focus on her experience at the library without being burdened by her past

260. The figurative comparisons in the closing lines ("she felt herself ache . . . recovered") chiefly serve to

(A) convey the incredible talent of a classical musician

(B) suggest that music, for Dina, is about becoming a "learned" (40) individual

(C) imply a connection between Dina's dedication to hearing music and her memory of her father

(D) emphasize the role music plays in making a "cold and inhospitable" (20) library more appealing

(E) present Dina as someone in great physical pain

261. Which of the following details most clearly demonstrates Dina's view of the library as "a sanctuary" (line 10)?

(A) "Everyone in there seemed so learned" (4)

(B) "The stately ceiling fans that hung from long poles swept the air with a comforting *whoosh*" (10–11)

(C) "rounding off the visit by sitting for a few minutes . . . one wanted it to" (16–17)

(D) "The modern libraries were equipped with music rooms" (18)

(E) "In the library, she selected records at random" (26)

262. It can be inferred from the passage that Dina's relationship with music is particularly influenced by

(A) a desire to become as "learned" (4) as the other library patrons

(B) a determination to learn about "names like Brahms, Mozart, Schumann, and Bach" (22)

(C) a desperate wish to escape her current reality

(D) childhood experiences with her father

(E) an obligation to please her father

263. The narration is most focused on

(A) Dina's sense of herself as uneducated
(B) Dina's goals to educate herself
(C) Dina's fascination with exploring the city independently
(D) Dina's obscure scholarly interests
(E) Dina's experiences in public libraries and their impact on her

Passage 26. R. A. Sasaki, "Driving to Colma"

In the following week, the focus of my life shrinks. All we can think about is: Will he eat? And then: What? My mother and I dig into the past for every old favorite we can remember. We count off calories and grams of protein, and make it through another day. My father had discovered a taste for lemonade. The exaggerated sweetness of it breaks through the drug-deadened tongue. We make it by   5
the half-gallon.

There are also his pills. It is as though we have entered a new world and must learn the language spoken there. We list the strange vocabulary on a chart, with little boxes to be checked off for each pill taken, so many times a day. There seems to be an inexhaustible supply of allopurinol. This gives me hope. He will   10
have to live a long time to finish all of those. Prednisone, four a day. Vitamins. There will be more names later: bleomycin, Oncovin, Decadron. Methotrexate and leucovorin. The names are strange, Russian-sounding. I roll the words around on my tongue. I suspect I will never forget them. I can fill my mind with recipes and names of drugs, and distract myself from the question that no one   15
can answer.

I collect books, and curl up in my favorite reading place halfway up the stairs. Except now, instead of horse stories or mysteries, instead of Russian novels, they are medical books, dictionaries of my new language. I look up the word: lymphoma. I look up allopurinol, prednisone, bleomycin, Oncovin, Decadron.   20
Methotrexate is poison; leucovorin, the antidote. I repeat names, effects, and side effects, like a child learning the Lord's prayer, or a new kind of catechism. I was always good in school.

At night, when I dream, I find myself back in my old Japanese house. The sliding wood-framed windows are opened wide to the trees outside, and the sun   25
is on the tatami. I am sitting on the window ledge, waiting for Matsumoto to come through the gate, up the stone steps, through the trees. But when I awaken, the fog is blanking out the small square window in the room where I slept as a child. I am back in the house where I grew up, in the life I have spent my life trying to escape, not because I hated it, but because it had simply become too   30
small.

264. Which of the following best describes the way the phrase "the focus of my life shrinks" (line 1) functions in the passage?

    (A) It serves as the thesis for an argument that the narrator proceeds to prove.
    (B) It refers only to the narrator's newly acquired understanding of medical terminology.
    (C) It connects the narrow focus of caring for a sick parent to the restricting feeling of living back at home.
    (D) It bookends the passage, reinforcing the narrator's perspective that her childhood was suffocating.
    (E) It conveys the narrator's singular focus on her father's health.

265. The narrator's comparison to a "new world" (line 7) suggests

    (A) she fears the unknown world of living without her father
    (B) she underestimates the gravity of her father's situation
    (C) she tries to make her mother feel better by turning the experience into an adventure
    (D) the shrinking and smallness of her life is also new and fascinating
    (E) she has discovered a new interest she wants to explore

266. The drugs mentioned in the second and third paragraphs serve which of the following functions for the narrator?

    (A) They incite hope and preoccupy and intrigue her.
    (B) They heal and intimidate, and offer respite.
    (C) They distract, poison, and overwhelm.
    (D) They soothe, sustain, and burden.
    (E) They mystify, console, and become scarce.

267. The "question" mentioned in line 15 is most likely a reference to

    (A) the meaning of life
    (B) all that is unknown about our futures
    (C) what the medicinal terms mean
    (D) the uncertainty of the father's recovery
    (E) what happens after death

268. A contrast between the narrator's present and past is developed by means of

   I. references to reading material
   II. comparisons between two homes
   III. a list of the father's medicines

   (A) I only
   (B) II only
   (C) I and II only
   (D) II and III only
   (E) I, II, and III

269. Which best conveys the effect of the sentence in lines 21–22 ("I repeat . . . catechism")?

   (A) A comparison presents the narrator's situation as sacred and holy.
   (B) A simile contrasts the frightening names of drugs with the soothing words of a prayer.
   (C) A metaphor suggests a strong connection between the healing powers of both medicine and prayer.
   (D) Comparisons emphasize the significance and ritual involved as the narrator immerses herself in learning something new.
   (E) Religious allusions contribute to the somber and austere tone of the passage.

270. By commenting that she "was always good in school" (line 23), the narrator most nearly means

   (A) studying gives her a sense of comfort and control during an ultimately uncertain time
   (B) she must justify spending time learning about her father's drugs
   (C) studying and acquiring knowledge is the best way to support her father
   (D) she hasn't changed much since childhood
   (E) she is resigned to study the names of medicines since there is nothing else she can do to help her father

271. Which of the following best explains the symbolic significance of the fog?

(A) It represents a memory of the smallness of her life in Japan.

(B) It represents the confining experience of living back at home, in comparison to the freeing open space around her Japanese home.

(C) It corresponds to the narrator's fear of the "new world" (7) described in the second paragraph.

(D) It is a metaphor for the narrator's somewhat comforting experience of coming back to her childhood home.

(E) It symbolizes the uncertainty the narrator feels about being home to help her parents.

272. Which of the following best describes the way the passage is narrated?

(A) A first person recollects an experience of returning home with a burdensome sense of guilt.

(B) A distant narrator describes the stress of caring for a sick parent.

(C) A narrator earnestly describes an experience returning to her suffocating childhood home.

(D) An ambivalent narrator describes the difficult but necessary obligation to help her parents.

(E) A narrator thoughtfully elaborates on how her life shrinks upon returning to her childhood home to care for a sick parent.

Passage 27. Zadie Smith, *White Teeth*

Children. Samad had caught children like a disease. Yes, he had sired two of them willingly—as willingly as a man can—but he had not bargained for this other thing. This thing that no one tells you about. This thing of *knowing* children. For forty-odd years, traveling happily along life's highway, Samad had been unaware that, dotted along that road, in the crèche facilities of each ser-   5 vice station, there lived a subclass of society, a mewling, puking underclass; he knew nothing of them and it did not concern him. Then suddenly, in the early eighties, he became infected with children; *other people's* children, children who were friends of *his* children, and then *their* friends; then children in children's programs on children's TV. By 1984 at least 30 percent of his social and cultural   10 circle was under the age of nine—and this all led, inevitably, to the position he now found himself in. He was a *parent-governor*.

By a strange process of symmetry, being a parent-governor perfectly mirrors the process of becoming a parent. It starts innocently. Casually. You turn up at the annual spring fair full of beans, help with the raffle tickets (because the pretty   15 red-haired music teacher asks you to) and win a bottle of whiskey (all school raffles are fixed), and, before you know where you are, you're turning up at the weekly school council meetings, organizing concerts, discussing plans for a new

music department, donating funds for the rejuvenation of the water fountains—
you're *implicated* in the school, you're *involved* in it. Sooner or later you stop   20
dropping your children at the school gates. You start following them in.

273. The context of the passage indicates that a "parent-governor" (line 12) is

    (A) a parent who is the primary teacher of their child
    (B) a teacher who educates with the nurturing style of a parent
    (C) a parent who oversees the administration of their child's school
    (D) a parent who is indifferent toward the affairs of their child's school
    (E) a parent who is particularly involved in the affairs of their child's
          school

274. The phrase "as willingly as a man can" (line 2) is intended as

    (A) a glib reference to Samad's partner
    (B) a comment on the unequal roles between men and women
    (C) a reminder that Samad did not have a say in having children
    (D) a wry suggestion that men are heavily influenced by their partners to
          have children
    (E) a simple clarification

275. The first paragraph relies on which of the following to portray children
from Samad's perspective?

    I. an extended metaphor
   II. colloquial diction
  III. an intentional emphasis on key words

    (A) I only
    (B) I and II only
    (C) II and III only
    (D) I and III only
    (E) I, II, and III

276. The "other thing" (line 3) is revealed to be

    (A) the experience of being a parent-governor
    (B) Samad's unplanned immersion in the world of children
    (C) Samad's indifference to a "subclass of society" (6)
    (D) the experience of parenting two children willingly
    (E) the imposed expectation to devote oneself to one's child's schooling

277. The "symmetry" referred to in line 13 emphasizes

(A) Samad's dedication to parenting his children
(B) Samad's unintentional engagement with the world of parenting
(C) the natural relationship between parenting and teaching
(D) Samad's reluctance to become a parent
(E) the difference between casual volunteering and onerous obligations

278. The "spring fair" (line 15) is mentioned to

(A) show that Samad does enjoy being a parent-governor
(B) present Samad as an involved parent
(C) highlight Samad's transformation to someone who loves children from someone who "knew nothing of them" (7)
(D) represent a casual interest that quickly evolves into full involvement
(E) mark the specific point at which Samad's life as a parent dramatically changes

279. The purpose of the list in lines 17–19 ("turning up . . . water fountains") is

(A) to detail all the ways that Samad helps his children's school
(B) to present the school as in need of parental support
(C) to mirror the ways Samad became "infected with children" (8)
(D) to present the role of parent-governor as important
(E) to subtly mock a school's unrealistic expectations of a parent-governor

280. The parenthetical phrases in the second paragraph primarily serve as

(A) helpful reminders
(B) historical and cultural context
(C) glimpses of the omniscient narrator's point of view
(D) details that reveal Samad's perspective
(E) essential background information

281. The italicized words throughout the passage function to

(A) accentuate Samad's voice and point of view in the narration
(B) underscore the narrator's perspective
(C) add dimension to the narrative by including colloquial diction
(D) emphasize the most odious aspects of parenting
(E) portray Samad as a caricature of a disinterested parent

282. The narrative point of view of the passage is best described as

(A) objective
(B) critical
(C) first-person
(D) stream of consciousness
(E) free indirect discourse

283. The "school gates" (line 21) can be interpreted as

(A) a symbol for the border between simply having children and "this other thing" (3)
(B) a literal point of no return for Samad
(C) a metaphor for the imprisonment of a domestic life
(D) an allusion to the entrance of heaven
(E) a metaphor for over-involved parents

284. The development of the passage is best described by which of the following?

(A) Illustrative comparisons show how Samad discovers the value of being a parent-governor.
(B) A shift from negative comparisons to positive ones shows how Samad comes to terms with being "infected with children" (8).
(C) A consistently negative tone describes the role of a parent-governor.
(D) A somewhat sarcastic tone conveys Samad's perspective on becoming a parent-governor.
(E) A wry narrator offers a glimpse into the humiliating experiences of a parent.

Passage 28. Upton Sinclair, *The Jungle*

Jurgis had made some friends by this time, and he sought one of them and asked what this meant. The friend, who was named Tamoszius Kuszleika, was a sharp little man who folded hides on the killing beds, and he listened to what Jurgis had to say without seeming at all surprised. They were common enough, he said, such cases of petty graft. It was simply some boss who proposed to add   5
a little to his income. After Jurgis had been there awhile he would know that the plants were simply honeycombed with rottenness of that sort—the bosses grafted off the men, and they grafted off each other; and some day the superintendent would find out about the boss, and then he would graft off the boss. Warming to the subject, Tamoszius went on to explain the situation. Here was Durham's,   10
for instance, owned by a man who was trying to make as much money out of it as he could, and did not care in the least how he did it; and underneath him, ranged in ranks and grades like an army, were managers and superintendents and foremen, each one driving the man next below him and trying to squeeze out

of him as much work as possible. And all the men of the same rank were pitted   15
against each other; the accounts of each were kept separately, and every man
lived in terror of losing his job, if another made a better record than he. So from
top to bottom the place was simply a seething caldron of jealousies and hatreds;
there was no loyalty or decency anywhere about it, there was no place in it where
a man counted for anything against a dollar. And worse than there being no   20
decency, there was not even any honesty. The reason for that? Who could say? It
must have been old Durham in the beginning; it was a heritage which the self-
made merchant had left to his son, along with his millions.

Jurgis would find out these things for himself, if he stayed there long enough;
it was the men who had to do all the dirty jobs, and so there was no deceiving   25
them; and they caught the spirit of the place, and did like all the rest. Jurgis
had come there, and thought he was going to make himself useful, and rise and
become a skilled man; but he would soon find out his error—for nobody rose
in Packingtown by doing good work. You could lay that down for a rule—if you
met a man who was rising in Packingtown, you met a knave. That man who had   30
been sent to Jurgis' father by the boss, he would rise; the man who told tales and
spied upon his fellows would rise; but the man who minded his own business
and did his work—why, they would "speed him up" till they had worn him out,
and then they would throw him into the gutter.

Jurgis went home with his head buzzing. Yet he could not bring himself to   35
believe such things—no, it could not be so. Tamoszius was simply another of the
grumblers. He was a man who spent all his time fiddling; and he would go to
parties at night and not get home till sunrise, and so of course he did not feel like
work. Then, too, he was a puny little chap; and so he had been left behind in the
race, and that was why he was sore. And yet so many strange things kept coming   40
to Jurgis' notice every day!

285. The word "this" in line 2 is likely a reference to all of the following *except*

    (A) Jurgis's low wages
    (B) "what Jurgis had to say" (3–4)
    (C) an incident involving unethical behavior
    (D) "the killing beds" (3)
    (E) the superintendent's behavior

286. The word "simply" in line 5 implies

    (A) the narrator's skepticism of Tamoszius's account
    (B) Tamoszius's dismay at the corruption around him
    (C) the obvious and overwhelming amount of graft in the company
    (D) Jurgis's realization of the company's true nature
    (E) the minor nature of the problems of the company

287. The image provided by the phrase "honeycombed with rotteness" (line 7) is apt because

    I. the author intends to liken the workers to bees

   II. the boss functions similarly to a queen bee

  III. the incidents of graft are ubiquitous and interconnected

  IV. there is a kind of sweetness to the unscrupulous structure of the factory

  (A) I and II only

  (B) II and III only

  (C) I and IV only

  (D) I, II, and III only

  (E) I, II, III, and IV

288. The phrase "like an army" (line 13) is primarily used to portray

  (A) the severity of the discipline in the plants

  (B) the fierce patriotism of the workers in the plants

  (C) the heroism involved in managing the plants

  (D) the significance of the hierarchical structure evident in the plants

  (E) the conscripted labor of the workers in the plants

289. The state of Durham's is attributed to all of the following causes *except*

  (A) inheritance of an unprincipled management system

  (B) desperation for advancement

  (C) disregard for humanity

  (D) ubiquitous venality

  (E) appreciation of a principled work ethic

290. According to the passage as a whole, the company being described seems to value workers who are

  (A) skilled, useful men

  (B) fast

  (C) fastidious

  (D) candid

  (E) unethical

291. The phrase "'speed him up'" (line 33) is in quotation marks because

    I. the implied speaker is quoting the bosses' euphemistic command
   II. the phrase is part of a dialogue
 III. the phrase is distinct from the implied speaker's voice

  (A) I only
  (B) II only
  (C) I and II only
  (D) I and III only
  (E) I, II, and III only

292. Which of the following best describes the way the third paragraph is narrated?

  (A) The third-person narration adopts the perspective and voice of Jurgis to portray his reactions to what he has heard about the plants.
  (B) Jurgis reacts to what he has heard about the plants through first-person narration.
  (C) Stream of consciousness presents Jurgis's anxious thoughts about the plants.
  (D) An omniscient narrator provides insights from the perspectives of several characters.
  (E) An unbiased and distant narrator describes events objectively.

293. Jurgis's response to Tamoszius's assessment of the company is most like the response of

  (A) someone who is firm in his or her beliefs
  (B) someone who has successfully been disabused of his or her initial perceptions
  (C) someone who is skeptical about unsettling information
  (D) someone corrupt
  (E) someone in complete denial

Passage 29. Ngugi wa Thiong'o, *The River Between*

The two ridges lay side by side. One was Kameno, the other was Makuyu. Between them was a valley. It was called the valley of life. Behind Kameno and Makuyu were many more valleys and ridges, lying without any discernible plan. They were like many sleeping lions which never woke. They just slept, the big deep sleep of their Creator.   5

A river flowed through the valley of life. If there had been no bush and no forest trees covering the slopes, you could have seen the river when you stood on top of either Kameno or Makuyu. Now you had to come down. Even then you could not see the whole extent of the river as it gracefully, and without any apparent haste, wound its way down the valley, like a snake. The river was called   10 Honia, which meant cure, or bring-back-to-life. Honia river never dried: it seemed to possess a strong will to live, scorning droughts and weather changes. And it went on in the same way, never hurrying, never hesitating. People saw this and were happy.

Honia was the soul of Kameno and Makuyu. It joined them. And men,   15 cattle, wild beasts and trees, were all united by this life-stream.

When you stood in the valley, the two ridges ceased to be sleeping lions united by their common source of life. They became antagonists. You could tell this, not by anything tangible but by the way they faced each other, like two rivals ready to come to blows in a life and death struggle for the leadership of this   20 isolated region.

294. To introduce the setting, the opening paragraph makes particular use of

    I. conditional statements
   II. objective description
  III. figurative comparisons

  (A) I and III only
  (B) I and II only
  (C) III only
  (D) II and III only
  (E) I, II, and III

295. The word "lions" (lines 4, 17) is used in the passage primarily to

  (A) symbolically represent the content valleys and their potential for conflict
  (B) metaphorically compare the mountains to predators to emphasize their danger
  (C) exaggerate the beauty of the valleys
  (D) subtly reveal that the scene takes place in Africa
  (E) develop a contrast between a peaceful valley and the restive ones nearby

296. By commenting that the valleys and ridges were "lying without any discernible plan" (line 3), the narrator

(A) portrays the valleys as chaotic
(B) suggests a lackadaisical approach to city planning
(C) conveys a sense of a region without any ambition
(D) alludes to a region suffering from isolation and neglect
(E) presents the other valleys as less defined than the valley of life

297. By "Now you had to come down" (line 8), the narrator most nearly means

(A) the slopes of the mountain are inhabitable
(B) you can't survive atop the mountains
(C) there is a better view of the river atop the mountains
(D) to see the river, you have to descend the mountains
(E) you must see what the valley has to offer

298. The effects of the second paragraph can be described by all of the following *except*

(A) a river is personified to emphasize its life-giving qualities
(B) the extent of the river is communicated with a conditional statement
(C) a simile illustrates the movement and shape of a river
(D) the meaning of a name casts doubt on a river's perceived qualities
(E) a river is described both by what it does and what it does not do

299. The form and structure of the third paragraph is distinct in that

(A) its brevity indicates its irrelevance to the passage
(B) its simple sentences convey a mundane idea
(C) three concise sentences reinforce a key portrayal of the river
(D) formal diction introduces Honia, a significant character in the passage
(E) the use of the past tense reveals that Honia no longer exists

300. The ridges appear as "antagonists" (line 18) primarily due to

(A) the drying up of Honia
(B) a change in perspective
(C) a life-and-death struggle for leadership
(D) their shared life-stream
(E) the scarcity of cattle, wild beasts, and trees

301. Which of the following best describes the way the passage is narrated?

  (A) A neutral observer presents the origins of a civilization.
  (B) A former resident exaggerates the qualities of a community.
  (C) An emotional narrator reminisces about their place of origin.
  (D) A skeptical historian questions the role that two mountains played in a community.
  (E) An informed storyteller establishes the significance of a setting.

302. The final paragraph presents a shift from

  (A) presenting Kameno and Mukuyu as combative to passive
  (B) describing the valley as arid to fruitful
  (C) neutral descriptions to biased conjectures
  (D) a placid, calm mood to a foreboding mood
  (E) vague diction to negative diction

Passage 30. Virginia Woolf, "An Unwritten Novel"

Such an expression of unhappiness was enough by itself to make one's eyes slide above the paper's edge to the poor woman's face–insignificant without that look, almost a symbol of human destiny with it. Life's what you see in people's eyes; life's what they learn, and, having learnt it, never, though they seek to hide it, cease to be aware of–what? That life's like that, it seems. Five faces oppo- 5
site–five mature faces–and the knowledge in each face. Strange, though, how people want to conceal it! Marks of reticence are on all those faces: lips shut, eyes shaded, each one of the five doing something to hide or stultify his knowledge. One smokes; another reads; a third checks entries in a pocket book; a fourth stares at the map of the line framed opposite; and the fifth–the terrible thing 10
about the fifth is that she does nothing at all. She looks at life. Ah, but my poor, unfortunate woman, do play the game–do, for all our sakes, conceal it!
As if she heard me, she looked up, shifted slightly in her seat and sighed. She seemed to apologise and at the same time to say to me, "If only you knew!" Then she looked at life again. "But I do know," I answered silently, glancing 15
at the *Times* for manners' sake. "I know the whole business. 'Peace between Germany and the Allied Powers was yesterday officially ushered in at Paris– Signor Nitti, the Italian Prime Minister–a passenger train at Doncaster was in collision with a goods train. . .' We all know–the *Times* knows–but we pretend we don't." My eyes had once more crept over the paper's rim. She shuddered, 20
twitched her arm queerly to the middle of her back and shook her head. Again I dipped into my great reservoir of life. "Take what you like," I continued, "births, death, marriages, Court Circular, the habits of birds, Leonardo da Vinci, the Sandhills murder, high wages and the cost of living–oh, take what you like," I repeated, "it's all in the *Times!*" Again with infinite weariness she moved her head 25
from side to side until, like a top exhausted with spinning, it settled on her neck.

The *Times* was no protection against such sorrow as hers. But other human beings forbade intercourse. The best thing to do against life was to fold the paper so that it made a perfect square, crisp, thick, impervious even to life. This done, I glanced up quickly, armed with a shield of my own. She pierced through my shield; she gazed into my eyes as if searching any sediment of courage at the depths of them and damping it to clay. Her twitch alone denied all hope, discounted all illusion.   30

303. According to the narrator, the "expression" referred to in line 1 is hard to avoid because
    (A) the woman is intrusive
    (B) there are no distractions
    (C) its sadness is overwhelming
    (D) the narrator is obsessed with sorrow
    (E) the narrator is confined on a train

304. The narrator defines "life" as
    (A) knowledge reluctantly gained from experience
    (B) that which people learn, seek to hide, and then disregard
    (C) experiences that appear in the news
    (D) that which is learned through living
    (E) shared experiences

305. Based on the first paragraph, it can be inferred that the "fifth" (lines 10, 11) person opposite is distinct in that she
    (A) plays the game
    (B) is older than the others
    (C) has a mark of reticence
    (D) conceals life
    (E) attempts to engage

306. The other four passengers are primarily characterized as
    (A) talkative
    (B) tenaciously secretive
    (C) cruelly indifferent
    (D) apathetic
    (E) observing custom

307. In line 12, "it" refers primarily to

(A) the game
(B) the woman
(C) life
(D) hope
(E) a secret

308. The author makes use of all of the following devices to develop the characterization of the woman *except*

(A) dialogue
(B) simile
(C) auditory imagery
(D) visual imagery
(E) subjective point of view

309. In the second paragraph, what does the narrator repeatedly imply she, and others, "knows" (line 19)?

(A) the events, details, and emotions that make up life
(B) the specific cause of the woman's unhappiness
(C) the details of the woman's life story
(D) that the woman is hoping for conversation
(E) the secret to happiness

310. The *Times* is portrayed as all of the following *except*

(A) a reservoir
(B) a shield
(C) a crutch
(D) impenetrable
(E) exhaustive

311. The narrator's point of view is developed primarily through

(A) exclamations
(B) third-person narration
(C) interior monologue
(D) personification
(E) dialogue

312. Over the course of the passage, the narrator experiences

    (A) curiosity, pity, compulsion, hope, and resignation
    (B) desperation, anger, resentment, fear, and hope
    (C) certainty, disgust, power, weakness, and regret
    (D) audacity, concern, annoyance, surrender, and hope
    (E) desperation, antipathy, empathy, and resolution

313. The figurative language in the last paragraph implies that, to the narrator, the woman appears as

    (A) a vulnerable citizen
    (B) a redoubtable foe
    (C) a calculating leader
    (D) a formidable ally
    (E) a pathetic inferior

314. The narrator's primary hope in the passage is best summarized as

    (A) a wish to avoid further interaction with any passengers
    (B) a wish that others would reveal their life experiences
    (C) a wish that the *Times* offered better comfort
    (D) a wish to learn the cause of the woman's unhappiness
    (E) a wish that the woman would conceal her unhappiness

315. The excerpt ends on a note of

    (A) ambivalence
    (B) mourning
    (C) optimism
    (D) capitulation
    (E) renunciation

CHAPTER 3

Pre-20th-Century Poetry

Passage 31. Anne Bradstreet, "The Author to Her Book"

Thou ill-form'd offspring of my feeble brain,
Who after birth did'st by my side remain,
Till snatcht from thence by friends, less wise than true,
Who thee abroad exposed to public view,
Made thee in rags, halting to th' press to trudge,   5
Where errors were not lessened (all may judge).
At thy return my blushing was not small,
My rambling brat (in print) should mother call.
I cast thee by as one unfit for light,
The visage was so irksome in my sight,   10
Yet being mine own, at length affection would
Thy blemishes amend, if so I could.
I washed thy face, but more defects I saw,
And rubbing off a spot, still made a flaw.
I stretcht thy joints to make thee even feet,   15
Yet still thou run'st more hobbling than is meet.
In better dress to trim thee was my mind,
But nought save home-spun cloth, i' th' house I find.
In this array, 'mongst vulgars may'st thou roam.
In critics' hands, beware thou dost not come,   20
And take thy way where yet thou are not known.
If for thy father askt, say, thou hadst none;
And for thy mother, she alas is poor,
Which caused her thus to send thee out of door.

316. In lines 1–6, the speaker addresses

    (A) a child in need of a reprimand
    (B) her harsh critics
    (C) her unborn child
    (D) a duplicitous colleague
    (E) a completed work

317. The "blushing" (line 7) is likely caused by
  (A) the press's unfounded criticism
  (B) friends' positive feedback
  (C) the speaker's lack of confidence
  (D) the book's obvious flaws
  (E) the speaker's "feeble brain" (1)

318. What is ironic about the effort the speaker puts forth to improve her book?
  (A) It is futile.
  (B) She is a worse writer than she thought.
  (C) It exacerbates the situation.
  (D) The "blemishes" (12) are actually amended.
  (E) She only partially improves it.

319. In which line does the speaker suggest she is without the skills and tools to improve her book?
  (A) "less wise than true" (3)
  (B) "I washed thy face, but more defects I saw" (13)
  (C) "Yet still thou run'st more hobbling than is meet" (16)
  (D) "But nought save home-spun cloth, i' the' house I find" (18)
  (E) "thou hadst none" (22)

320. The speaker implies her book is all of the following *except*
  (A) unfinished
  (B) disseminated prematurely
  (C) fallible
  (D) irreparable
  (E) polemical

321. The tone of the poem is
  (A) academic
  (B) nurturing
  (C) self-deprecating
  (D) vengeful
  (E) acerbic

322. Based on the poem as a whole, the speaker's relationship to her critics can best be described as

(A) formal
(B) productive
(C) oppressive
(D) unconventional
(E) acrimonious

323. Which of the following best characterizes the development of the poem as a whole?

(A) An inconsistent rhyme scheme magnifies delusional theories.
(B) Harsh adjectives present the publishing industry as unjust.
(C) An apt comparison is fully developed to reveal a point of view.
(D) A playful rhyming pattern softens the poem's message about the trials of parenting.
(E) A morbid simile highlights the speaker's insecurity.

324. The relationship between the speaker and her addressee is most similar to the relationship between

(A) a teacher and a student
(B) a nurturing father and a child
(C) a boss and an employee
(D) a fastidious artist and her painting
(E) a director and an actor

325. The main topic of the poem is

(A) an artist's relationship with her work
(B) an artist's dislike for her work
(C) the need for editing before publication
(D) unreasonable critics
(E) the hardships of motherhood

326. The speaker's instructions in the closing lines (19–24) imply all of the following *except*

(A) the speaker views some audiences as less discerning than others
(B) the speaker has given up on improving her work
(C) the speaker hopes an anonymous readership will be more generous
(D) the speaker views the work as beyond repair
(E) the speaker's decision is motivated in part by her financial state

Passage 32. Emily Dickinson, "Success is counted sweetest ..."

Success is counted sweetest
By those who ne'er succeed.
To comprehend a nectar
Requires sorest need.

Not one of all the purple host   5
Who took the flag to-day
Can tell the definition,
So clear, of victory,

As he, defeated, dying,
On whose forbidden ear   10
The distant strains of triumph
Break, agonized and clear!

327. In context, the word "comprehend" in line 3 most likely means

   (A) to eat
   (B) to solve
   (C) to determine
   (D) to analyze
   (E) to truly know

328. According to the speaker, who can best understand the definition of "victory" (line 8)?

     I. "the purple host" (5)
    II. "those who ne'er succeed" (2)
   III. "he, defeated, dying" (9)

   (A) I and II only
   (B) I and III only
   (C) II and III only
   (D) III only
   (E) I, II, and III

329. Based on the poem, it can be inferred that the color purple is symbolic of

   (A) jealousy
   (B) royalty
   (C) camaraderie
   (D) victory
   (E) compensation

330. The words "agonized" (line 12) and "strains" (line 11) are used in reference to "triumph" (line 11) because

    (A) those who do not win long for a second chance

    (B) the joy of victory is tainted by the jealousy of others

    (C) the sounds of victory are emotionally hard to hear for those who have lost

    (D) the triumph was not rightfully earned

    (E) competition inevitably creates antipathy

331. The poem as a whole presents a contrast between

    (A) those with and without success

    (B) a well-earned and undeserved victory

    (C) competition and collaboration

    (D) soreness and sweetness

    (E) clear and distant

332. The structure of the poem consists of

    (A) a hypothesis, reasoning, and a solution

    (B) a proposition and evidence

    (C) a maxim and illustrations of that maxim

    (D) a theory and examples

    (E) a question answered by hypothetical situations

333. The overall tone of the poem is

    (A) sorrowful

    (B) sanctimonious

    (C) moralistic

    (D) adagelike

    (E) envious

334. The poem can be summarized by which of the following sentences?

    (A) Only those who have achieved success understand its sweetness.

    (B) Success comes only to those who risk and persevere.

    (C) Success is best won through hard work.

    (D) Only those who have not achieved success understand its sweetness.

    (E) The victor is always better off.

Passage 33. Jayadeva, Excerpt from *Gita Govinda*

Beautiful Radha, jasmine-bosomed Radha,
All in the Spring-time waited by the wood
For Krishna fair, Krishna the all-forgetful,—
Krishna with earthly love's false fire consuming—
And some one of her maidens sang this song:—   5

I know where Krishna tarries in these early days of Spring,
When every wind from warm Malay brings fragrance on its wing;
Brings fragrance stolen far away from thickets of the clove,
In jungles where the bees hum and the Koil flutes her love;
He dances with the dancers of a merry morrice one,   10
All in the budding Spring-time, for 'tis sad to be alone.

I know how Krishna passes these hours of blue and gold
When parted lovers sigh to meet and greet and closely hold
Hand fast in hand; and every branch upon the Vakul-tree
Droops downward with a hundred blooms, in every bloom a bee;   15
He is dancing with the dancers to a laughter-moving tone,
In the soft awakening Spring-time, when 'tis hard to live alone.

Where Kroona-flowers, that open at a lover's lightest tread,
Break, and, for shame at what they hear, from white blush modest red;
And all the spears on all the boughs of all the Ketuk-glades   20
Seem ready darts to pierce the hearts of wandering youths and maids;
Tis there thy Krishna dances till the merry drum is done,
All in the sunny Spring-time, when who can live alone?

Where the breaking forth of blossom on the yellow Keshra-sprays
Dazzles like Kama's sceptre, whom all the world obeys;   25
And Pâtal-buds fill drowsy bees from pink delicious bowls,
As Kama's nectared goblet steeps in languor human souls;
There he dances with the dancers, and of Radha thinketh none,
All in the warm new Spring-tide, when none will live alone.

Where the breath of waving Mâdhvi pours incense through the grove,   30
And silken Mogras lull the sense with essences of love,—
The silken-soft pale Mogra, whose perfume fine and faint
Can melt the coldness of a maid, the sternness of a saint—
There dances with those dancers thine other self, thine Own,
All in the languorous Spring-time, when none will live alone.   35

Where—as if warm lips touched sealed eyes and waked them—all the bloom
Opens upon the mangoes to feel the sunshine come;

And Atimuktas wind their arms of softest green about,
Clasping the stems, while calm and clear great Jumna spreadeth out;
There dances and there laughs thy Love, with damsels many a one,   40
In the rosy days of Spring-time, for he will not live alone.

335. The first verse serves as the poem's

    (A) overture
    (B) invocation
    (C) climax
    (D) denouement
    (E) coda

336. The appositives in lines 1–5 provide

    (A) epithets for Radha and Krishna
    (B) examples to support a claim
    (C) additional details about the setting
    (D) stereotypical descriptions
    (E) the problem that will be discussed in the poem

337. The simile in line 25 serves to

    (A) imply that nature can be destructive
    (B) emphasize Krishna's infidelity
    (C) compare the season to a war
    (D) compare flowers to people
    (E) highlight the commanding powers of spring

338. The setting is described using

    (A) sensory imagery to convey a motivation for Krishna's actions
    (B) amorous images to praise Krishna
    (C) personification to suggest nature is controlling
    (D) inappropriate comparisons to emphasize Krishna's inappropriate behavior
    (E) excessive imagery that reflects Radha's extreme devotion

339. In line 27, "Kama's nectared goblet steeps in languor human souls" most likely refers to

    (A) the drunken feeling of love
    (B) the smallness of human ambition
    (C) the awakening of desire
    (D) the wetness of springtime
    (E) the intoxicating effects of alcohol

340. The consistent repetition of the word "alone" emphasizes the contrast between

    (A) celibacy and marriage
    (B) loneliness and companionship
    (C) independence and submission
    (D) monogamy and polygamy
    (E) the speaker and Radha

341. The poem's refrain serves to

    (A) describe spring
    (B) reinforce the speaker's empathy for Krishna
    (C) make Radha feel lonelier
    (D) introduce new characters
    (E) question Krishna's intentions

342. The maiden's song implies that Krishna's attitude toward Radha is

    (A) scornful
    (B) oblivious
    (C) ambivalent
    (D) coy
    (E) calculating

343. In line 34, "thine other self, thine own" refers to

    (A) Krishna
    (B) Radha
    (C) Mâdhvi
    (D) Mogra
    (E) Kama

344. The maiden's attitude toward Krishna can best be described as

    (A) mercurial
    (B) ambivalent
    (C) sanctimonious
    (D) incriminating
    (E) apologetic

345. We can infer from the poem's context that words like "Kroona," "Ketuk," "Keshra," "Pâtal," and "Mogras" (lines 18, 20, 24, 26, 31) are all

(A) allusions
(B) names of characters
(C) names of gods
(D) names of types of foliage
(E) names for spring

346. The implication from the maiden's song is that Krishna is all of the following *except*

(A) faithful
(B) promiscuous
(C) dexterous
(D) charming
(E) indulgent

347. The overall mood of the poem can best be described as

(A) jealous
(B) exultant
(C) reticent
(D) admonishing
(E) conciliatory

Passage 34. Andrew Marvell, "To His Coy Mistress"

Had we but world enough, and time,
This coyness, lady, were no crime.
We would sit down and think which way
To walk, and pass our long love's day;
Thou by the Indian Ganges' side   5
Shouldst rubies find; I by the tide
Of Humber would complain. I would
Love you ten years before the Flood;
And you should, if you please, refuse
Till the conversion of the Jews.   10
My vegetable love should grow
Vaster than empires, and more slow.
An hundred years should go to praise
Thine eyes, and on thy forehead gaze;
Two hundred to adore each breast,   15
But thirty thousand to the rest;
An age at least to every part,
And the last age should show your heart.

For, lady, you deserve this state,
Nor would I love at lower rate.   20

But at my back I always hear
Time's winged chariot hurrying near;
And yonder all before us lie
Deserts of vast eternity.
Thy beauty shall no more be found,   25
Nor, in thy marble vault, shall sound
My echoing song; then worms shall try
That long preserv'd virginity,
And your quaint honour turn to dust,
And into ashes all my lust.   30
The grave's a fine and private place,
But none I think do there embrace.

Now therefore, while the youthful hue
Sits on thy skin like morning dew,
And while thy willing soul transpires   35
At every pore with instant fires,
Now let us sport us while we may;
And now, like am'rous birds of prey,
Rather at once our time devour,
Than languish in his slow-chapp'd power.   40
Let us roll all our strength, and all
Our sweetness, up into one ball;
And tear our pleasures with rough strife
Through the iron gates of life.
Thus, though we cannot make our sun   45
Stand still, yet we will make him run.

348. The actions described by the speaker throughout the first stanza
(lines 1–20) are

(A) regrettable
(B) currently happening
(C) in the future
(D) hypothetical
(E) inevitable

349. The speaker uses the word "coyness" in line 2 to refer to his addressee's

(A) sedentary lifestyle
(B) hurried state
(C) procrastination
(D) seduction
(E) modesty

350. The speaker references the "Indian Ganges" (line 5), the "Humber" (line 7), the "Flood" (line 8), and the "Jews" (line 10) to

(A) impress his addressee with his knowledge
(B) intimidate his addressee with obscure references
(C) elaborate on how, with "world enough, and time" (1) he would not mind his addressee's "coyness" (2)
(D) add historical context to his argument
(E) tempt his addressee to change her mind by invoking travels they could take together

351. The phrase "vegetable love" (line 11) is

(A) indicative of the speaker's duplicity
(B) meant to undermine the speaker's integrity
(C) intended to emphasize the speaker's immediate desire
(D) a symbol of the seductive powers of the natural environment
(E) a metaphor for the speaker's strong love

352. It can be inferred that the phrases "the rest" (line 16) and "every part" (line 17) are references to

(A) the speaker's other emotions
(B) the addressee's desirable qualities
(C) other attractive women
(D) romantic acts
(E) the speaker's lust

353. The second stanza (lines 21–32) differs from the first in that

I. the imagery changes from lustful to dark
II. the tone changes from arrogant to desperate
III. the flattery is reduced

(A) I and II only
(B) I and III only
(C) II only
(D) II and III only
(E) I, II, and III

354. The effect of the device used in the phrase "Time's winged chariot hurrying near" (line 22) is

(A) the power of time is undermined
(B) time is portrayed as a savior
(C) the speed of time's passage is dramatized
(D) time is portrayed as negligent
(E) the speaker's argument is called into question

355. The word "quaint" in line 29 hints at the speaker's

(A) respect for his addressee's prudence
(B) disdain for chastity
(C) admiration for his addressee's steadfastness
(D) immodest proposition
(E) true view of his addressee's virginity

356. The simile in line 34 serves to

(A) impress the addressee
(B) underscore the addressee's ephemeral youth
(C) distract the addressee
(D) point out the addressee's natural beauty
(E) question the addressee's beauty

357. The speaker presents time as all of the following *except*

(A) fleeting
(B) the reason why they should not delay
(C) easily defeated
(D) threatening
(E) a juggernaut

358. The final stanza is distinct from the other stanzas in that

(A) it ends with a proposition
(B) it implies a parallel between chastity and death
(C) it makes significant use of figurative language to compel the addressee
(D) it references the present instead of the past
(E) the tone changes from confident to desperate

359. The speaker's strategy in the passage as a whole consists of

    (A) an introduction to a problem, weighing the pros and cons of a solution, and a call to action

    (B) soothing sounds, cogent examples, and personal anecdotes

    (C) seduction, accurate data, and historical examples

    (D) a major premise, minor premise, and conclusion

    (E) agreement and contradiction

Passage 35. Christina Rossetti, "Winter: My Secret"

I tell my secret? No indeed, not I;
Perhaps some day, who knows?
But not today; it froze, and blows and snows,
And you're too curious: fie!
You want to hear it? well: 5
Only, my secret's mine, and I won't tell.

Or, after all, perhaps there's none:
Suppose there is no secret after all,
But only just my fun.
Today's a nipping day, a biting day;   10
In which one wants a shawl,
A veil, a cloak, and other wraps:
I cannot ope to everyone who taps,
And let the draughts come whistling thro' my hall;
Come bounding and surrounding me,   15
Come buffeting, astounding me,
Nipping and clipping thro' my wraps and all.
I wear my mask for warmth: who ever shows
His nose to Russian snows
To be pecked at by every wind that blows?   20
You would not peck? I thank you for good will,
Believe, but leave the truth untested still.

Spring's an expansive time: yet I don't trust
March with its peck of dust,
Nor April with its rainbow-crowned brief showers,   25
Nor even May, whose flowers
One frost may wither thro' the sunless hours.

Perhaps some languid summer day,
When drowsy birds sing less and less,
And golden fruit is ripening to excess,   30
If there's not too much sun nor too much cloud,
And the warm wind is neither still nor loud,
Perhaps my secret I may say,
Or you may guess.

360. The questions in lines 1 and 21 indicate the speaker

    (A) is inquisitive
    (B) is confused
    (C) is responding
    (D) is dubious
    (E) is hopeful

361. The tone of line 6 is best understood as

    (A) juvenile
    (B) hostile
    (C) aggressive
    (D) vexing
    (E) irritable

362. The main purpose of the first stanza is to

    (A) introduce a premise
    (B) establish the rhyme scheme
    (C) describe the setting
    (D) characterize the speaker as power-hungry
    (E) develop the relationship between the speaker and addressee

363. The "wraps" mentioned in lines 12 and 17 serve, for the speaker, mainly as

    (A) a way to rhyme with "taps"
    (B) a physical embodiment of her secret
    (C) a metaphorical friend
    (D) a figurative refuge
    (E) a means for staying chaste

364. In lines 13–17, the speaker is doing which of the following?

    (A) using a jovial tone to match her perspective on winter
    (B) creating rhythm to distract her addressee
    (C) using figurative language and repetition to dramatize a threat
    (D) using synonyms to emphasize a point
    (E) using esoteric terms to intimidate her addressee

365. According to the speaker, spring differs from winter and summer in its

(A) steadfastness
(B) monotony
(C) interminability
(D) capriciousness
(E) uniformity

366. Winter, spring, and summer are treated in the poem

(A) objectively, to indicate the best temperature for revealing a secret
(B) absurdly, to further exasperate the addressee with random digressions
(C) rhythmically, to establish a musical tone
(D) figuratively, to illustrate pestering meddlers
(E) symbolically, to portray people's inquisitiveness as a result of nature

367. It can be interpreted that the speaker withholds her secret for all of the following reasons *except*

(A) her addressee is overzealous
(B) she does not actually have one
(C) she values privacy
(D) it will hurt others if revealed
(E) withholding something coveted is playfully powerful

368. It can be inferred that the speaker's attitude toward her addressee is mainly one of

(A) mild amusement
(B) censorious disapproval
(C) fond appreciation
(D) willingness to engage
(E) sincere avoidance

369. The speaker gives symbolic significance to

I. the weather
II. a house
III. clothing
IV. a nose

(A) I only
(B) I and III only
(C) II, III, and IV only
(D) I, II, and III only
(E) I, II, III, and IV

370. In response to the final line of the poem, the addressee most probably feels

(A) attacked
(B) passionate
(C) resentful
(D) satisfied
(E) hopeful

371. Which of the following best describes the effect of the final stanza's syntactical structure?

(A) The end rhymes and steady beat correspond to the eventual revelation that will conclude the poem.
(B) The repetition of the word "Perhaps" highlights the speaker's antipathy.
(C) The uncommon adjectives modify ordinary nouns, which presents the secret as exclusive.
(D) The stanza is made up of a periodic sentence, which heightens the sense of anticipation.
(E) The final stanza is written in passive voice, which shows the speaker is in control of her secret.

Passage 36. Phyllis Wheatley, "An Hymn to the Evening"

SOON as the sun forsook the eastern main
The pealing thunder shook the heav'nly plain;
Majestic grandeur! From the zephyr's wing,
Exhales the incense of the blooming spring.
Soft purl the streams, the birds renew their notes,   5
And through the air their mingled music floats.

Through all the heav'ns what beauteous dies are spread!
But the west glories in the deepest red:
So may our breasts with ev'ry virtue glow,
The living temples of our God below!   10

Fill'd with the praise of him who gives the light,
And draws the sable curtains of the night,
Let placid slumbers sooth each weary mind,
At morn to wake more heav'nly, more refin'd;
So shall the labours of the day begin   15
More pure, more guarded from the snares of sin.

Night's leaden sceptre seals my drowsy eyes,
Then cease, my song, till fair Aurora rise.

372. The verbs in lines 1–6 are notable because they are

(A) passive
(B) mundane
(C) repetitive
(D) literal
(E) sensory

373. The speaker consistently responds to her observed environment with

(A) restrained awe
(B) unabashed reverence
(C) fearful respect
(D) whimsical enthusiasm
(E) sincere shock

374. Line 9 marks a transition in the poem from

(A) objectivity to subjectivity
(B) a focus on nature to a focus on people
(C) exclamation to consternation
(D) daybreak to nightfall
(E) dramatic description to tempered praise

375. What do the "living temples of our God below" (line 10) symbolically represent?

(A) devout souls
(B) churches erected in honor of God
(C) "beauteous dies" (7)
(D) secularism
(E) "all the heav'ns" (7)

376. Considering the poem as a whole, the speaker implies that slumbers are placid as a result of

(A) quietude
(B) drawn curtains
(C) "labours of the day" (15)
(D) "Night's leaden sceptre" (17)
(E) our piety

377. The speaker indicates that sleep can have all of the following effects *except*

(A) to restore
(B) to mollify
(C) to stimulate
(D) to ready
(E) to purify

378. The speaker most probably views the "leaden sceptre" (line 17) with

(A) anxiety
(B) some skepticism
(C) nervousness
(D) ambivalence
(E) reverence

379. The speaker attributes which of the following behaviors to God?

  I. regulates
 II. inspires
III. intimidates

(A) I only
(B) I and II only
(C) II and III only
(D) III only
(E) I, II, and III

380. The alliteration in the poem's final couplet primarily functions to

(A) contrast the poem's earlier lines
(B) create a sense of foreboding
(C) evoke the sound of slumber
(D) disrupt the rhyme scheme
(E) present God as harmonious

381. The context of the poem suggests that "Aurora" (line 18) is symbolic of

(A) a companion
(B) the speaker's muse
(C) music
(D) light
(E) the morning

382. In the final two lines, the speaker seeks to convey a feeling of

(A) intimidation
(B) threat
(C) captivity
(D) grandeur
(E) repose

383. In order to convey its central message, the poem relies repeatedly on all of the following *except*

(A) understatement
(B) exclamation
(C) couplets
(D) metaphor
(E) sensory images

Passage 37. Walt Whitman, "O Captain! My Captain!"

O Captain! my Captain! our fearful trip is done!
The ship has weathered every wrack, the prize we sought is won.
The port is near, the bells I hear, the people all exulting,
While follow eyes the steady keel, the vessel grim and daring.

But, O heart! heart! heart!   5
Leave you not the little spot
Where on the deck my Captain lies,
Fallen cold and dead.

O Captain! my Captain! rise up and hear the bells!
Rise up! for you the flag is flung, for you the bugle trills: 10
For you bouquets and ribboned wreaths; for you the shores a-crowding:
For you they call, the swaying mass, their eager faces turning.

O Captain! dear father!
This arm I push beneath you.
It is some dream that on the deck   15
You've fallen cold and dead!

My Captain does not answer, his lips are pale and still:
My father does not feel my arm, he has no pulse nor will.
But the ship, the ship is anchored safe, its voyage closed and done:
From fearful trip the victor ship comes in with object won!   20
Exult, O shores! and ring, O bells!
But I, with silent tread,
Walk the spot my Captain lies,
Fallen cold and dead.

384. The best paraphrase of line 4 is

    (A) all eyes are watching the formidable vessel

    (B) witnesses are focused on the vessel's departure

    (C) bystanders are concerned about the vessel's arrival

    (D) we follow the eyes of all these people as we pull into the port

    (E) people are in awe of the damage done to our vessel

385. Lines 5–8 can best be summarized as

    (A) I should never forget the moment of my captain's death.

    (B) I love my captain.

    (C) My heart is breaking upon seeing my captain die.

    (D) I will never leave this spot where my captain has died.

    (E) I will never forget this moment.

386. It can be inferred that the "bells," "flag," "bugle," "wreaths," and crowds (lines 9–12)

    (A) are meant to be ironic

    (B) are part of the speaker's hallucination

    (C) describe both a victory celebration and a funeral

    (D) are metaphors for the captain

    (E) are similes for the captain

387. In lines 19–20, the ship is like the captain in all of the following ways *except*

    (A) they have both ended their heroic journeys

    (B) they have achieved their goals

    (C) they are both potentially metaphorical

    (D) they have both arrived home safely

    (E) they are both celebrated

388. Which of the following best conveys the effect of the speaker's shift in tone when referencing the captain?

    (A) The shift from exclamations in the first and third stanzas to calm statements in the fifth stanza corresponds to the speaker's acceptance of his captain's state.

    (B) The shift to direct addresses in the fifth stanza reveals the speaker's growing concern for his captain's state.

    (C) The shift from exclamations to internal thoughts in the fifth stanza indicates the speaker has become more withdrawn from the experience.

    (D) The shift from direct addresses to dialogue implies that the speaker's remorse is shared by others.

    (E) The shift from addressing the captain by his title to claiming him as "my Captain" in the fifth stanza emphasizes the extent of the speaker's pain.

389. The three segments (stanzas 1, 3, and 5) of the poem are divided according to
    (A) the speaker's shock, anger, and disbelief
    (B) the speaker's discovery, denial, and acceptance
    (C) death, funeral, and denial
    (D) theory, research, and conclusion
    (E) argument, counterargument, and solution

390. The repetition of the phrase "O Captain! my Captain" contributes to
    (A) the uplifting tone of the poem
    (B) the elegiac tone of the poem
    (C) the idea that mourning is musical
    (D) the poem's rhyme scheme
    (E) a sense of the speaker's exultation

391. In the final stanza, there is a contrast between
    (A) the speaker and the ship
    (B) land and sea
    (C) noisy rejoicing and quiet mourning
    (D) splendid victory and regrettable surrender
    (E) life and death

392. Based on the poem as a whole, which of the following could the captain most likely symbolize?
    (A) a nation's beloved leader
    (B) an excellent seafarer who has suddenly died
    (C) a controversial leader
    (D) the mighty naval industry
    (E) the speaker himself

393. The poem's style and content are most similar to those of
    (A) a limerick
    (B) a satire
    (C) a screed
    (D) an ode
    (E) an elegy

394. The poem ends with the speaker in a state of
    (A) optimism
    (B) disappointment
    (C) celebration
    (D) denial
    (E) mourning

Passage 38. William Wordsworth, "The world is too much with us"

The world is too much with us; late and soon,
Getting and spending, we lay waste our powers:
Little we see in nature that is ours;
We have given our hearts away, a sordid boon!
This Sea that bares her bosom to the moon;   5
The Winds that will be howling at all hours
And are up-gathered now like sleeping flowers;
For this, for every thing, we are out of tune;
It moves us not—Great God! I'd rather be
A Pagan suckled in a creed outworn;   10
So might I, standing on this pleasant lea,
Have glimpses that would make me less forlorn;
Have sight of Proteus coming from the sea;
Or hear old Triton blow his wreathed horn.

395. In context of the poem as a whole, the "powers" referred to in line 2 are

    (A) grossly exaggerated; our powers are minimal

    (B) ironic; the speaker means we are actually powerless

    (C) hypothetical; the speaker imagines a world where we have powers

    (D) misdirected; we should use them differently

    (E) forsaken; we have squandered them on unworthy things

396. The subject of "Getting and spending" in line 2 is

    (A) the world

    (B) we

    (C) God

    (D) nature

    (E) our powers

397. In the context of the poem, the phrase "sordid boon" (line 4) is

    (A) a call for an end to industry

    (B) a sarcastic expletive that mocks our "hearts" (4)

    (C) a paradox that deplores human nature

    (D) an oxymoron that captures the opinion expressed in lines 1–4

    (E) a celebration of nature's benefits

398. The function of the figurative language in lines 5 and 6 is

(A) to dramatize the potential danger of the world
(B) to alleviate the speaker's regret
(C) to underscore the majestic qualities of nature
(D) to question the relationship between man and the sea
(E) to create an intimidating tone

399. The image created in lines 5 and 6 coincides with the image from which of the poem's other line(s)?

(A) line 2
(B) line 4
(C) lines 7–8
(D) line 10
(E) lines 13–14

400. Which of the following best describes the structure of the poem as a whole?

(A) An alternating rhyme scheme expresses nature's positives and negatives.
(B) Allusions and imagery present opposing viewpoints about nature's value.
(C) A problem presented in the sestet is exacerbated in the octave.
(D) An octave presents a dire problem and the sestet ponders a hypothetical alternative.
(E) A regular rhyme expresses loss that is alleviated by an uplifting closing couplet.

401. In context of the poem as a whole, we can infer that the word "world" means

(A) humanity
(B) London
(C) the man-made world
(D) nature
(E) people

402. The metaphor in line 10 compares

(A) a religion to a mother's breast
(B) Paganism to an outdated belief system
(C) beliefs to mothers
(D) religion to breast milk
(E) Pagans to mothers

403. The allusions in lines 13–14 illustrate

    (A) the speaker's optimism
    (B) the speaker's predicament
    (C) the speaker's desire
    (D) the speaker's knowledge
    (E) the speaker's solution

404. The theme of the poem as a whole can best be stated as

    (A) nature is better than technology
    (B) the natural world has more to offer than people
    (C) the natural world is a panacea for our troubles
    (D) it is regrettable that we have immersed ourselves in industry and lost touch with the natural world
    (E) we can forget our sins by personifying nature as godlike

Passage 39. Countee Cullen, "I Have a Rendezvous with Life"

I have a rendezvous with Life,
In days I hope will come,
Ere youth has sped, and strength of mind,
Ere voices sweet grow dumb.
I have a rendezvous with Life,   5
When Spring's first heralds hum.
Sure some would cry it's better far
To crown their days with sleep
Than face the road, the wind and rain,
To heed the calling deep.   10
Though wet nor blow nor space I fear,
Yet fear I deeply, too,
Lest Death should meet and claim me ere
I keep Life's rendezvous.

405. The word "Ere" (line 3, 4) most nearly means

    (A) until
    (B) before
    (C) when
    (D) after
    (E) because

406. The statements in lines 1–4 are similar to the one in lines 5–6 in that
   I. they reference time
   II. they create a mood of anticipation
   III. they allude to the poem's theme
   (A) I only
   (B) II only
   (C) III only
   (D) I and III only
   (E) I, II, and III

407. The rhyme between "hum" (line 6) and "dumb" (line 4) serves to
   (A) highlight the speaker's conscience
   (B) communicate God's ominous voice
   (C) create the sound of vexing insects buzzing in spring
   (D) emphasize the need to relish the sounds of life that signal spring's arrival
   (E) portray the speaker's imagined heaven

408. The poem indicates that "some" (line 7) are inhibited by their
   (A) obliviousness to what "Life" has to offer
   (B) tendency to take risks
   (C) inclination to avoid challenges
   (D) self-consciousness
   (E) proclivity for introversion

409. In comparison to "some" (line 7), the speaker indicates he, too, is
   (A) fearsome
   (B) frightened
   (C) resistant
   (D) brave
   (E) audacious

410. The speaker's use of the word "space" (line 11) is in response to
   (A) stormy obstacles he may encounter
   (B) his eagerness for "Spring's first heralds hum" (6)
   (C) his fear of death
   (D) his anticipation for his rendezvous with life
   (E) the "road" (9) feared by "some" (7)

411. Based on the poem as a whole, the word "Life" is best interpreted to mean

(A) romantic love
(B) the speaker's desired mate
(C) breathing
(D) all that the world has to offer
(E) strictly the pleasures of youth

412. The word "rendezvous" (lines 1, 5, 14) can be replaced with all of the following *except*

(A) encounter
(B) meeting
(C) engagement
(D) date
(E) interview

413. The words "Life" and "Death" are capitalized most likely to

(A) portray them as intimidating the speaker
(B) capture the speaker's view that life and death hold sway over him
(C) personify them as menacingly influential
(D) allude to them as Greek gods
(E) humanize them to decrease their formidable qualities

414. The speaker's main concern is

(A) the inevitability of dying young
(B) the drawbacks of aging
(C) the temporality of the seasons
(D) the crippling fear that prohibits people from experiencing life
(E) the need to make the most of life

Passage 40. Kahlil Gibran, "Defeat"

Defeat, my Defeat, my solitude and my aloofness;
You are dearer to me than a thousand triumphs,
And sweeter to my heart than all world-glory.

Defeat, my Defeat, my self-knowledge and my defiance,   5
Through you I know that I am yet young and swift of foot
And not to be trapped by withering laurels.
And in you I have found aloneness
And the joy of being shunned and scorned.

Defeat, my Defeat, my shining sword and shield,
In your eyes I have read   10
That to be enthroned is to be enslaved,
and to be understood is to be leveled down,
And to be grasped is but to reach one's fullness
and like a ripe fruit to fall and be consumed.

Defeat, my Defeat, my bold companion,   15
You shall hear my songs and my cries and my silences,
And none but you shall speak to me of the beating of wings,
And urging of seas,
And of mountains that burn in the night,
And you alone shall climb my steep and rocky soul.   20

Defeat, my Defeat, my deathless courage,
You and I shall laugh together with the storm,
And together we shall dig graves for all that die in us,
And we shall stand in the sun with a will,
And we shall be dangerous.   25

415. The poem as a whole is written as a(n)

   (A) allegory of the trials and tribulations of life
   (B) anecdote about the speaker's experience with failure
   (C) letter to an old friend and mentor
   (D) speech about valor, humility, and honesty
   (E) apostrophe to a personified experience

416. In the second stanza, the speaker reveals that

   (A) "Defeat" is characteristic of the young
   (B) "Defeat" is an actual person
   (C) he sees value in "Defeat" because it pushes him to succeed
   (D) he sees value in "Defeat" because it teaches him to disregard accolades
   (E) he has a sarcastic attitude toward "Defeat"

417. The parallel structures in the third stanza serve to

   (A) portray "Defeat" as unrelenting
   (B) present "Defeat's" messages as overwhelming
   (C) communicate the cohesion of "Defeat's" messages
   (D) create rhythm with a discordant sound
   (E) create a regular beat with a predictable sound

418. The metaphor of the "sword and shield" (line 9) is meant to

(A) emphasize "Defeat's" emboldening powers
(B) characterize the speaker as invincible
(C) contradict the previous stanza's imagery
(D) change the poem's tone from sarcastic to laudatory
(E) emphasize "Defeat's" valiant nature

419. The third stanza reveals that the speaker thinks success is

(A) hypocritical
(B) unimaginable
(C) overrated
(D) easily obtained
(E) better than "Defeat"

420. The simile in lines 13–14 compares

(A) "ripe fruit" to falling
(B) "Defeat" to fruit
(C) ripeness to satisfaction
(D) "ripe fruit" to "one" who is understood
(E) royalty to freedom

421. The speaker characterizes "Defeat" as all of the following *except*

(A) enviable
(B) distinct
(C) useful
(D) brave
(E) bold

422. The poem's refrain

(A) is found in lines 1, 4, 9, 15, and 21 and characterizes "Defeat" as independent
(B) is found in all lines beginning with "And" and highlights the theme
(C) is found in all lines beginning with "And" and provides evidence for a claim
(D) is found in lines 1, 4, 9, 15, and 21 and enhances the poem's ode-like quality
(E) is the entire last stanza and contains the theme

423. The speaker's address to "Defeat" as his "deathless courage" (line 21) emphasizes

(A) the poem's dark and morbid message
(B) the speaker's appreciation of death
(C) that courage and death are opposites
(D) that with "Defeat" comes immortality
(E) that with "Defeat" he has the courage to face any obstacle

424. The speaker sees "Defeat" primarily as his

(A) friend
(B) valued companion
(C) adversary
(D) obstacle
(E) parent

425. The mood that is established by the end of the poem is one of

(A) confidence
(B) cynicism
(C) desire
(D) destruction
(E) wistfulness

CHAPTER 4

20th-Century/Contemporary Poetry

Passage 41. Pamela Hart, "Kevlar Poem"

The woman who invented Kevlar
liked to walk in the woods with her father
naming trees and plants
She collected leaves
to press and save   5
She sketched the sky and fern beds
the rocks along streams
The woman who discovered Kevlar
liked to sew clothing for her dolls
thought she might be a fashion designer   10
Her father died when she was ten
and there was no Kevlar for heart disease
or her sadness
The woman who discovered
Kevlar loved the messy   15
astonishing world
She contemplated chemicals
while spinning strands
of a polymer brew
to concoct   20
something synthetic and strong
fine enough to be woven
into the reed of a woodwind instrument
or the panel of a bulletproof vest

426. The poem characterizes the woman through

    I. references to her bond with her father

    II. actions that establish her lifelong sense of curiosity

    III. her motivation to invent something that would change the world

  (A) I only

  (B) II only

  (C) I and II only

  (D) II and III only

  (E) I, II, and III

427. Which best conveys the effect of lines 17–21 ("She contemplated . . . strong")?

  (A) Figurative language portrays the inventor's scientific experimentation as intentional and extraordinary.

  (B) Visual imagery explicitly compares the woman's experimenting to witchcraft.

  (C) A metaphor presents the Kevlar invention as the result of an accidental process.

  (D) Alliteration underscores the soothing effects that experiments have on the woman.

  (E) Vivid and precise verbs detail the process of inventing Kevlar.

428. At a point in the poem, Kevlar is treated

  (A) euphemistically; it stands in for the dangers in the world like war and death

  (B) symbolically; it represents a type of protection

  (C) poetically; the lyrical and rhythmic sound of the word contributes to the poem's form

  (D) neutrally; it is another substance that the woman enjoys working with

  (E) reverentially; it is the woman's only significant accomplishment

429. The poem suggests that a likely influence for the woman's eventual discovery of Kevlar is

    I. walking with her father

    II. her father's death

    III. an urge to make a difference

  (A) I only

  (B) II only

  (C) II and III only

  (D) I and II only

  (E) I, II, and III

430. By commenting that "there was no Kevlar for heart disease/ or her sadness" (lines 12–13), the speaker

   (A) hints at the irony that the woman's eventual invention of a protective material could not protect her from her personal pain

   (B) implies that death is inevitable

   (C) emphasizes the father's death as a motivating factor for the invention of Kevlar

   (D) exaggerates the pain of losing a parent

   (E) alludes to the woman's ultimately unsatisfying invention

431. Which of the following best describes the development of the poem as a whole?

   (A) a meditation on the origins of important inventions

   (B) a biography of a renowned inventor

   (C) an exploration of one inventor's experiences and influences

   (D) a metaphorical representation of an invention

   (E) a lyrical treatment of the bond between fathers and daughters

432. The woman's father is presented as all of the following *except*

   (A) loved

   (B) missed

   (C) influential

   (D) companionable

   (E) a scientific mentor

433. The poem's tone

   (A) is mournful and remains constant

   (B) alternates between sympathetic and mournful

   (C) shifts around line 12 from repertorial to almost mystical

   (D) changes from reverential to spiritual

   (E) shifts in line 10 from reflective to pitying

Passage 42. David Hernandez, "I Made a Door"

Took a plank and sawed it in half, the pieces
small, horizontal, I painted them white,

then drilled the hinges in. Outside the house
I climbed a ladder, up to the fold of roof

over roof, gap to the attic.   5
I took a hammer. I took the door,

my homespun contraption, one-way
swinging thing, and drove in the nails,

forbade for once raccoons and possums
from entering the darkest of rooms,   10

but not from leaving. Or so I believed.
Sounds over my head the following week,

paws on wood, the tapping claws, slow rasp
of fur scraping against the air ducts.

Next morning I walked the perimeter   15
of the house, I turned in right angles,

eyes to the eaves. One thought.
Two. How did he slip in? What other errors

will my muddling hands make?
Failure enters the mind, finds a fissure   20

and burrows into the marrow of me.
Says I am flawed from head to heels.

Says I am all mistakes down to my cells,
then amends my serotonin.

I was wrong from the start: 25
The door made me.

434. A shift in the poem is most evident

(A) in line 6; the speaker becomes more involved in making a door
(B) in line 9; the speaker reveals the motivation behind the project
(C) in line 11; the speaker transitions to revealing the unexpected outcome of the project
(D) in line 15; the speaker transitions from problem to solution
(E) in line 23; the speaker first reveals his waning sense of confidence

435. Which of the following best conveys the effect of lines 12–14?

   I. sensory imagery illustrates the speaker's rising concern
  II. a list written as a sentence fragment reveals the clues that alert the speaker to an unexpected outcome
 III. descriptions provide context for the speaker's subsequent thoughts about his abilities

(A) I only
(B) I and II only
(C) III only
(D) II and III only
(E) I, II, and III

436. The questions in lines 18–19 function in all of the following ways *except*

(A) they emphasize the shift in the speaker's perspective about his accomplishment
(B) they develop the speaker's sense of self-doubt
(C) they contrast the confidence conveyed earlier in the poem
(D) they mirror the way the speaker's actions are presented in lines 1–10
(E) they demonstrate the process described in lines 20–21

437. The poem implies parallels between all of the following *except*

(A) failure and rodent invaders
(B) "a homespun contraption" (7) and self-worth
(C) rodents' actions and the speaker's self-doubt
(D) a door and the speaker
(E) serotonin and rodents

438. The phrase "amends my serotonin" (line 24) most nearly means

(A) makes me happy
(B) permanently changes my brain
(C) alters my mood
(D) improves my capacity to learn
(E) heightens my emotional state

439. The actions attributed to "Failure" (line 20) are distinct in that

    I. they mark a shift in the poem's subject from the speaker to Failure, showing the speaker's sense of self as dependent on outside circumstances

    II. they are confused with the actions of the raccoons and possums in order to suggest that the speaker is not at fault

    III. they personify Failure in order to illustrate the command it has on the speaker's sense of self

(A) I and II only

(B) II only

(C) III only

(D) I and III only

(E) I, II, and III

440. The effect created by the final statement is best described by which of the following?

(A) An ironic twist on the title reveals the speaker's important discovery that his attempt to change a situation has actually changed him.

(B) A witty pun lightens the mood of an otherwise dark poem about failure.

(C) A play on the word "made" reveals that the speaker has lost control over his project.

(D) A sentence fragment reveals the speaker's fragmented sense of his own accomplishment.

(E) A sentence written in the active voice positions the speaker as powerful.

441. Which of the following best characterizes the development of the poem as a whole?

(A) Heroic couplets convey an amusing anecdote.

(B) Simple action verbs contrast the complexity of solving a difficult problem.

(C) A metaphorical treatment of an experience that shapes the speaker.

(D) A lyrical treatment of man's struggle with the natural world.

(E) Sensory imagery helps narrate a traumatic experience in hindsight.

Passage 43. David Tomas Martinez, "To the Young"

black male dressed
like a punk rock

hipster club kid
with teddy bears

tied to his sneakers: 5
you too are split

down the middle,
like your mother,

bent in front
of the kitchen table   10

with New Edition
in the background

for three hours
as she sews your gray

and pink acid wash   15
jeans at the crotch

to make a new,
mixed breed.

Only Chicano rockers
moshing in a corner   20

with leather jackets
and skin head pins,

and white boys
banging Crip

with dirty blonde corn   25
rows held with gel

can know
your pain.

And their mothers,
too.   30

442. The poem is addressed to

(A) those young people who defy stereotypes
(B) all young people who idolize fashion
(C) those who dress like they're young
(D) families who support their children
(E) people who cross socioeconomic barriers to befriend others

443. A parallel is suggested between all of the following *except*

(A) a black male and Chicano rockers
(B) a son and his mother
(C) "gray/ and pink acid wash/ jeans" (14–16) and one's identity
(D) teddy bears tied to sneakers and dirty blonde cornrows held with gel
(E) the speaker and "the young"

444. Which of the following best describes the effect of lines 17–18 "to make a new/ mixed breed"?

  I. A metaphorical phrase develops the experience of representing multiple identities.
 II. An intentional line break emphasizes the sense of division and mixing.
III. A phrase is used to convey more than one meaning.

(A) I only
(B) I and II only
(C) III only
(D) II and III only
(E) I, II, and III

445. Chicano rockers and white boys are mentioned in the poem in order to

(A) contrast the music and fashion choices of the black male addressed in line 1
(B) give examples of young people who conform to society's expectations
(C) highlight just how unique the black male rocker and his mom are
(D) show the variety of modern fashion styles
(E) develop the portrayal of those young people who are "split/ down the middle" (6–7)

446. The "pain" in line 28 is an implied reference to

    (A) the physical pain the mother experiences "bent in front/ of the kitchen table . . . for three hours" (9–13)

    (B) the challenges that come with identifying with a social group in which you are a minority

    (C) the difficulties with procuring your desired clothes and accessories

    (D) suffering from parental disapproval

    (E) physical discomfort from wearing trendy but ill-fitting clothes to look a certain part

447. The tone of the poem is best described as

    (A) pitying

    (B) idealistic

    (C) hopeful

    (D) attentive

    (E) laudatory

448. Which of the following best describes the development of the poem as a whole?

    (A) an amusing look into the lives of a variety of music fans

    (B) a meditation on the impact music has on young lives

    (C) a lyrical celebration of mothers and sons

    (D) a philosophical consideration of identity

    (E) a poetic expression of a plight experienced by some young people

449. The poem presents the relationship between mothers and their kids as

    (A) codependent

    (B) somewhat resentful

    (C) supportive

    (D) inappropriate

    (E) lacking boundaries

Passage 44. Dorothy Parker, "Men I Am Not Married To"

No matter where my route may lie,
No matter whither I repair,
   In brief—no matter how or why
Or when I go, the boys are there.
   On lane and byways, street and square,   5
On alley, path and avenue,
   They seem to spring up everywhere—
The men I am not married to.
   I watch them as they pass me by;
At each in wonderment I stare,   10
   And, "but for heaven's grace," I cry,
"There goes the guy whose name I'd wear!"
   They represent no species rare,
They walk and talk as others do;
   They're fair to see—but only fair—   15
The men I am not married to.
                        {2}

   I'm sure that to a mother's eye
Is each potentially a bear.
   But though at home they rank ace-high,
No change of heart could I declare.   20
   Yet worry silvers not their hair;
They deck them not with sprigs of rue.
   It's curious how they do not care—
The men I am not married to.
   L'ENVOI   25
   In fact, if they'd a chance to share
Their lot with me, a lifetime through,
   They'd doubtless tender me the air—
The men I am not married to.

450. The repetition in the first six lines serves to emphasize

    (A) the speaker's relief that she is single
    (B) the speaker's desire to marry
    (C) the speaker's insistence that no man is for her
    (D) the ubiquitous presence of men
    (E) the speaker's frustration that temptation surrounds her

451. The phrase "spring up" (line 7) is most likely intended to

(A) mock single men

(B) create a bawdy and illicit tone

(C) compare the attractiveness of single men to the beauty of flowers

(D) reference the unpredictable nature of men

(E) stress the pervasive presence of men

452. The word "wonderment" (line 10) is notable because

(A) it contrasts the earlier suggestion that men are everywhere

(B) it reveals the speaker actually wants to marry the men she sees

(C) it symbolizes the speaker's desire

(D) it references the speaker's thoughts about seeing the men referred to previously

(E) it is intended wryly

453. The qualification in line 15 supports which of the following statements?

(A) The men are single for a reason.

(B) The speaker dislikes the men because they are homely.

(C) The speaker insists on not marrying these men only because they are "fair" (15).

(D) The speaker is seeking someone exceptional.

(E) The men are not estimable in the speaker's eyes.

454. Line 21 is best summarized by which of the following statements?

(A) The men do not care about women.

(B) The men stay young because they do not worry about marrying.

(C) The men are unconcerned about the speaker's unavailability.

(D) Worrying ages us.

(E) The men are "only fair" (15) because of their silver hair.

455. Lines 23–24 are distinct from the rest of the poem in that

(A) they hint at the speaker's indifference to the men around her

(B) they matter-of-factly state the speaker's intention not to marry

(C) they reveal the men's inner state

(D) they hint at the speaker's disappointment

(E) they undermine the speaker's conviction

456. The final stanza serves primarily to

(A) address any critics who might assume the speaker is not desirable
(B) criticize the men referred to in lines 23–24
(C) justify the speaker's decision not to marry
(D) confirm the speaker does not care for the men she's not married to
(E) counter any disinterest suggested by the men's lack of worry

457. The tone of the poem as a whole is best described as

(A) polemical
(B) silly
(C) sarcastic
(D) jolly
(E) playful

Passage 45. Tracy K. Smith, "The Good Life"

When some people talk about money
They speak as if it were a mysterious lover
Who went out to buy milk and never
Came back, and it makes me nostalgic
For the years I lived on coffee and bread,   5
Hungry all the time, walking to work on payday
Like a woman journeying for water
From a village without a well, then living
One or two nights like everyone else
On roast chicken and red wine.   10

458. The speaker suggests "some people" (line 1) are

(A) indifferent toward money
(B) looking for love
(C) wistful about money
(D) suffering from dire conditions
(E) desperate for money

459. The comparison between money and a lover in line 2 is meant to be

(A) comical; the image is ridiculous
(B) dark; poverty is unjust
(C) absurd; there is no comparison between being poor and being single
(D) intriguing; money is desirable but hard to retain
(E) weak; losing money is far worse than losing a lover

460. In context of the poem as a whole, the reference to "coffee and bread" (line 5) is most likely meant to evoke

    (A) a life of poverty
    (B) a sense of getting by
    (C) a sense of regret
    (D) economic inequality
    (E) an artistic sensibility

461. In the poem, a parallel is drawn between "a village without a well" (line 8) and

    (A) a slum
    (B) a home with basic sustenance
    (C) an impoverished soul
    (D) roast chicken and red wine
    (E) a mysterious lover

462. From the point of view of "some people" (line 1), "everyone else" (line 9) likely appears

    (A) rude
    (B) deserving
    (C) ostentatious
    (D) snobby
    (E) fortunate

463. The poem suggests that, for the speaker, money is

    (A) still coveted
    (B) more troublesome now
    (C) well-earned
    (D) no longer an issue
    (E) always scarce

464. The speaker explicitly compares herself to

    (A) a mysterious lover
    (B) "some people" (1)
    (C) someone in need of basic sustenance
    (D) "everyone else" (9)
    (E) her younger self

465. The poem as a whole is best understood as a(n)
- (A) eulogy for a lover who never returned
- (B) plea for financial assistance
- (C) vindication of hard work that has led to financial independence
- (D) reminiscence of a humbler time
- (E) ode to luxurious pleasures

466. Which best describes the effect of the poem's form?
- (A) A consistent rhyme scheme conveys a consistent need for money.
- (B) Obscure adjectives and verbs articulate a rare experience.
- (C) Casual, informal diction expresses a simple memory.
- (D) One extended comparison makes an unconventional point about poverty.
- (E) A long sentence broken into ten lines emphasizes the complexity of a desire.

Passage 46. Rabindranath Tagore, "The Home"

I paced alone on the road across the field while the sunset was
hiding its last gold like a miser.

The daylight sank deeper and deeper into the darkness, and the
widowed land, whose harvest had been reaped, lay silent.

Suddenly a boy's shrill voice rose into the sky. He traversed   5
the dark unseen, leaving the track of his song across the hush of
the evening.

His village home lay there at the end of the waste land, beyond
the sugar-cane field, hidden among the shadows of the banana and
the slender areca palm, the cocoa-nut and the dark green   10
jack-fruit trees.

I stopped for a moment in my lonely way under the starlight, and
saw spread before me the darkened earth surrounding with her arms
countless homes furnished with cradles and beds, mothers' hearts
and evening lamps, and young lives glad with a gladness that   15
knows nothing of its value for the world.

467. The simile in line 2

    (A) compares gold to a cheapskate to emphasize the town's poverty

    (B) compares the sun to a scrupulous saver to convey the disappearance of sunlight

    (C) contrasts the gold to a miser to show the town's poverty

    (D) contrasts the sun to a miser to show how dark it has become

    (E) symbolizes darkness

468. Line 3 creates emphasis in part through

    (A) repetition of a key phrase

    (B) personification of the darkness

    (C) hyperbolic description of the dark

    (D) soft and soothing sounds

    (E) alliteration that calls attention to the darkness

469. The phrases "widowed land" (line 4) and "her arms" (line 13) are best understood as

    (A) commentary on harsh agricultural practices

    (B) conflicting references to the speaker's society

    (C) metaphors for the tribulations of women

    (D) personifications of a depleted yet nurturing earth

    (E) symbols of the speaker's longing

470. The sentence that comprises the second stanza of the poem differs from that of the first in that

    (A) it evokes a mood of stillness instead of movement

    (B) it relies on figurative comparison to establish mood

    (C) it emphasizes light instead of darkness

    (D) it develops the setting through auditory imagery

    (E) it is focused on the speaker's actions

471. The third stanza contains a contrast between

    (A) night and day

    (B) boy and sky

    (C) boy and man

    (D) sound and silence

    (E) light and dark

472. The phrase "waste land" (line 8) serves to

    (A) portray the setting as hellish

    (B) present the "home" (8) as in the middle of nowhere

    (C) suggest a war has just taken place

    (D) portray the people of this town as deprived and devastated

    (E) emphasize the stark contrast between the boy's home and the "widowed land" (4) nearby

473. What is the primary function of the fourth stanza?

    (A) to provide the precise location of the speaker

    (B) to develop the characterization of the boy

    (C) to provide a glimpse into the culture and background of the people

    (D) to illustrate the home as distinct from its surroundings

    (E) to emphasize the remoteness of the home

474. The poem's final sentence can best be paraphrased as

    (A) Happy families are unaware of how valuable their bliss is to the world.

    (B) The dark, lonely earth is lit up by the people who inhabit it.

    (C) I wish I were part of one of these families.

    (D) Home is where the heart is.

    (E) The natural world protects families from the harsh environment.

475. The list in lines 14–15 conveys the speaker's feeling of

    (A) exclusivity

    (B) envy

    (C) mild satisfaction

    (D) indulgence

    (E) reassurance

476. Which of the following best describes the structure of the poem?

    (A) The first half focuses on the speaker and the second half on the environment.

    (B) Alternating stanzas depict the speaker and his environment.

    (C) Increasingly longer stanzas add complexity to a dilemma.

    (D) An octave and sestet present a problem and its solution.

    (E) Stanzas written in free verse reveal a speaker's meditation upon observing a scene.

Passage 47. Sara Teasdale, "From the Woolworth Tower"

Vivid with love, eager for greater beauty
Out of the night we come
Into the corridor, brilliant and warm.
A metal door slides open,
And the lift receives us.   5
Swiftly, with sharp unswerving flight
The car shoots upward,
And the air, swirling and angry,
Howls like a hundred devils.
Past the maze of trim bronze doors,   10
Steadily we ascend.
I cling to you
Conscious of the chasm under us,
And a terrible whirring deafens my ears.

The flight is ended.   15

We pass thru a door leading onto the ledge—
Wind, night and space
Oh terrible height
Why have we sought you?
Oh bitter wind with icy invisible wings   20
Why do you beat us?
Why would you bear us away?
We look thru the miles of air,
The cold blue miles between us and the city,
Over the edge of eternity we look   25
On all the lights,
A thousand times more numerous than the stars;
Oh lines and loops of light in unwound chains
That mark for miles and miles
The vast black mazy cobweb of the streets;   30
Near us clusters and splashes of living gold
That change far off to bluish steel
Where the fragile lights on the Jersey shore
Tremble like drops of wind-stirred dew.
The strident noises of the city   35
Floating up to us
Are hallowed into whispers.
Ferries cross thru the darkness
Weaving a golden thread into the night,
Their whistles weird shadows of sound.   40

We feel the millions of humanity beneath us,—
The warm millions, moving under the roofs,
Consumed by their own desires;
Preparing food,
Sobbing alone in a garret,   45
With burning eyes bending over a needle,
Aimlessly reading the evening paper,
Dancing in the naked light of the cafe,
Laying out the dead,
Bringing a child to birth—   50
The sorrow, the torpor, the bitterness, the frail joy
Come up to us
Like a cold fog wrapping us round.
Oh in a hundred years
Not one of these blood-warm bodies   55
But will be worthless as clay.
The anguish, the torpor, the toil
Will have passed to other millions
Consumed by the same desires.
Ages will come and go,   60
Darkness will blot the lights
And the tower will be laid on the earth.
The sea will remain
Black and unchanging,
The stars will look down   65
Brilliant and unconcerned.

Beloved,
Tho' sorrow, futility, defeat
Surround us,
They cannot bear us down.   70
Here on the abyss of eternity
Love has crowned us
For a moment
Victors.

477. Compared with the diction in the rest of the first stanza, the words in
     lines 1–3

     (A) reference the speaker's companion
     (B) describe a setting with sensory adjectives
     (C) contribute to a dreadful tone
     (D) convey a sense of promise
     (E) create anticipation

478. The effect created in lines 8–9 is best described by which of the following?

(A) The air is personified as a violent attacker, creating a dark mood.

(B) A simile dramatizes the intensity of the wind's sound.

(C) Obscure adjectives create a sense of wild confusion.

(D) An ironic comparison sheds light on the poem's theme.

(E) A threatening tone is softened by a description of the air.

479. The "terrible whirring" (line 14) is a reference to which of the following lines?

(A) Line 4 ("A metal door slides open")

(B) Line 7 ("The car shoots upward")

(C) Line 9 ("Howls like a hundred devils")

(D) Line 13 ("the chasm under us")

(E) Line 15 ("The flight")

480. The function of line 15 can be described as all of the following *except*

(A) its separation from the previous stanza emphasizes the speaker's emotional shift

(B) its brevity highlights the relief the speaker feels

(C) its simple and concise diction contributes to an uncomplicated and calm feeling

(D) its tense shifts from the previous stanza to indicate a pivotal transition in the mood

(E) it serves as its own stanza to call attention to the significance of the ride ending

481. In context, the questions in lines 19, 21, and 22 suggest the speaker is

(A) thinking out loud

(B) speaking to her partner

(C) lamenting her choice

(D) being overly dramatic

(E) on the verge of a breakdown

482. The phrase "the edge of eternity" (line 25) is meant

(A) as an exaggeration

(B) sarcastically

(C) earnestly

(D) figuratively

(E) literally

483. The figurative language used to describe light

(A) contributes to a sense of fear and doom
(B) suggests the speaker is hallucinating
(C) is muddled with contradictory images and nonsensical comparisons
(D) helps answer the questions posed in lines 19–22
(E) communicates the variety of ways the light appears to the speaker

484. The end of the third stanza (lines 35–40) marks a shift in the poem from

(A) fear to acceptance
(B) dread to tolerance
(C) hope to dismay
(D) excitement to surrender
(E) cacophony to quiet

485. By describing the "warm millions" as "consumed by their own desires" (line 43), the speaker means to

(A) critique their way of life
(B) contrast her sense of purpose with their aimless actions
(C) present them as selfishly unconcerned with their environment
(D) imply their obliviousness to the temporality of their existence
(E) preface a list of routine behaviors she sees as meaningless

486. The comparison to "a cold fog" (line 53) emphasizes

(A) the extremity of the weather
(B) the harsh conditions experienced by the speaker on the journey described in the first stanza
(C) the speaker's desire to be with her companion
(D) the chilling reminder of life's temporality
(E) the speaker's sense that the "warm millions" (42) are in danger of dying

487. The speaker most likely uses the phrase "other millions" (line 58) to

(A) suggest that the "anguish, the torpor, the toil" (57) are just a few of the many things that people experience
(B) serve as a contrast to "these blood-warm bodies" (55)
(C) foreshadow the fate of the lights and the tower
(D) create continuity with the "warm millions" (42)
(E) highlight the wonder of the life cycle

488. The significance of lines 60–62 can best be described by which of the following?

(A) The speaker definitively states the inevitable demise of two creations she previously portrayed as powerful.

(B) An idea that was previously suggested is now supported with evidence.

(C) A worry expressed earlier in the poem is now laid to rest.

(D) The speaker personifies lights and the earth to show their weakness.

(E) The tower, which was once threatening, will reach an inexorable doom.

489. The final stanza is distinct in all of the following ways *except*

(A) It articulates a theme.

(B) Its tone is uplifting.

(C) The speaker is empowered.

(D) A figurative reference to eternity evokes uncertainty.

(E) The speaker addresses her companion directly.

Passage 48. William Butler Yeats, "That the Night Come"

She lived in storm and strife.
Her soul had such desire
For what proud death may bring
That it could not endure
The common good of life,   5
But lived as 'twere a king
That packed his marriage day
With banneret and pennon,
Trumpet and kettledrum,
And the outrageous cannon,   10
To bundle Time away
That the night come.

490. It can be inferred from the poem as a whole that "She" views "the common good of life" (line 5) as all of the following *except*

(A) unappreciated

(B) undesirable

(C) unappealing

(D) unendurable

(E) not enjoyable

491. The subject(s) of the poem is/are

(A) "a king" (6)
(B) "She" (1)
(C) "the common good of life" (5)
(D) "Time" (11)
(E) "She" and "a king"

492. Line 1 is distinct from each of the other lines in the poem in that it

(A) exaggerates a problem
(B) describes the subject of the poem
(C) contains figurative language
(D) is comprised of an independent clause
(E) is objective

493. The word "it" in line 4 refers to

(A) "death" (3)
(B) "Her" (2)
(C) "soul" (2)
(D) "desire" (2)
(E) "She" (1)

494. The main difference emphasized in the poem between "She" (line 1) and the "king" (line 6) is

(A) their gender
(B) their way of living
(C) the object of their desire
(D) their attitude
(E) their class status

495. The speaker's point of view is most like that of

(A) a harsh critic
(B) an indifferent observer
(C) an indulgent friend
(D) a mentor
(E) an omniscient narrator

496. The structure of lines 2–12 is best described by which of the following?

    (A) A complex sentence's many clauses are broken into ten lines to convey the woman's anticipation of night.

    (B) A run-on sentence exaggerates the severity of the woman's problem.

    (C) The subtle rhyme scheme makes light of the woman's predicament.

    (D) A comparison between love and death is developed over ten lines to emphasize its importance.

    (E) The idea expressed in lines 2–12 contradicts the less developed idea from line 1.

497. The simile in line 6 reveals

    (A) the king's superiority to the woman

    (B) the king's love for his wife

    (C) the woman's anticipation of her wedding night

    (D) the woman's regret that she did not marry

    (E) the woman's excitement about death

498. The nouns included in lines 8–10 serve as

    (A) symbols of the woman's desire

    (B) details to emphasize the king's power

    (C) opposites to "the common good" (5)

    (D) examples of extreme desires

    (E) objects that signify night

499. The poem characterizes night as

    I. coveted

    II. foreboding

    III. interminable

    (A) I only

    (B) II only

    (C) I and III only

    (D) II and III only

    (E) I, II, and III

500. The phrase "To bundle Time away" (line 11) means

    (A) to endure time

    (B) to protect time

    (C) to enjoy time

    (D) to save time

    (E) to ignore time

ANSWERS

Chapter 1: Pre-20th-Century Prose

Passage 1. Louisa May Alcott, "An Old-fashioned Girl"

1. (D) Tom's indignant resolution is that he proclaims he will never "bother" (32) about with Fanny's friends without her being there, but this decision is not the source of the humor (A). In this assertion, he does not directly attack Fanny (B) and his comment in reference to "bothering about [her] friends" is hardly biting (C). What is funny, however, is that Tom's decisive words and his "air of indignant resolution" (12) are "somewhat damaged by a tousled head, and the hunched appearance of his garments generally" (13–14). The tousled head alone (E) does not create the humor; rather, it is the juxtaposition of the disheveled appearance with the intended authoritative declaration that is comical (D).

2. (A) The narrator appears to know that Fanny is "hoping to soothe [Tom's] ruffled feelings" (17) when she offers something to Tom in return for his picking up Polly—I. The narrator appears to know that Tom "regarded girls as a very unnecessary portion of creation" (22–23)—III. These are both instances where the narrator reveals her access to characters' internal thoughts, as these details could not be gleaned from the characters' actions or speech alone. The description of Tom rising from the sofa (11–14) does not reveal the narrator's access to the characters' internal thoughts. There is no reference to Tom's internal state. Any objective viewer could observe his "air" and how it contrasts with his appearance—II. The narrator herself observes that "Boys are apt to think so . . ." (23). These lines provide commentary from the narrator about boys in general, so they do not reveal the narrator's access to characters' thoughts—IV.

3. (A) The somersaults are used literally to indicate a movement/exercise boys of Tom's age enjoy and **figuratively** to indicate the complete reversal these boys will experience in a few years when they often become infatuated with the same girls they now loathe. The narrator does not intend to convey arrogance with this observation; it is meant to be an insightful observation about the nature of some boys of Tom's age (B), (C). She does not regret this behavior or see it as negative (D). She is not intending to educate (E) the reader about boys, either; she is providing context for and insight on the events in the story.

4. (E) The phrases are not part of a dialogue or conversation (B) and they are not specialized vocabulary terms that require background knowledge (D). The narrator does not use these phrases sarcastically to point fun at the boys who say these expressions (A), nor is she quoting an expert (C). The quotations indicate that these phrases are distinct from the narrator's voice. They likely belong to Tom himself or more generally to boys of Tom's age (E).

5. (E) After Fanny says that she described Tom's appearance to her friend Polly, Tom "gave a hasty smooth to his curly pate and a glance at the mirror, feeling sure that his sister hadn't done him justice. . ." (34–35). The context reveals that Tom is certain Fanny has underestimated his attractiveness, since sisters always do. His actions demonstrate this wariness—he does one quick touch-up and check in the mirror to make sure to contradict what he assumes Fanny has said to describe him, whatever it may have been. Tom is not looking in the mirror because he is overly concerned with his appearance (C), nor is he overly confident and arrogant about his good looks (D). Fanny's actual opinion of Tom's appearance is never provided in the passage, so it cannot be confirmed or belied (A), (B).

6. (D) While Fanny is working on her hair and refuses to accompany Tom because the rain will damage its "crimp" (3), she is not *primarily* concerned with her hair. She qualifies this behavior by explaining, "I want to look nice when Polly comes" (4) (E). Later, she adds that Polly is "ever so nice; and I shall keep her as long as she's happy" (20–21), which shows her intent to please Polly. When it appears that Tom will likely be late to meet Polly, Fanny cries, "'what *will* Polly think of me?'" (37). Tom jokes that Fanny appears to care more for her hair than for Polly (E), but Fanny consistently expresses a desire to please Polly. Fanny is annoyed that her brother is stubborn about going by himself and begs him to hurry (A), (B), but these concerns fall under the larger desire to make Polly's visit a happy one. Nowhere does the passage indicate that Fanny is in competition with Polly over their looks (C).

7. (C) The revelation in lines 42–44 that Tom "ran himself off his legs to make up for it afterward" (44) is significant to the portrayal of Tom because, for the first time, it is suggested that Tom intends to do what is expected, despite all his ornery resistance. Before he runs, though, he is careful to affect a "leisurely" (42) saunter because he "is bent on not being hurried while in sight" (43–44) of Fanny. Perhaps he is posturing (adopting an affected or artificial manner) and does not want to give her the privilege of thinking she holds sway over his actions. Perhaps he wants to punish her in some small way for not accompanying him as she had said she would. Or, more likely, he knows that being late would only add to the awkwardness and discomfort of the whole experience, but he does not want Fanny to know he is that concerned. The posturing works, as Fanny observes his "slouchy" strolling and declares boys to be "'the most provoking toads in the world'" (46).

8. (C) See question 7. While in Fanny's sight, Tom intentionally acts as if he intends to be late ("sauntered") as a way of hiding his true intention of hurrying. When out of sight, "as soon as he turned the corner, his whole aspect altered" (48–49). The description in lines 49–51 reveals the contrast between Tom's true intention and his feigned one. (A) provides a parallel action, not a contrasting one.

9. (A) It is stated throughout the passage that Tom's hesitation to meet Polly hinges around his fear of interacting with "strange girls" (29) by himself, equating Fanny's delightful friend to "a wild woman of Australia" (7). It is meeting them alone that utterly frightens him, as he apparently agreed to go when Fanny was planning to accompany him (10). Once Tom arrives at the station, he feels "rather daunted at the array of young ladies who passed" (57). The narrator puts the word "chig-non" (61) in quotation marks and makes sure to attribute this pronunciation to Tom alone (E). We can assume his pronunciation is incorrect since he seems overall very unfamiliar with and flustered by "such a flapping of sashes, scallops, ruffles, curls and feathers" (64). The added detail of his comical mispronunciation adds to the development of his intense anxiety and awkwardness around young girls. They wear hairstyles he does not even know how to pronounce. The narrator does not intend to portray Tom as laughably uncultured or ignorant (B), (C) because such a portrayal would not develop the wider characterization of him as "utterly" (67) fearful of the opposite sex.

10. (D) There are two **similes** in these lines: "panting *like* a race horse, and as red *as* a lobster" (52–53). Both comparisons add to the revelation that Tom truly intends to do what is expected of him, despite his posturing while in Fanny's view. The similes provide a strong image of Tom having run incredibly fast to make up for his earlier posturing ("sauntered leisurely . . . while in sight"). There is no **personification** or **metaphor** in these lines (A), (C). These similes do create dynamic visual imagery (B), but they are not indicative of his posturing since they reveal Tom's true intention to be on time.

11. (B) See question 9. Tom initially agreed to meet Polly when he thought his sister would accompany him (10). As soon as he discovers this is not the case, the fear and anxiety set in. He is "arrested at the awful idea that he might have to address several strange girls before he got the right one" (29–30), he runs "himself off his legs" (44) to avoid being late, which would only add to his anxiety, he repeats that it is "too bad of Fanny" (55) to send him alone when he views the daunting "array of young ladies" at the station (57), and he has the "air of a martyr" (59) while "nerving himself" (62) to approach a damsel that appears, from Tom's perspective, as strange and foreign as an exotic bird ("flapping of . . . feathers"). Tom does appear to want to follow orders (A) and arrive on time since he runs "himself off his legs" (44), but that intention is framed by his larger nervousness around interactions with girls. He does not want to be late and perhaps miss Polly because that would mean he would have to "nerve" himself to approach a "daunting array" (57) of strange girls. He does antagonize Fanny (C) when he discovers she is not accompanying him to meet Polly, but this reaction also falls under the purview of (B). He does not hurry because he is concerned with appearing to be a gentleman (D) who pleases girls (E). The dominant portrayal of Tom is that he is almost crippled ("utterly quenched") by his fear of interacting with strange girls, and his speech and actions serve this portrayal.

12. (A) See question 11. Tom's nervousness about approaching "the damsel" (63) is carefully articulated. We see him "nerving himself to the task" (62) as he "slowly" (63) approaches what appears to him as strange, unpredictable, and forbidding as a wild and delicate bird ("such a flapping of . . . feathers"). His discomfort is perhaps exacerbated by the stranger's "breezy" (66) and "cool" (67) demeanor, which stands in stark contrast to flustered and "meek" (65) Tom, who was just now "panting" (52) and "red as a lobster with the wind and the run" (53). Tom is earlier described as "arrested by the awful idea that he might have to address several strange girls before he got the right one" (29–30) and here we see this feared exchange occur. Once Tom gathers up the nerve to approach her, the young lady responds, "'No,'" with a "cool stare" that "utterly quenched him" (67–68). When used in context of thirst and drinking, quench carries a positive connotation of satisfying and appeasing. The context here, however, does not support this usage of the word as Tom is nowhere near satisfied that he now must repeat this dreaded interaction with yet more strange girls. In this context, "quenched" carries a connotation of extinguished, overcome, quelled. He gathered up all that nerve to no avail. (E) is not wrong, but "frustration" is not as apt a word as "anxiety" to describe Tom's emotional state. Choice C is incorrect because the quoted phrase is not meant to emphasize a point about all "young ladies" and "young men," and the word "cruel" is too extreme.

Passage 2. Frances Burney, *Evelina*

13. (A) The mercers in the shops "took care by bowing and smirking, to be noticed" (6–7) because they are eager to be noticed by the patrons, perhaps so that they may receive more business, making them solicitous (anxiously concerned, eager to please). The speaker even notices, "they recommended them all [the silks] so strongly" (10), indicating that their primary motivation is to persuade customers to "buy everything they showed" (10–11). While there are "six or seven men belonging to each shop" (6), which may imply they are excessive and redundant (B), (C), the question asks for the *primary* characterization and this is secondary to their solicitous manner. The mercers are "bowing" (6) and pleasing in order to make a sale, not because they are guided by principle and doing what is right (E).

14. (C) The speaker is most "diverted" (14) by the fact that the women are served by men who "seemed to understand every part of a woman's dress better than" (16–17) they do themselves. She is surprised and confused as to how and why this can be the case, indicated also by the exclamation point. There are no details to indicate she views these men negatively (D), (E), (A), (B). In fact, she is more impressed by their knowledge than bothered.

15. (A) The word "affected" means assuming or pretending to possess that which is not natural. The speaker finds it unusual that "such men!" (15–16) exist, men who know women's clothes better than women. She finds this unusual, unnatural, affected.

16. (C) The speaker remarks, "The dispatch with which they work in these great shops is amazing, for they have promised me a complete suit of linen against the evening" (20–21). The word "dispatch" means haste, speed, efficiency. While the shops are accommodating her need to have her garments by "this evening," it is their efficiency that impressively allows them to accommodate her, making (C) more specific than (E).

17. (E) The speaker is disoriented; she finds her hair "odd" (22), and does not recognize herself, which is an unsettling feeling. Even the terminology to describe her new hair style is unfamiliar. She sees it as "entangled" while "they" euphemistically call it "frizzled" (26). She *fears* it will be difficult to comb it. (C), though true, does not encapsulate the unsettling feelings the speaker conveys. She is confused, perplexed, and a little bewildered by this strange new style.

18. (D) The speaker is insecure about dancing well in front of different people, outside of her "school" (28). She is apprehensive (nervous, fearful) and wishes "it was over" (28) despite reassurances from Miss Mirvan. (E) indicates that her dance skills are actually poor, and this may not be the case. When considering *the passage as a whole*, it is clear that the speaker suffers from a more general insecurity and apprehension. The speaker's aforementioned reference to her "fear" (26) about her frizzled hair, along with an earlier admittance that she "was almost afraid to go on" (8) while shopping reveal her apprehension toward the strangeness of these new experiences.

19. (B) It is stated that the speaker may "improve by being in this town" (30). She claims that once she has improved, her letters will not contain this "wretched stuff" (29) and "will be less unworthy" (30). The wretched stuff likely refers to the subject matter of the letter we have been reading, which reflects her confusion and naiveté about her upper-class environment. Since she suggests she might improve and she describes her experiences only with shopping and balls, we can infer that she is here to become more refined, sophisticated, cosmopolitan. The reference to being "less unworthy" (30) may lead to (C), but the purpose of her being here is not solely to please the reader of her letter.

20. (D) Evelina qualifies her feelings with the word "almost" two times when describing her experience "a-shopping." She does find the shops "very entertaining," but she is also somewhat bewildered by the newness and strangeness of the experience. There was "so much ceremony" (8) that she was "almost afraid to go on" (8) and "almost ashamed" (12) she could not "buy everything" (3) the mercers showed her. The combination of entertainment, overwhelming attention from the mercers, and the amount of fine clothes makes her feel hesitant—but not so much that she needs to leave.

21. (B) Evelina closes her letter, "Your dutiful and affectionate, though unpolished, Evelina" (31–32), which emphasizes her perception of herself. She acknowledges her strengths and what she perceives to be a temporary weakness, her unrefined nature, which she is currently considering improving (see question 19).

22. (D) In the passage, the speaker describes what she has seen and experienced and how she felt about it. She reveals emotions such as "half afraid" (27), "almost afraid" (8), and "almost ashamed" (12) to express her reactions to what she has experienced. While she does appear to be tenacious (determined) because she is open to "improving" (30) herself, she is not characterized as wise (E) because she is naive and new to the environment. She is merely recording all that is new and weird to her, not insightful analyses or criticism of her society (A). Also, while she does appear guileless (open, honest), she does not appear uncouth (bad-mannered, rude). This adjective is too extreme (B).

Passage 3. Miguel de Cervantes, *Don Quixote*

23. (D) Nowhere in this passage is it indicated that Don Quixote feared his chivalric ambitions were too great (E). Quixote does leave his home "without giving notice of his intention to anyone" (4–5) (A); and he indeed doesn't know exactly where he is going since "he pursued his way, taking that which his horse chose" (22) (B). Also, later in the passage, we learn that an integral part of his heroic fantasy is the "grievous wrong" (42) that Princess Dulcinea has done him (C). Nevertheless, the best answer is (D), since the elucidation of the "terrible thought" (11) arrives immediately in the next sentence: that it "occurred to him that he had not been dubbed a knight" (12–13). The legitimacy of his entire adventure depends on his being a knight.

24. (B) All of the following are true: one, Quixote was unable to reason coherently (A), "his craze being stronger than any reasoning" (17); accordingly, two, he had a tenuous grasp on reality (C); three, he had faith in his good fortune (D), since he was willing to take a path "which his horse chose" (22); and four, he was unwilling to go home (E), given the fact that "he made up his mind to have himself dubbed a knight by the first one he came across" (18–19). Yet it is this last detail that confirms that the best answer is (B), his fantasizing was resourceful. In this instance where he encounters an obstacle to the carrying out of his "grand purpose" (10), it is the resourcefulness of his imagination that provides a way of overcoming that obstacle. His fantasy, in effect, offers both problem and solution.

25. (E) Quixote, as the speaker, believes that his adventures are and will be entirely veracious, or truthful. He is emphatic about this, making multiple references to the "sage magician" who will be "the chronicler of this wondrous history" (39).

26. (D) In keeping with the playful layering of voices typical of *Don Quixote* as a whole, this sentence is a quotation within a quotation, where Don Quixote speaks in the anticipated voice of his future "sage" chronicler. Quixote is imitating the lofty, pretentious style of medieval **heroic epic**. Some might describe this rhetorical style as sophisticated (C), but the best answer is (D), grandiloquent, because the language is courtly and lofty to the point of being bombastic and arrogant, which is not exactly sarcastic (B) or neutral (E).

27. (D) In the sentence, Quixote addresses his anticipated chronicler, which is, slyly, a reference to the writer himself, Cervantes, since he is, in fact, Quixote's chronicler, making (D), the narrator, the best answer. Quixote addresses the "sage chronicler" with, "whoever thou art, to whom it shall fall to be the chronicler" (38–39), indicating he does not have a specific chronicler in mind (E) and it could not be Dulcinea (B) or himself (A), whom he obviously knows.

28. (C) From the passage, it is clear that Quixote sees self-flattery and extreme confidence as an acceptable and perhaps necessary quality for a knight to possess, which means he does not see humility (humbleness) as a necessary trait. For Quixote, a knight must not travel directly and purposefully (A), but rather he should pursue "his way, taking that which his horse chose, for in this he believed lay the essence of adventure" (22–23). Quixote obviously does not value plain, succinct speech, preferring instead the grandiloquent, lofty rhetoric of heroic romance (B). A knight must embrace romance (D), as Quixote does in swearing his undying fealty to Princess Dulcinea. Although Quixote finds creative ways of circumventing the rules he imposes on himself ("he made up his mind to have himself dubbed a knight by the first one he came across"), he certainly claims to make every effort to observe his own chivalric code (E).

29. (A) Don Quixote thinks of himself in the most grandiose and epic terms. He fancies himself a heroic knight whose adventures, though they have not yet begun, will undoubtedly be chronicled by a "sage magician" (38). He almost calls off the adventure due to the color of his armor being inappropriate, but "being crazed" he is able to reason that scrubbing his armor shall do. Humorous details like this, along with the stark absence of any other characters who can legitimize Quixote's vision of himself, alert a careful reader to the farcical **tone** of the passage. There is no indication that Quixote is deserving of such exalted speech.

30. (A) The narrator's attitude toward his protagonist is neither belittling (B) nor spiteful (C), since he describes Quixote in sympathetic terms. He refers to him as a "novice knight" (15) and "our new-fledged adventurer" (24), both being expressions that Quixote thought of himself. Because the narrator does show some sympathy for Don Quixote's idealistic spirit, neither can he be said to be entirely dispassionate (unemotional, detached) (E). Although Quixote fails to give "notice of his intention to anyone" (4–5), he has a "grand purpose" (10) that includes "wrongs he intended to right, grievances to address, injustices to repair, abuses to remove, and duties to discharge" (3–4). By implication, the narrator endorses his ambitions but questions his methods and their likelihood of success. The best answer is (A), magnanimous (fair, generous). Even though the narrator pokes fun at his hero's folly, he demonstrates a subtly generous attitude toward his noble enterprise.

Passage 4. Kate Chopin, "The Kiss"

31. (E) Even though the setting appears to be romantic (A, B) because of the fire, darkness, and the word "ardently" (5), a closer look at the **imagery** of the opening paragraph reveals a surreptitious (sneaky, underhanded) atmosphere, especially with the phrases "uncertain glow" (2) and "deep shadows" (2–3). The shadows alone evoke darkness and deception, but their depth evokes an even more extreme trickery. These deep shadows added to the "uncertain glow" further cement a surreptitious **tone** to the story. We cannot be certain that the glow is even a glow. These phrases conjure up doubt, skepticism, mystery, and perhaps even fraud.

32. (D) Brantain is meek compared to the more up-front and audacious Harvy, who "pressed an ardent, lingering kiss upon" Nathalie's lips (22–23), confidently responds to her angry questions (37–41), and "with an insolent smile" (75) rejects her kiss (81). Brantain, on the other hand, is less confident in expressing his desire for Nathalie. In the second paragraph, he is relieved by and thankful for the dark shadows because they allow him to develop the "courage to keep his eyes fastened as ardently as he liked upon the girl" (5–6). While the word "ardent" is used to describe Harvy's kiss, it merely describes Mr. Brantain's stare, further contrasting their personalities. Brantain is also hesitant in confessing his feelings for Nathalie, unlike the more up-front Harvy: "She was confidently waiting for him [Brantain] to declare himself . . ." (14). Brantain also unquestioningly believes and accepts Nathalie's dubious explanation of her kiss with Harvy (55–56, 67).

33. (D) Up until these lines, we may have still assumed that Nathalie is genuinely attracted to and sexually interested in Brantain because of her occasional "slow glance into the shadow where [he] sat" (9–10) and the fact that "she was confidently waiting for him to declare himself and she meant to accept him" (14–15). However, the next sentence (15–17) reveals that she is primarily interested in Brantain for "the entourage which [his] wealth could give her" (16–17). Her flirtations suggest that she is opportunistic (one who seeks opportunities for advancement without regard for morals or principles). She is not frank or honest about her true intentions (C), open to bribery (F), or passionate about Brantain (B).

34. (E) Physical gestures (I) communicate characters' intentions and desires: Brantain keeps "his eyes fastened as ardently as he liked upon" (5–6) Nathalie. Nathalie sends a "slow glance" (9) occasionally in Brantain's direction while "idly" (8) stroking the satiny coat of her cat, showing her intentional efforts to appear interested in Brantain so that she can marry him for "his millions" (82). Harvy walks with a confident "stride" (20) and "pressed an ardent, lingering kiss upon" (22–23) Nathalie's lips, which characterizes him as bold and confident. Their dialogue shows idiosyncrasies that coincide with their characters (II): Brantain stammers (27), which adds to the portrayal of him as awkward and "without guile (12)." Harvy uses casual, colloquial terms like "'Hang me'" (32) and "'deuced awkward,'" (32) which adds to the portrayal of him as cavalier. Nathalie speaks with completely different **tones** and registers when she speaks with Harvy ("'Don't touch me; don't come near me'") and Brantain ("'Will you let me . . . Perhaps I should not have . . .'"), which coincides with the portrayal of her as someone who has a plan for getting what she wants. The light (III) that opens the scene is described as "dim" (2) and "uncertain" (2) with "deep shadows (2–3)," an appropriate backdrop for a scene with three characters who don't know what each other really wants: Brantain is flummoxed by Harvy's appearance, Harvy and Nathalie's relationship doesn't have clear boundaries, etc. When the passage introduces Brantain, he sits comfortably in the shadows, which "lent him courage to keep his eyes fastened as ardently as he liked upon the girl who sat in the firelight" (4–6). Nathalie, more confident in her intentions than Brantain, is appropriately lit up by the warm lighting.

35. (E) The adjective "delicious" (45) is not usually paired with the noun "frankness" (45), and this pairing makes the reader question the authenticity of Nathalie's frankness. The adjective "delicious" conjures up an image of Nathalie licking her lips, eagerly anticipating approaching Brantain with such a deceptively frank manner. It depicts Nathalie as more wily (cunning, strategic) than frank. She clearly has some ulterior motive in approaching Brantain; perhaps it has to do with her desire to marry him for his "wealth" (16). Also, the question asks about the phrase in context of the passage. Later it is confirmed that Nathalie is not being frank and candid with Brantain. She is like a chess player "who, by the clever handling of his pieces, sees the game taking the course intended" (76–77).

36. (C) In her explanation to Brantain, Nathalie contextualizes Harvy's bold kiss by explaining that he is her brother's friend and "often fancies that he is entitled to the same privileges *as the family*" (60). She means to imply that he assumes he can be affectionate toward her the way a brother or cousin would.

37. (B) A careful read of Nathalie's speech to Brantain reveals that she never actually admits to any wrongdoing herself. She cleverly assuages him with a logical explanation (A) (see question 32), a tactful evasion (55) so as not to remind Brantain of the details of the embarrassing scene (C), the trappings of genuine concern and remorse ("an engaging but perturbed smile," "almost weeping") (D), and appealing to his ego when she insists "'it makes so much difference to me what you think of—of me'" (61–62) (E).

38. (B) While Brantain's face is "radiant" (67), Nathalie's is "triumphant" (67). The word "triumphant" implies that she has achieved something great, that she is happy because she has accomplished a task or goal and not because she is genuinely pleased to make Brantain happy. The word helps to characterize Nathalie as someone who is guileful (sly, cunning) and has ulterior motives beyond love and affection when flirting with men.

39. (E) In contrast to her "delicious frankness" (45) and "triumphant" (67) face when speaking with Brantain, Nathalie's face is now "bright," "tender" (77), and "hungry" (78) in front of Harvy. With Brantain, she uses trickery and deception to convince him that she genuinely cares what he thinks and is honestly interested in him when she is, in fact, interested only in his "wealth" (16) (see questions 37 and 38). However, with Harvy, she abandons such ruses, and her face is described with straightforwardly honest emotion. Also, it is never mentioned that Harvy has wealth, which would indicate that is not Nathalie's primary motivation (C).

40. (A) In the **simile** in lines 76–77, Nathalie feels as if she is a chess player who has cleverly handled her pieces and sees her triumph is imminent. This same feeling is also revealed when she is described as having a triumphant face in line 67, after it is clear that she has assuaged Brantain's doubts and restored his interest in her, as she had cleverly planned to do.

41. (D) After Harvy rejects Nathalie's kiss, she recovers by reminding herself that "she had Brantain and his million left" (82). She does not mind that she cannot have "everything" (82), meaning both Brantain's money (financial needs) and Harvy's kiss (emotional needs), because she at least has secured her financial stability.

42. (E) In the final paragraph, the narrator adopts Nathalie's voice and thoughts. It is Nathalie who reacts to Harvy's news with the resignation to "Brantain and his millions" (82). Because there are no indications that Nathalie is speaking these lines, there is no clear distinction between the narrator's voice and the character's, which makes these lines examples of **free indirect style**. The **third-person narration** is not merely omniscient (A) because the narration actually adopts Nathalie's own speech style. There is not enough context or evidence provided in the passage to justify choice C.

Passage 5. William Congreve, *The Way of the World: A Comedy* (1895)

43. (D) In line 10, we learn that Fainall is related to Sir Wilfull Witwoud ("you have the honour to be related to him"). Mirabell is incredulous that Sir Wilfull Witwoud is traveling abroad at his age. Fainall's response reveals his low opinion of his distant relative, whom he refers to as a "blockhead." The comment is sarcastic: it is not actually "for the honour of England" that they send blockheads like Sir Wilfull Witwoud abroad to Europe. Fainall's later comments do acknowledge Sir Wilfull Witwoud has some redeeming qualities ("loving," good nature"), revealing his own complicated feelings toward his relative (E), but the comment quoted in the question (lines 17–18) is best interpreted as a mocking comment.

44. (E) When he learns that Sir Wilfull Witwoud will be traveling at his age, Mirabell compares him to an exported good and jokingly suggests that Parliament should save the "credit of the nation" (19–20) and prohibit exporting fools. Here, "credit" can be meant both as an economic term and as the reputation of England. Fainall continues the economic comparison to join in the banter about Sir Wilfull Witwoud's low reputation. He adds that it is better for England to trade its fools and deal with that "loss" than to suffer from an overstock of them. While this teasing does provide some background information about how Sir Wilfull Witwoud is perceived (B), the specific words quoted in the question do not describe him directly. Their primary function is to develop the humorous metaphorical comparison between him and an unwanted good.

45. (A) Mirabell asks Fainall if the "follies of this knight-errant" (23) (meaning the afore-mentioned, soon-to-be-traveling fool Sir Wilful Witwoud) are similar to those of his brother, Witwoud, who is referred to as the knight's "squire" to continue the **metaphor**. Fainall replies with another figurative expression, comparing Witwoud to a medlar (a juicy fruit that grows on a bush), which "will melt in your mouth" and is "all pulp (27)." Sir Wilfull Witwoud (the knight) is a "crab" that will "set your teeth on edge" and is "all core (26–27)." These comparisons do not highlight positive traits (B, C, D); rather, they describe how both brothers are distasteful but in different ways. A fruit that melts and is all pulp might be less unpleasant than a crab that sets your teeth on edge, but the descriptions present them both as offensive.

46. (C) Sir Wilfull Witwoud is certainly portrayed as irritating: he is a "blockhead" (18), a "fool" (35) who should be exported to Europe (A). It is suggested that he is connected to a noble family (line 7) and that Fainall is related to him by marriage. Mirabell, if he marries Millamant, would be his cousin as well. Mirabell responds that he would "rather be his relation than his acquaintance" (14), suggesting that it is useful to be related to him, but he would not choose his company without the benefit of being connected to a noble family (B). Fainall presents him as tolerable and redeemable because he "has something of good-nature and does not always want [lack] wit" (32–33). Mirabell mentions that his conversation "is now and then to be endured" (37) (D, E). There are several references to him not being clever ("blockheads," "a fool with a good memory and some few scraps of other folks' wit"), making C the only incorrect description and the correct answer.

47. (C) Fainall says Sir Wilfull "has something of good-nature, and does not always want wit" (32–33), which in this context means he does not always *lack* wit, so Fainall indicates that he has some sense of wit. Mirabell agrees ("Not always") but elaborates on this small sense of wit by explaining that Sir Wilfill is simply "a fool with a good memory and some few scraps of other folks' wit" (35–36). Even more, he "so passionately" tries to look as though he understands "raillery" (39) (good-humored teasing) that he won't raise an objection ("he is not exceptious" (38)) to an "affront" (40) or even "downright rudeness and ill language" (40–41), instead treating such ill humor as jests and fiery satire.

48. (A) Mirabell has been going on at length about the subtleties of Sir Wilfull Witwoud's flaws, so Fainall's comment that he can "finish his picture" of him "at full length" (43) means that he can continue this portrait because "the original" subject of the discussion has arrived ("Behold"). Fainall does not indicate or suggest that Mirabell's impressions are false or that he disagrees with them, making B, C, D, and E incorrect.

49. (B) Sir Wilfull Witwoud is initially described as a "chief of that noble family" (7) and "extraordinary" (9), and it is an "honour" (10) to be related to him, mostly because of his familial connection. These descriptions have truth to them, so they are not fully sardonic (E) or belittling (D). In context of the passage as a whole, the flattery takes on a hint of sarcasm once Fainall and Mirabell reveal a rather low impression of Sir Wilfull Witwoud. Fainall compares him to a crab that will "set your teeth on edge" (26–27), and Mirabell describes him as "a fool . . . now and then to be endured" (37).

50. (C) Fainall and Mirabell are clearly well acquainted and enjoy a witty banter, picking up each other's clever comparisons and developing them with further insights, all related to their shared acquaintance, Sir Wilfull Witwoud. Fainall compares him to an unwanted export, and Mirabell develops the comparison. Fainall also compares Sir Wilfull to a crab, and Mirabell adds that he is "rotten without ever being ripe at all" (28–29). While their banter does indirectly portray Sir Wilfull, the passage is not best described as an introduction to a character we do not even meet (D). The focus is more on the two characters we do observe.

Passage 6. Hannah Cowley, "The Belle's Strategem"

51. (B) Once he is informed that his cousins are coming to town, Courtall "paints them" in his mind (since he has not seen them yet) as "Hebes . . . made up of rusticity, innocence, and beauty" (15–16). Knowing that they are "from the farthest part of Northumberland" (14–15) and have never "been in town" (15), he imagines they fit his stereotyped image of country dwellers as innocent, simple, and beautiful, an image that will be challenged once he meets them in person. He is not intending to disparage (belittle) them (A) because "innocence, and beauty" have a flattering tone. Choice D is similar to B, but Courtall does not *create* his cousins as much as he imagines them to be a certain way.

52. (A) While the word "Hebes" has been used as a contemptuous term for Jewish people, a careful look at the context reveals that Courtall uses the word in a flattering way to describe how he (mistakenly) imagined his country-dwelling cousins to be "made up of rusticity, innocence, and beauty" (15–16). The use of the word as a slur did not actually appear until the 1900s, after the publication of this eighteenth-century play. The slur is an intentional shortening of the word "Hebrew," so the actual definition of "Hebe" is unrelated to the meaning of the slur. In the eighteenth century, the word would have referred to the Greek goddess of youth and spring. While knowledge of the word's etymology is certainly useful, a careful reader's attention to context would eliminate (B), (C), and (E) as options because Courtall does not intend the word negatively. Lovingly (D) is too extremely positive.

53. (E) Courtall first imagines his cousins fit his stereotyped image of country dwellers as innocent, simple, and beautiful (see question 51), an image that will be challenged once he meets them in person. Instead of being beautiful, he describes them as "maypoles" (19), which conjures an image of awkward, towering height and rail-like thinness, not graceful stature and slenderness—III. Instead of "being made up of rusticity [and] innocence" (16), they want to escape their rustic culture and embrace the "fine" city in hopes of "leaving it—Wives" (28). Their bold demands to have access to "the first circles" (45), by way of their cousin Courtall, contradict his expectation that they are innocently content rustics—I. Courtall's breakfast with his cousins does not serve to contrast his initial expectations of them—II.

54. (D) The word "fallow" is defined as "not in use, unseeded." Courtall's first mention of his "cousins Fallow" (11) is in line with his initial image of them as rustic and innocent, meaning unmarried and virginal. (E) is too negative and not supported by the context of Courtall's positive tone. The word does allude to the cousins' being "virginal" (unseeded) but "fallow" does not imply they are particularly moral (A). It is also entirely possible that their last names happen to be Fallow, which is why he refers to them as "my cousins Fallow" with a capital "F." However, a careful reader cannot overlook how apt the name is for the virginal rustic cousins.

55. (C) The cousins "bounced" in with a "violent bustle" and "opened at once, like hounds on a fresh scent" (21) with a series of exclamations, greetings, and entreaties, making them audacious (E), eager, and talkative (not demure, shy, reserved—C). They are referred to as "from the farthest part of Northumberland" (14–15) and never having "been in town" (15), making them country dwellers (B). Courtall discovers that they have "come to town with the hopes of leaving it—Wives" (27–28), and they ask to be escorted to "all the fine places" (24–25) in order to meet "Knight-Baronights" (28), making them opportunistic and aspirational (A), (D).

56. (D) Almack's is mentioned in context of Courtall listing "all the fine places" his cousins want him to take them in order to leave the city as "Wives" (28). Saville laughs at the mere idea of gallant Courtall damaging his reputation by being seen "at Almack's, with five aukward country cousins!" (37–38). Almack's is clearly an exclusive place for those who are deemed appropriately "fine" (24).

57. (E) Saville's reference to Courtall as a "Man of Gallantry" (39) cannot be seen as entirely sincere since the instances Courtall is regaling him with only seem to show him as the opposite of gallant. "Gallant" means "chivalric, gentlemanly, gracious, munificent," but Courtall is possessive of his corner of society from which he excludes his cousins, he lies to avoid interacting with them and is embarrassed to be seen with them. Saville does not necessarily intend to use the phrase ironically, but a careful reader would notice the nuanced insincerity suggested by the term's application to Courtall—I. Courtall tells Saville that he avoided his cousins by "complaining of [his] hard, hard fortune that obliged [him] to set off immediately for Dorcetshire" (35). He follows this with a hearty "ha! ha! ha!" indicating that there is no hard fortune or that the claim was merely an excuse—II. Courtall views the "cousins of our days" with distaste because they are not content to innocently sightsee but "boldly demand their entrees in the first circles" (45). His cousins "come up Ladies—and, with the knowledge they glean from magazines and pocket-books, Fine Ladies" (42–44). Here, the aside reveals Courtall's insincerity in calling them "Fine" because a true sophisticated "first circle" lady would not "glean" the proper demeanor, pedigree, and education from a magazine. He is poking fun at the rustics who assume they can put on "fine" airs by gathering tips from magazines—III.

58. (C) See question 56. The cousins want to be escorted to "all the fine places" in order to leave the city as "Wives" (28). These are places they are likely to meet "Knight-Baronights." Courtall makes up excuses to avoid being seen at these places with his "five aukward country cousins" because it would damage his reputation. He says if they were "like the rustics of the last age" (40–41) who were content with visiting "Paul's, the Lions, and the Wax-work" (41) he would be "at their service (41–42)." He goes on to explain that the cousins "boldly demand their entrées into the first circles," which indicates that it is the exclusivity that makes the "fine places" (24–25) something to avoid when with his cousins. Paul's, the Lions, and the Wax-work, then, must be places that do not belong to the "first circles" (45), since he would be content to take them there, and so are better suited to country folk (C).

59. (E) Early in the passage, Courtall does not genuinely mean that it would have been a "treat" (9) for Saville to have met his cousins as he may have been courted by them or trapped into accompanying them on their hunt for husbands (A). Courtall also knows that it is not genuinely "heroic" of him to stay for merely an hour with his cousins, but it feels heroic to him due to his intense dislike of their intentions and attitudes (B). Courtall tells Saville that he "gets off" (30) the hook to accompany his cousins to "all the fine places" (24–25) by pleading "a million engagements" (31) (D). He follows this by admitting, "However, conscience twitched me," and Courtall reveals his brief moment of sincerity when he decides to actually arrange a meeting with his cousins, but at a location he deems more appropriate (and less damaging to his reputation): "the most private place in town" (33). After this engagement, however, his insincerity returns as he takes "a sorrowful leave, complaining of [his] hard, hard fortune" (34–35), the mention of which induces him to laugh ("ha! ha! ha!") (C).

60. (D) Courtall is concerned for his reputation as a "Man of Gallantry" (39) and would prefer to not be seen "with five aukward country cousins" (37–38) who "boldly demand their entrées into the first circles" (44–45). He is likely concerned they might embarrass him with their general "bouncing" and "violent bustle," along with their hound-like scents (21) and bold attempts to court a "fine" (24) husband (C). (A) implies that Courtall prefers privacy in general, but he only prefers privacy when associating with his embarrassing (to him) cousins. Courtall does not specifically want to prevent his cousins from meeting men (C); rather, he does not want to help them do it or serve as their ticket into the "first circles" (45).

61. (E) If his cousins had "come to town, like the rustics of the last age" (40–41) to see the sights, and not assume the airs of "Fine Ladies" (43–44), Courtall would be "at their service" (41–42). Instead, they "laugh at the bashfulness of their grandmothers, and boldly demand their entrées into the first circles" (44–45). We already know that Courtall is vexed by his cousins' boldness and does not want to assist them in their attempts to become "Wives" of "Knight-Baronights" (28). He longs for the bashful cousins of the last age (the current grandmothers), who were content as rustics. Though Courtall clearly values cosmopolitanism, the question focuses on his comparison between cousins of the past (who were rustic and stayed in their place) and the cousins of his day who want to climb the social ladder. Since he's comparing two kinds of cousins, the best answer is the one that shows what he actually prefers about the cousins of the past (they are content to remain country rustics), making (C) not as good as (E).

62. (C) While a reader/viewer might not find Courtall and Saville's pompous joking all that funny, the scene is written as a comedy and the source of humor is Courtall's interactions with his cousins. The comic **tone** of the passage is created by Courtall's detailed depictions of his rustically awkward and out-of-place cousins. Courtall first laughs at the idea of Saville arriving "half an hour sooner" because he would "have given [Saville] such a treat, ha! ha! ha!" (8–9). The laughter here is at the expense of the cousins because Courtall uses the word "treat" sarcastically. It is implied that Saville would have been equally vexed by the cousins' behavior had he met them. Later, Saville laughs at Courtall's narrow "escape" from having to accompany his rustic cousins to Almack's. The laughter here is not directed at Courtall, but to the "five aukward country cousins! ha! ha! ha!" (38) (E). This humor would fall flat were it not for Courtall's illustrative portrayals of his gauche cousins, including their actual speech, specifics about where they would like to be taken, descriptions of their unattractive appearance, and a contrast to what he had initially imagined them to be. Courtall does not have distaste for all country girls, since he contrasts his cousins to the more appealing "rustics of the last age" who are more "bashful" (40–45) (A), (D). These "rustics" are lauded as opposed to belittled so they cannot be the primary source of humor in the passage (B).

63. (B) Saville appears to share the sensibilities of Courtall. They both find the "five aukward cousins" (37–38) humorous, they both agree that it would be embarrassing and tragic to be seen with them, and they both laugh at the casual lying and deception used to escape them. Choosing (A) would indicate a misread of the passage's humorous **tone** (see question 62). (D) implies that Saville servilely laughs along with Courtall in an attempt to please him, but this is not supported by the text.

Passage 7. Fyodor Dostoyevsky, *Crime and Punishment*

64. (D) The paragraph opens with the declaration that the protagonist "had successfully avoided meeting his landlady on the staircase" (4). In this paragraph, the narrator proceeds to describe the protagonist's living situation and how he always felt "a sick, frightened feeling" (9) when passing his landlady. This feeling is clarified by the last sentence of the paragraph: "He was hopelessly in debt to his landlady, and was afraid of meeting her" (10–11). This sentence could have been placed at the start of the paragraph, but delaying this clarification creates some suspense and curiosity for the reader.

65. (C) The third paragraph elaborates on the precise reason why the protagonist avoids his landlady. It does not refute (A) the analysis provided previously because the previous paragraph only hints that his fear may be due to his owing rent. There is no question explicitly raised in the second paragraph that the third can respond to (B). Both paragraphs mention the same characters (the protagonist and the landlady) (D), and the **tone** is constant throughout the passage (see question 73) (E). The second paragraph is more focused on establishing setting and context for the protagonist's feelings; it describes his room, introduces the landlady, and briefly mentions his fear. The third paragraph, however, expands on the reasons behind the protagonist's emotional state. It explains his "overstrained irritable condition" (13) by describing how he has isolated himself from others and "has lost all desire to" attend to "matters of practical importance" (17–18) (C).

66. (D) The second paragraph may lead a reader to believe that the protagonist avoids his landlady because he has a "sick, frightened feeling" (9) due to his "debt" (10) to her. However, the third paragraph elaborates on this fear. His fear is not due to his being "cowardly or abject" (12) but more a result of being "so completely absorbed in himself, and isolated from his fellows that he dreaded meeting, not only his landlady, but anyone at all" (14–16).

The debt he owes her is not troubling to him, as he "had given up attending to matters of practical importance; he had lost all desire to do so" (17–18). He is not actually fearful of her because "nothing that any landlady could do had a real terror for him" (18–19). Instead, it is the torture of "trivial, irrelevant" pestering, "threats and complaints" (20–21) that he wants to avoid. The subsequent paragraph will elaborate on what is preoccupying the protagonist to the point of complete self-absorption that makes simple interaction with his landlady so odious.

67. **(B)** The **axiom** is: "'all is in a man's hands and he lets it all slip from cowardice'" (26–27), which paraphrases as a man's cowardice causes a man to squander opportunities (let it all slip).

68. **(A)** The two sentences are **chiastic** because the order of words in one of two parallel clauses is inverted in the other. In the first clause "chatter" is the *cause,* and in the second clause "chatter" is the *result,* but the grammar and phrasing are parallel in both clauses. The sentences are not axiomatic (B) or veracious (truthful) (C) because they do not contain self-evident truths. The protagonist is not necessarily exaggerating, so the sentences are not **hyperbolic** (D). Perhaps he is in denial or deluding himself, but there is no evidence to suggest this, and the statements themselves are not delusional statements (E).

69. **(C)** In these lines, the protagonist thinks to himself about "his fears" (24). He says he wants "to attempt a thing like that" but is frightened by "these trifles" (25). We are not told what "that" and "these" are, and he goes on to refer to this deed as "there" (32), "that" (32), and "it" (32), keeping us in suspense and confusion over what he is actually contemplating that is so fear-inducing. In addition to creating a sense of mystery (A, D, E) the vague language characterizes the protagonist's own fear (B) because he clearly cannot even *say* what it is he is contemplating; he is afraid even of the words. The vague language definitely does not elucidate (clarify) the protagonist's actual desire (C)—we are purposely made unaware of what he actually wants to do.

70. **(B)** The detailed descriptions of Petersburg's "airlessness," "bustle," "stench," and "drunken men" show how the environment "worked painfully upon the young man's already overwrought nerves" (35–38). The setting, though not directly, does provide some justification—I—for the protagonist's isolation from others (14–15) and his overall state of petulance (irritability). The **imagery** used to communicate the odor, heat, and noise of the city "complete the revolting misery of the picture," undoubtedly adding to the overall tone of misery—II. There are no details to make III a viable answer.

71. **(A)** The final paragraph focuses on describing the putrid, squalid conditions of the protagonist's environment. The "heat in the street was terrible," and "that special Petersburg stench . . . worked painfully upon the young man's already overwrought nerves" (36–38). The "drunken men" in the streets only "completed the revolting misery of the picture" (41). The contrast between beauty and ugliness is apparent in the next sentence: "An expression of the profoundest disgust gleamed for a moment in the young man's refined face" (41–43). The narrator goes on to describe the man as "exceptionally handsome, above the average in height, slim, well-built, with beautiful dark eyes . . . ." The contrast between the ugly city and the beautiful man makes it more understandable why the protagonist "walked along not observing what was about him . . . not caring to observe it" (46–47). The contrast provides some understanding of his chosen isolation and indifference to people and "matters of practical importance" (17). While the details do focus on the filth in the city, the filth is not explicitly contrasted with cleanliness the way it is contrasted with the protagonist's "refined" (42) and "handsome" (43) face, making (A) a better choice than (C).

72. (E) The protagonist is not bold; he avoids meeting his landlady and "anyone at all" (15–16). He creeps "down the stairs like a cat" (22) to slip out unseen. He is also "acutely aware of his fears" and admits to being "'frightened by these trifles (25).'" He muses about how he talks too much and whether his idle "chatter" (29) is the cause or result of his doing nothing. He is emotionally detached (A) from his environment: "He had become so completely absorbed in himself, and isolated from his fellows that he dreaded meeting . . . anyone at all" (15). He "had given up attending to matters of practical importance; he had lost all desire to do so" (17–18). He "walked along not observing what was about him and not caring to observe it" (46). The protagonist has given up on life; he even ceased to care that he is "crushed by poverty" (16) (D). He is clearly not well (C), as he has "been in an overstrained irritable condition, verging on hypochondria" and "he was very weak," having not "tasted food" (50) for two days. The protagonist stands out amid his putrid environment, "exceptionally handsome, above the average in height" (43) (B).

73. (A) The narrator observes the protagonist throughout the passage. He does not pity the protagonist (D) because he describes him as beautiful, and perhaps the protagonist would not describe himself that way. While the narrator does agree that the city is putrid when he describes it as such in the final paragraph, these descriptions are more indicative of his being observant (A) than empathetic (E) because he is merely noticing the "heat . . . airlessness . . . and dust" (35–36), where the stench has come from ("pothouses") and why the city appears "revolting" (41) and not necessarily indicating that he feels the protagonist's pain. The narrator describes events and the protagonist's inner state through an **omniscient point of view**, not from a distant, aloof perspective (C). The narration does not offer commentary disapproving (B) of the protagonist's avoidance of his landlady, his abject poverty, his hypochondria, or his verbal musings.

74. (C) The protagonist admits, "'I want to attempt a thing like that and am frightened by these trifles'" (24). The "thing" is also referred to as "that" and "a plaything . . . a fantasy." He does make a reference to "Jack the Giant-killer" (31–32), but the reader never fully discovers exactly what he is "thinking" of while "lying for days in [his] den" (31). He avoids his landlady because "he had given up attending to matters of practical importance" and "had become so completely absorbed in himself. . .that he dreaded meeting, not only his landlady, but anyone at all" (14–18) (A). He is physically weak because "for two days he had scarcely tasted food" (50) (B). The final paragraph provides the protagonist's impression of his environment (see question 72) (D) and a description of his "handsome" (43) appearance (E).

Passage 8. Euripides, *Medea*

75. (D) In the first paragraph, Medea explains that she has come forth "from the house" out of "fear lest [the ladies will] be blaming" her, meaning if she were to stay in her house, "showing pride," she would gain an "ill name and a reputation for indifference" (3–4). She leaves and speaks to the "Corinthian ladies" so that they will not "blame" or judge her. She is trying to mitigate their judgment of her. Though she does say that "there is no just discernment in the eyes of men" (6), labeling the people as unjust is not her purpose in leaving her house (B).

76. (C) Medea says that there is "no just discernment in the eyes of men" because they "loathe [a person] at first sight, though never wronged by him" (8), making I incorrect.

People will form unrelenting judgments of others even if they are "stranger[s]" (8). Regarding II, Medea says that she does not wish to commend a citizen who "resents the city's will" (11) and out of "stubbornness of heart" (10) refuses to hate those whom the city hates.

77. (B) In the first paragraph, Medea introduces the topic of her speech. She is here to persuade the Corinthian women not to blame her. She explains why she needs to leave her house to lessen their hatred for her. In the second paragraph, she develops this topic by explaining how she was wronged, perhaps to help them understand her situation and the reasons for her crime or sin. She says, "on me hath fallen this unforeseen disaster, and sapped my life; ruined I am . . ." (12–13). Both paragraphs are addressed to the "Corinthian ladies" (A). No questions are posed in the first paragraph (C). Both paragraphs contain specifics (D); the first gives examples of the men's unjust discernment, and the second gives examples of why "women are the most hapless creatures" (16). While the first paragraph does contain some mild criticism of the unjust discernment of men, it also contains understanding of such judgment (9–10) as well as explanations of why she has come forth from her house, so it is not primarily a diatribe. Medea explains the hardships women have to endure, which indirectly allows her to present her desire for vengeance as warranted, but the justification here does not address any harsh criticism in the first paragraph, making (E) not as good as (B).

78. (C) Medea's commentary on women's lives opens with an arguable claim (thesis): "Of all things that have life and sense, we women are the most hapless creatures" (15–16). She uses transitions like "first" and "Next" to lay out her reasons and examples, which constitute lines 17–29. The transition "And yet" (30) leads to a counter-argument ("they say we live secure at home, while they are at the wars"), which she claims is "sorry reasoning" and swiftly offers a rebuttal: "I would gladly take my stand in battle array three times o'er, than once give birth" (31–32). There is no optimism in her commentary (D) and the examples do not appear to be ranked according to severity (E). She alludes to the privileges men have, but the commentary is not equally focused on men and women's experiences (B). There is certainly logic to her list of complaints (A).

79. (D) Medea's opening argument introduces the idea of misfortune and fate. She says "we women are the most *hapless* creatures" (16). They are unlucky, first, in that they were even born female, and this misfortune continues when they marry because their future depends on this choice being "good or bad" (19). Furthermore, a woman would have to have a "diviner's eye to see how best to treat the partner of her life" because she "hath not learnt the lesson in her home" (22). While Medea does say that marital bliss might be possible "if haply we perform these tasks" (23–24), this observation comes directly after Medea explains that the most important factor is a woman's choice in husband being "good or bad"and that a woman would need a "diviner's eye" to even know what her husband wants. It is only by remote chance that a woman would be able to discover the ways to satisfy her husband. Even if a woman performs the tasks a husband wants, marital bliss is still dependent on the chances that he "live with us, without resenting the yoke" (25). Marital bliss depends on pleasing your husband, which initially (as the question asks) depends on fate, making (D) a better choice than (A). While (B), (C), and (E) would certainly help to improve a woman's condition, they all hinge on good fortune, according to Medea.

80. (E) According to Medea, when a man "is vexed with what he finds indoors, he goeth forth and rids his soul of its disgust, by taking him to some friend or comrade of like age"

(26–28), whereas women "must needs regard his single self" (28–29), which means they are expected to stay at home and only have their husband as a companion—I. Medea points out that the pain of childbirth far outweighs the pain incurred in battle (30–32)—II. Women's happiness in a marriage is, in part, dependent on their ability to "best treat the partner of her life" (23), making her submissive to the man. Also, she states that women cannot "disown [their] lords" (20), which indicates that only a man has the power to divorce a woman—III.

81. (C) In the second paragraph, Medea cites examples of women's unfortunate lot in life. She says they have to "buy a husband at a great price" (17) (B), and if they make a bad choice in spouse, they cannot be unfettered (E) from a bad marriage because "divorce is not honourable to women" (20), and while the husbands have the option to leave the house and seek the company of friends, women "must needs regard his single self" (28–29), which means they do not have that same option (A). A woman, according to Medea, also must "have a diviner's eye" (22–23) to be able to determine how best to please her husband since she has not been taught how to do this. All these examples imply that women's submission to men causes their haplessness (D), but nowhere does she mention their obligation to *raise* children (she does indicate that she would rather fight in war than bear the pain of childbirth)(C).

82. (A) See question 78. As part of Medea's argument that "women are the most hapless creatures" (16), she uses the phrase "And yet" (30) to transition into an anticipated counter-argument: "they say we live secure at home, while they are at the wars" (30–31). Men view themselves as more hapless because of the danger they incur on the battlefield. Medea calls this "sorry reasoning" (31) and provides a rebuttal by citing child birth as a more painful experience. (C) does not mention the counter-argument and (B) and (E) suggest this is a digression; however, addressing a likely counter-argument actually strengthens one's claim.

83. (C) Medea says, "But enough!" (32) after she has gone on complaining about the plight of women for nearly the whole passage. She is about to change the focus from general women to herself by admitting, "this language suits not thee as it does me" (33). She acknowledges that she is the one in a compromised position, not them. This acknowledgment serves as a transition to her current quest for revenge and appeal for their tacit acceptance. Her detailed argument in support of her claim that "women are the most hapless creatures" (16) was not a digression (D); rather, it was essential in order for her to garner sympathy from the Corinthian ladies in order to persuade them to grant her her wish: their "silence" (39). Also, perhaps by addressing concerns that can apply generally to all women, she hopes her audience may feel that her quest for vengeance is partly theirs, increasing the chances that they will grant her their "silence."

84. (D) In lines 33–38, Medea says that she should stop griping about the lot of women because it applies only to her situation and not to the women she is addressing. She goes on, "thou hast a city here, a father's house . . . but I am destitute, without a city . . . a captive . . . ." (33–36). Medea distinguishes between herself and them by assuming they all have what she does not. Though she does mention she is without a family or husband (A, B) she is assuming they still have these things, making (D) the better answer choice.

85. (E) Medea acknowledges that though women are "timorous" and "coward[s] at the mere sight of steel" (43), she abandons this timorous nature and fills her heart with deadly thoughts.

86. (C) Of the options, the best choice is (C) because Medea is filled with deadly thoughts she intends to pursue, since she has just attempted to convince the Corinthian ladies to grant her their vows of silence. Her deadly plan means she is not undecided about her next steps (E) or entirely hopeless (A), despite her earlier focus on her hapless lot in life. She is not lecturing or moralizing here (D).

87. (B) Medea says women are "timorous in all else . . . a coward at the sight of steel" (42–43). She has already equated herself with all women in the first 29 lines, so Medea certainly does not view herself as innately courageous. She does not take responsibility for her situation, attributing it to the "hapless" (16) state of womanhood (A). She is inciting sympathy and cooperation from the Corinthian ladies by detailing the sad misfortunes they all share as women (C, D), and she makes several references to being alone ("without a city . . . a captive . . . with no mother, brother, or kinsman") (E).

Passage 9. Gustave Flaubert, *Madame Bovary*

88. (E) The narrator and his peers "rose as if just surprised at [their] work" (3), which indicates that they were *not* actually engaged with their work. In fact, some "had been asleep." As opposed to the "new fellow," who is "so attentive as if at a sermon" (17–18), the other boys have no difficulty tearing themselves away from the lesson to "fall into line" (19). They also carelessly throw their "caps on the floor" (21–22), in a manner that would purposely make "a lot of dust: it was the thing" (23–24). The boys are habituated to the routines and customs of their school, as opposed to the "new fellow," who appears in stark contrast to the others in his rapt attention and upright behavior. The narrator is intrigued by the new fellow and how he differs from the rest of them; he doesn't express a sense of exclusivity about his right to attend the school (D).

89. (B) The narrator perhaps describes the new fellow's clothing to emphasize how awkward he appeared among the other boys in the school, how he does not fit in. We have already learned that he was "not wearing the school uniform" (2) and that "his short school jacket of green cloth with black buttons must have been tight about the armholes, and showed at the opening of the cuffs red wrists accustomed to being bare" (12–14). The jacket appears not to fit properly, and the red wrists imply that the new fellow is not used to wearing any kind of school uniform, unlike the other boys in the school. The narrator also notices his boots were "ill-cleaned" (16), suggesting further that the new fellow does not fit in. The school servant does mention that he "recommends" the new student to the headmaster's "care" (6), but the narrator's description of the new fellow's clothing does not suggest his academic potential (E). (D) is incorrect because even though the boy may feel apprehensive and uncomfortable in his clothes, the narrator's intention is to convey his own (and the students') impressions of the new fellow based on his clothing, and what he seems to point out repeatedly is how he does not match everyone else and looks out of place.

90. (C) The new fellow is described as "attentive as if at a sermon" (17–18) during the lesson, which means he is careful to follow the rules and meet the expectations, "not daring even to cross his legs or lean on his elbow" (18). The teacher "was obliged to tell him to fall into line with the rest" (19–20) because he is so preoccupied with paying attention to the lesson that he does not notice the others have lined up. Though the teacher has to tell him to follow what the others are doing, (A) and (B) misunderstand the teacher's intention; the new fellow is not being reprimanded for not following the others. The narrator is carefully describing the observations he had of this fellow. There is a greater purpose to all these observant details; they are meant to characterize the new fellow, not to belittle him (E) (see question 94). While the new fellow does not fit in with his classmates, it is too extreme to say he is an outcast (D).

91. (B) The phrase "'the thing'" (24) is in quotation marks because it is what the students call the action to which "the thing" refers (throwing their hats). It is their own vernacular, a colloquial phrase, an **idiomatic expression** to describe an action they take regularly.

92. (B) The narrator notices the cap is ugly, "one of those poor things" but still "full of expression" (28–29). The fact that it is full of expression shows that the cap carries meaningful significance as a **symbol**. It is poor but full of expression, just as the new fellow appears to be poor because of his "ill-cleaned" (16) boots and "short school jacket" (12) that does not quite fit. However, like the cap, the fellow is also "full of expression"; he is "attentive as if at a sermon" (17–18) and he "looked reliable, but very ill at ease" (11–12). The narrator goes on to describe the cap's "composite order" (27), every type of material, color, and texture that made up the cap. Since this detailed description of the cap follows other speculations and conjectures about the new fellow, we can infer that the cap is potentially symbolic of him. After all, the paragraph ends with a statement that easily suggests the cap's symbolism for the fellow: like him, "the cap was new; its peak shone" (34). The previous paragraphs have detailed exactly how the new fellow himself sticks out from the other boys, how his "peak shone." Though he notes how the new fellow is markedly different from others, and though he refers to his hat as having "dumb ugliness" (29), the narrator is not harshly judgmental of the fellow in all his descriptions of his cap, nor does he intend to describe it purely to ridicule him (D).

93. (A) (See question 92). The final sentence is notable for its simplicity in comparison to the prior sentence. This closing line contains two simple independent clauses that reiterate a basic description of the new fellow's cap. The **repetition** here calls attention to the features of the cap that potentially signify the fellow himself. Like the cap, he is new, and his peculiar appearance and behavior make him stand out from his new peers. He does not quite blend in; like his cap, he "shone."

94. (C) The passage as a whole is devoted entirely to characterizing the new fellow. Each paragraph contributes to this characterization primarily through the narrator's (who speaks for his classmates) observations. We do learn a little about the culture of this school, but those details are in service to the characterization of the new fellow—I. While the passage does suggest class differences between the new fellow and the schoolmates, this is certainly not the primary purpose of the passage—II.

95. (E) The narrator observes and comments on the new fellow for the entire passage, beginning with the moment he first sees him. He describes his attire in great detail, along with the behaviors that appeared most distinctive to him. His impressions are purely subjective, from his own point of view. Since he was a classmate, he cannot be said to be unreliable (A). The style and content of the passage do not resemble that of a biography; even so, biographers may take liberties in their descriptions of their subjects, and the narrator's descriptions are not definitively unfair (D).

96. (D) The new fellow differs from the narrator in his attire/clothing (2, 12–16, 24–33), his height (10), his deportment/manner/behavior (17–25), and his attitude (17–20). Their environment is the same: the classroom and school (D).

Passage 10. Nathaniel Hawthorne, *The Scarlet Letter*

97. (E) The narrator repeats the phrase "It may seem marvellous that . . ." several times in the opening paragraph to denote the strange, baffling (E), intriguing, unexpected nature of Hester Prynne's choice to remain in the town where "she must needs be the type of shame" (9–10). The amazement at her choice is communicated through the narrator's list of alternative settings that Hester could have chosen as her home.

98. (D) The comments set off by dashes suggest other paths Hester Prynne could have taken instead of staying "within the limits of the Puritan settlement" (2). She could have returned to "her birth-place, or to any other European land" (3) or "the passes of the dark, inscrutable forest" (5–6).

99. (C) After the series of clauses beginning with "It may seem marvellous that . . ." Hester Prynne would stay at the location of her crime and punishment, the narrator responds to the assumption of it being "marvellous" with a generality of human nature. It is not so marvelous because, he explains, "there is a fatality, a feeling so irresistible and inevitable that it has the force of doom, which almost invariably compels human beings to linger around and haunt, ghost like, the spot where some great and marked event has given colour to their lifetime" (10–13). He goes on to qualify the apparently marvelous decision by saying that "the darker the tinge that saddens" one's life, the more irresistible the urge to remain at that spot.

100. (B) The "marked event" is explained in the following sentence to be "[h]er sin, her ignominy" (14), her transgression. This sin was committed with "one with whom she deemed herself connected in a union that . . . would bring them together before the bar of final judgment . . . for a joint futurity of endless retribution" (25–28).

101. (A) The **metaphor** comparing Hester's sin to "the roots which she had struck into the soil" (14–15) helps us imagine why she would choose to remain in "that place" (9), the scene of her transgression. The "chain that bound her here" (20) is also metaphorical—she is not actually in chains (I). A **simile** describes "a new birth" (15) converting the forest "into Hester Prynne's wild and dreary, but life-long home" (17), more suitable to her now than her childhood home in a rural English village where her "stainless maidenhood" (19) is long gone, "like garments put off long ago" (19)—II. These descriptions enhance the narrator's theories of why Hester might have chosen to stay, but they do not *prove* the theories correct, which makes III incorrect.

102. (E) As opposed to the previous paragraph that articulates the narrator's generality about how sin anchors human beings, the second paragraph explores Hester's secret justifications for why she continues "a resident of New England" (31–33). According to the narrator, she privately longs for "a joint futurity of endless retribution" (28) with her accomplice. She also reasoned that she should stay for "retribution" (28), for "her earthly punishment" (35), to purge her soul (36), and to become more "saint-like" (37). The paragraph does refer to her sin (B), and her fatal choice to remain at the location of her crime (A), but these references are not unique to the second paragraph. Her predicament (staying at the scene of her crime) and chosen setting (the setting of her crime) are also thoroughly discussed in the first paragraph (C) (D).

103. (E) Since this person is described as one who will join Hester Prynne "before the bar of final judgment . . . for a futurity of endless retribution" (27–28), we can assume he has been her partner (accomplice) in sin.

104. (D) The second paragraph explains that Hester likely stays in New England, in the town where she committed her crime, to endure punishment, cleanse her soul, and achieve a "saint-like" "purity," and "martyrdom" (36–37). (A) and (C) are false and not mentioned in the passage. (E) is mentioned in the first paragraph, so it is not suggested by the second paragraph as the reason Hester remains in New England. Hester may have felt ambivalent about remaining, but the question asks why she decides to stay. Ambivalence would not be a reason to stay (B).

105. (B) The second paragraph introduces Hester's secret: another reason she may have decided to stay in New England is in order to be near her accomplice, "one with whom she deemed herself connected in a union that . . . would bring them together before the final bar of judgment, and make that their marriage-altar, for a joint futurity of endless retribution" (25–28). Hester cannot marry her accomplice "on earth" (26), so she secretly longs to be joined with him in eternity by their shared retribution for their crime. The "tempter of souls had thrust this idea upon Hester's contemplation, and laughed at the passionate and desperate joy with which she seized, and then strove to cast it from her" (28–31).

106. (E) The narrator conjectures that "another feeling kept Hester within the scene and pathway that had been so fatal" (24–25). The feeling is described as a "secret" (22) hope that she and the "one with whom she deemed herself connected" (26) by their sin would be brought "before the bar of final judgment . . . for a joint futurity of endless retribution" (27–28). She seizes this idea with "passionate and desperate joy" but hastens to "bar it in its dungeon" (31). She is not actually marrying someone (A), nor does she hope to actually marry her accomplice (B, C). The idea that brings her joy is the thought of being united with her accomplice for eternity, even if it is one of retribution and not actual marriage.

107. (D) The narrator actively theorizes about Hester's motives, fears, thoughts, emotions, etc., showing curiosity about the character. He does not excessively praise or admire her (C). He acknowledges and is intrigued by her sins and quest for redemption. He is not aloof (E); on the contrary, he appears almost to be sitting on her shoulder as he observes her battle with a secret and attempts to "cast it from" (30–31) herself. There are no details that depict the narrator as condescending or critical of Hester's actions and thoughts (A, B).

Passage 11. Mary Shelley, *Frankenstein*

108. (E) The speaker observes, "There was a sense of justice in my father's upright mind which rendered it necessary that he should approve highly to love strongly" (3–4). The narrator goes on to reason that perhaps his father had suffered before due to loving someone who was not worthy of his devotion, "and was so disposed to set a greater value on tried worth" (6). His love is not unconditional; a person must have proven herself worthy in order to be loved by the father. The father felt "a desire to be the means of . . . recompensing her for the sorrows she had endured" (9–10) (A)(D), he is "inspired by reverence for her virtues" (8) (B), and the "considerable difference between the ages . . . seemed to unite them only closer in the bonds of affection" (1–3) (C).

109. (D) The question asks for the *primary* characterization of the mother. She is first described as loved by the father who is "inspired by reverence for her virtues" (8). She is described as having to endure sorrows, as a "fair exotic" (12) because of her delicate health and "weakened frame" (19). Her mind is "benevolent" (14), which is also seen through the "inexhaustible" (23) stores of affection she has for her son, the narrator, and how she sees it as a "necessity" (38) to "act in her turn the guardian angel to the afflicted" (40). While she sees it as a necessity to help the poor, it is too extreme to say she is dependent on children for happiness (C). While she is captivating because of her virtue, choice B is incorrect because the father's affection differs "wholly from the doting fondness of age" (7–8) and has more to do with his desire to recompense her "for the sorrows she had endured" (9–10) and his "reverence for her virtues" (8). She is captivated by the appearance of the girl in the cottage, but there is not sufficient evidence to suggest that it is beauty alone that catches her eye or that she is partial to beauty in other circumstances (E).

110. (C) While the comparison of the father to a gardener and the mother to a fair exotic might imply that the father is officious (overbearing and fussy) in his protection of the mother, the **tone** of the lines does not indicate that the speaker intends to portray the father in such a negative way. The speaker makes the comparison, more likely, to emphasize how his father nurtures his mother the way an attentive gardener would care for a rare flower. The comparison does imply that the mother is in need of care and attention, but the positive tone does not imply that she is needy, clingy, pathetic, or dependent on the father's care (A).

111. (D) The first paragraph gives helpful background for comprehending the details in the second paragraph. The first paragraph explains the relationship between the speaker's parents and characterizes the mother. These details are useful in interpreting the second paragraph, in which we see the mother's specific actions and behavior (she helps the poor). The background from the first paragraph helps us understand the motives and reasons behind her actions.

112. (A) The **metaphor** compares the parents' love to a mine from which they extract unlimited amounts of affection for their son. The narrator implies that, even though they expended so much love and devotion on each other, their capacity to love was so inexhaustible that they still were able to love him without conservation.

113. (E) The speaker mentions that his parents saw him as "their plaything and their idol . . ." (25–26), implying that they adored him so much it was as if they worshipped him the way an acolyte (a religious follower, a worshipper at an altar) might worship a religious idol.

114. (D) The sentence contains a series of explanatory dependent clauses, one of which contains a list describing the factors contributing to his "train" of childhood enjoyment: "With this . . . added to the . . . it may be imagined that while . . . I received *a lesson of* *patience, of charity, and of self-control,* I was so guided by a silken cord . . ." (29–33). The "train" of enjoyment is a **metaphor**, but the comparison to a train does not clearly communicate that the influence was excessive. The narrator describes it as "enjoyment," making (E) incorrect. There is no allegory (A) or anecdote (C) in the sentence. There is no evidence to suggest the narrator's perspective is delusional (B).

115. (E) The narrator provides context to the visit to the abode. He explains that his mother "desired to have a daughter" (34) and that their "benevolent dispositions often made them enter the cottages of the poor" (37–38). The narrator then goes into great detail describing the distinctive and impressive qualities of the young girl who "attracted [his] mother far above all the rest" (46–47). This context suggests that the girl might become involved in their lives in a pivotal way. The anecdote does highlight another example of his mother's benevolence, but its purpose is not to simply add to a list of her generous deeds (D).

116. (E) The girl is characterized as visually striking by the words "very fair" (48) and by the contrast made between her and her "dark-eyed, hardy little vagrant" (48) peers. Her gold hair "set a crown of distinction on her head" (50)—I. She is otherworldly; she is described in line 53 as heavenly, celestial, and "of a distinct species." Her distinguishing qualities evoke strong emotions in the narrator and the mother: "none could behold her without looking on her as of a distinct species, a being heaven-sent . . ." (52 53)—III.

117. (C) The **tone** is not factual; the speaker speculates and recalls his impressions of his parents (B, E). It is not resentful but rather exceedingly praiseworthy of his parents (D). It is not grave (serious); he mostly recalls sweet, sentimental moments (A). Even his mother's physical weakness is described in the context of how much his father loved and cared for her. The tone is best stated as earnest because the speaker appears to genuinely feel the emotions his word choice suggests he feels. There is no hint of irony, sarcasm, humor, self-deprecation, hostility, regret, remorse, etc.

118. (D) The passage opens with the narrator speculating about the father's past, his reasons for loving the mother, and details about his devotion and sacrifice. In doing so, the narrator touches on the remarkable characteristics of his mother that have earned the devotion of his father. This background is necessary in order for readers to comprehend the parents' devotion to their son and the descriptions of the young girl in the abode, who we can imagine may become his sister. The narrator does recount some fond memories, but the passage as a whole does not focus on memories that are best described as simply fond. The narrator has a purpose with sharing his "first recollections" (25) and the anecdote about the girl in the abode; they support his analysis of his family's relationships, motivations, and characteristics, making (E) a better choice than (A).

Passage 12. Jonathan Swift, *Gulliver's Travels*

119. (C) In the first paragraph, the speaker mentions that he "obtained [his] liberty" in the past "fortnight," indicating that he has been recently emancipated (B). He mentions that he was willing to give Reldresal his time "on account of his quality and personal merits, as well as of the many good offices he has done [him] . . . ," making him grateful (A). He shows that he is gracious when he "offered to lie down, that he [Reldresal] might the more conveniently reach [the speaker's] ear" (D). Since the speaker has to either lie down so Reldresal can speak into his ear or hold Reldresal in his hand, it is clear that the speaker may be quite large (E).

Though he accommodates Reldresal and expresses gratitude, it is too extreme to say he is obedient, making (C) the only incorrect choice (and the correct answer).

120. (E) The word "it" in the phrase refers to the speaker's "liberty" (1), indicating that Reldresal will pretend that the speaker entirely earned his liberty but does not actually believe he did. He "added, that if it had not been for the present situation of things at court, perhaps [the speaker] might not have obtained it so soon" (11).

121. (C) In lines 24–25, the speaker says, "We compute the *Tramecksan*, or high heels, to exceed us in number; but the power is wholly on *our side*," implying that he is a member of the opposing party, that of the low heels, also called "*Slamecksan.*"

122. (D) Reldresal explains that his majesty is partial to the "low heels": he makes use "only of low heels in the administration of the government" (19–20) and "his majesty's imperial heels are lower . . . than any of his court" (21–22). His majesty's shoes and partiality to the low heels are not what's worrying, however. The problem discussed in lines 23–28 is that his majesty's *heir* has "some tendency towards the high heels," which is suggested by his "gait" resulting from "one of his heels [being] higher than the other" (27–28). The heir appears partial to the high heels, which suggests a problem of potential defection to the opposing party: *Slamecksan* (high heels) instead of *Tramecksan* (low heels).

123. (D) "These intestine disquiets" (29) that the speaker has been describing have been the domestic (existing within their home country) problems and strifes (struggles) between opposing factions in the empire. No one has actually been found to have committed treason (C); there are merely speculations about potential defection. There is no mention of elections (B).

124. (E) The speaker explains that the empire is skeptical about the truth of the addressee's claims "that there are other kingdoms and states in the world, inhabited by human creatures as large as [himself]" (32–33) because their "philosophers . . . would rather conjecture that [he] dropped from the moon" (33–34) (B). The word "rather" suggests that the philosophers find it more convenient to formulate a cursory dismissal of the addressee's claims than to have to contend with the frightening certainty "that an hundred mortals of [the addressee's] bulk would, in a short time, destroy all the fruits and cattle of his majesty's dominions" (35–36). Their reasoning is not research-based (B) (D) or even that logical (A), as it stems from avoidance and fear. They are willing to believe something even more absurd—that he dropped from the moon or stars—than to engage with his assertions that "there are other kingdoms and states in the world" with creatures of his large size.

125. (A) The word "fomented" means goaded (motivated, encouraged). The speaker goes on to explain that the monarchs of Blefuscu contributed to the war's continuance by providing "refuge" (49) to Lilliput's "exiles" (62). By doing so, they keep the enemy protected, which allows the rebellions to continue.

126. (D) Reldresal mentions the *Blundecral*, which contains "a fundamental doctrine of our great prophet Lustrog" (56–57), to explain that the emperors of Blefuscu, their opponents, accuse them (Lilliput) of "making a schism in religion" by "offending" the edict that, as written in the *Blundecral*, "*true believers break their eggs at the convenient end*" (59). Reldresal asserts that this accusation is not well founded. He believes their claim is "a mere strain upon the text" and that the *Blundecral's* words suggest it should "be left to every man's conscience" (60–61). He mentions the *Blundecral,* then elaborates on Blefuscu's role in inciting conflict.

127. (D) The argument between Blefuscu and Lilliput is an argument about conflicting interpretations, because both nations interpret the words of the "great prophet Lustrog" (56–57) differently. The words "the convenient end" are interpreted by one nation to be the "big end" and by the other nation to be the "small end" (45). The speaker says, " . . . which is the convenient end, seems, in my humble opinion, to be left to every man's conscience" (59–61).

128. (C) All of the words printed in italics ("*Slamecksan,*" "*Tramecksan,*" "*drurr,*" "*Alcoran,*" and "*Blundecral*") refer to objects or names in Lilliput and Blefuscu's language. (A) is incorrect because a "drurr" is not a person or a place. It is also not that important (B)—it is a unit of measure.

129. (C) At the start of the passage, prior to explaining the current predicament, Reldresal mentions that the speaker of lines 1–11 would not have obtained his liberty so soon "if it had not been for the present situation of things at court" (10–11)—II. After explaining the situation, Reldresal announces that "his imperial majesty, place[es] great confidence in [the first paragraph's speaker's] valor and strength" (70)—I. This strength will come in handy, Reldresal implies, for the imminent battle with Blefuscu, who "are just preparing to make a descent upon us [Lilliput]" (69)—II. Choice III (and D and E) is incorrect because Reldresal and "his imperial majesty" belong to the *Slamecksan* party (24–25) and are not fighting against it.

130. (A) The passage as a whole carries an ironic and satirical **tone**, with the absurd conflicts serving as a satirical take on political conflicts in general. Essential to a satirical tone, though, are characters who genuinely participate in the imagined and farcical world. Reldresal, a character in this world, authentically describes Lilliput's problems in a grave tone to persuade his addressee to assist the nation in its war against Blefuscu.

Passage 13. Sophocles, *Oedipus the King*

131. (D) The passage begins with Oedipus asking three questions. He asks why his "children," the citizens of his land, carry "suppliant branches" in prayer and entreaty (1– 4). He also inquires whether the priest stands there in "dread or sure hope" (12). He then asks if the priest knows that he is there for them "'gainst all" (13). As these are all actual questions directed to another person who is about to answer in the following lines, they are not **rhetorical questions** (B). An **invocation** is a call to someone else for assistance. The priest invokes Oedipus, but Oedipus does not invoke the priest in these opening lines (C).

132. (C) The **personification** in these lines characterizes the city and its people as desperately in need of assistance. The city "breathes/ Heavy with incense, heavy with dim prayer/And shrieks to affright the Slayer" (4–6). A city cannot actually breathe, pray, and shriek; these actions all personify the city as pleading for help. While the technique of personification does imply that the object is alive (D), that is not the sole purpose of the device. It presents things as alive for a reason, and in these lines the city is given human qualities to emphasize its desperation. The incense and prayer may lead to choosing (E), but the personified "shrieks" and the heaviness of the breathing make (C) the best choice.

133. (C) Oedipus makes sure to mention that he is so moved by the citizens' plight that he has "scorned withal/ Message or writing" (7–8) once he knew that he was called by his people—II. He calls himself "world-honoured Oedipus" (9), clearly characterizing himself as venerable, deserving of great honor and respect—I. In lines 12–14, he emphasizes that he is there for the citizens above all else; his "will is [theirs]" (12–13). He reiterates how moved he is by their hardships by saying only "stern" hearts would not feel for "so dire a need" (14), indicating that he is not preoccupied but is here to assist the people—III.

134. (D) Oedipus was summoned (C) by the people, but he makes a point of saying that he has "scorned withal/ Message or writing" because "this [their plight] so moves [him]" (7–10). Instead of merely responding in writing, he implies that he has come in person to demonstrate his deep concern for their well-being.

135. (A) Oedipus first says that he notices how the city "breathes," is heavy with "dim prayer," and "shrieks"; then he says "this moves me" (7). The word "this" refers to the city's heavy breathing, dim prayers, and shrieks; in other words, what concerns him is the city's plight.

136. (B) The people appeal to Oedipus because he "came to Thebes so swift, and swept away/ The Sphinx's song, the tribute of dismay/ . . . That made [them] free" (39–41). They do not see him as a peer to God (34) (C), and do not believe he knows more than they know (42) (D). It is true that "the world saith" (44) Oedipus saved their lives, but the people are not relying on rumors, as they "say" and can confirm this themselves (E). Oedipus is described as filled "by God's breath" (43)(A), but his record of success is their primary motivation for appealing to him now.

137. (B) The priest explains that "A burning and a loathly god hath lit/ Sudden, and sweeps our land, this Plague of power" (30–31). Another word for a plague is disease.

138. (A) The **metaphor** compares the ship to the city and its woes. Like the city, the ship is "weak and sore" (24). The ship is "shaken with storms" (25), and the city is shaken by the "Plague of power" (31). The ship cannot keep "her head above the waves whose trough is death" (26), like the citizens of the city who are dying in droves.

139. (D) Oedipus has previously addressed the people as the "fruit of Cadmus' ancient tree" (1), which indicates that Cadmus is the founder of Thebes and that its people are all his children. The priest's reference to Cadmus' house reinforces their vulnerability: the "children" of Thebes are dying "hour by hour" (32), leaving their house, their city where they lived together as one family, empty. Their new "house" is Hell, now populated by the "steam of tears and blood" (33).

140. (C) In closing, the priest again refers to Oedipus as their Lord and Chief before declaring, "we lay our grief/ On thy head, if thou find us not some aid" (47–48). Oedipus is their lord and chief, and so he is responsible for helping them with their turmoil. If he cannot offer aid, their grief is on his "head," meaning he will carry the burden of their grief because he has not fulfilled his duty as their lord and chief to assuage it. The fault will lie with him. While the other choices do indicate feelings the people may have toward Oedipus, they are not correct summaries of the indicated lines.

141. (A) The priest's **tone** is grave as he explains to Oedipus the severity of the situation the citizens are in—they are suffering from a "Plague of power" (31). Oedipus's tone, on the other hand, is mostly compassionate. He urges the priest to tell him what causes them to approach him with "suppliant branches" (4), and he insists that their hardship "moves [him]" (7), that his "will/ Is [theirs] for aid 'gainst all" (12–13). (E) is an understandable answer choice, but the priest's tone is not entirely laudatory (full of praise). While the priest does praise Oedipus for freeing the people in the past, and for being full of "God's breath" (43), the main purpose of his speech is to convey the seriousness of the city's turmoil, which his tone reflects.

142. (A) Cadmus is the name of the founder of the city of Thebes, the setting of the passage. In the opening line of the passage, Oedipus addresses his city's citizens as his "children, fruit of Cadmus' ancient tree" (1). Here, he uses a **metaphor** to compare the people of the land to fruit that has been born from a tree, implying that the citizens have been born from Cadmus; Cadmus is the father of the people the way a tree fathers its fruit. The second reference to Cadmus is also a metaphor. The priest now compares the city and the citizens to "Cadmus' house" and family. As the plague festers, "Cadmus' house grows empty, hour by hour/ And Hell's house rich with steam of tears and blood" (32–33). The dead citizens leave their land ("Cadmus' house") and enter Hell. In line 39, the city's name is revealed to be Thebes, making (A) correct.

Passage 14. Oscar Wilde, *The Picture of Dorian Gray*

143. (B) The shadows of "birds in flight" (9–10) on the curtains make Lord Henry recall the Japanese painters who "seek to convey the sense of swiftness and motion" in the "immobile" medium of art (12–14). The context suggests Lord Henry likely recalls this art form because the birds in motion are in contrast to the "oppressive" stillness of the room (16) the way that the immobile art form is at odds with the motion it attempts to convey.

144. (B) The first two paragraphs include **sensory images**, like descriptions of the scents in the studio (rich odor of roses, heavy scent of the lilac, perfume of the pink-flowering thorn), sounds (sullen murmur of the bees, dim roar of London), and figurative descriptions of what Lord Henry sees (the gleam of the honey-sweet and honey-colored blossoms, tremulous branches, a beauty so flamelike, and a momentary Japanese effect). The descriptions include ornate adjectives, not common ones (A). There are accurate descriptions of plants, but the entire description of the setting does not consist primarily of botanical facts (D). The narration is not objective, because the scents, sounds, and views are described figuratively (E). The lavish beauty does appear oppressive (16) from Lord Henry's perspective, but there is only one **simile** ("like the bourdon note")—not multiple ones—and it is not that surprising (C).

145. (A) Upon hearing that Basil does not plan to send his painting anywhere, Lord Henry "elevated his eyebrows and looked at him in amazement" (36–37) and exclaims, "'What odd chaps you painters are!'" (39). He does ask Basil questions, but they are not sarcastic; he is sincerely wondering, "'Have you any reason?'" (39) (E).

146. (B) Upon seeing Basil's impressive work of art, Lord Henry comments that it is his "best work" and immediately insists he "'must send it next year to the Grosvenor'" (28–29). His reasoning suggests he goes to the Grosvenor partly to "'see the people'" (32). He is shocked when Basil announces he will not send it anywhere, exclaiming painters are odd and adds, "'there is only one thing in the world worse than being talked about, and that is not being talked about'" (41–42). He thinks Basil should display his painting for influential people to see in order to set himself "far above the young men in England, and make the old men quite jealous'" (43–44).

147. (C) After 19 lines of rich descriptions of the setting (see question 144), Basil Hallward is introduced as the artist of the painting of "a young man of extraordinary personal beauty" (18–19). From here, the passage moves from descriptive details about the setting to dialogue between Lord Henry and Basil that serves to present Basil as an artist who warrants but does not desire critical acclaim. While line 39 does show Lord Henry transitioning from a casual to a more surprised and confused tone, it is too extreme to say that he is angry (E).

148. (D) Lord Henry is not humble (D) when he asserts that the Grosvenor is the perfect place for the painting and that the academy is too vulgar, citing the witty observation about its patrons in lines 30–33 (A). He flatters Basil, calling his painting his "best work" (C), urging him to send it to the Grosvenor (E); he is incredulous when Basil declares he will not send it anywhere ("Lord Henry elevated his eyebrows . . . looked at him in amazement") (B).

149. (B) After Basil is described as pleasurably smiling at "the gracious and comely form" he had painted, the narrator (not Lord Henry [C]), describes a different reaction that contrasts ("But . . . ") his previous smile, casting doubt on his satisfaction. This reaction is not straightforward; we do not know why he is "placing his fingers upon the lids" (A), and it does not indicate that he is *certainly* unstable (E). It is odd, but not in the way that Lord Henry declares in line 39 (D).

150. (C) The dialogue in the passage is predominantly comprised of Lord Henry's exhortations (urgings) to Basil Hallward to display his painting. In his speech, Lord Henry expresses his views on artists, the academy, the Grosvenor, reputation, and the art industry. It is worth noting that Lord Henry's appreciation of Basil's impressive painting does not go beyond his recognition of it as worth sending to the Grosvenor. This is curious given that earlier Lord Henry makes subtle and astute observations about the birds' movement as similar to a "necessarily immobile" (13) art form that seeks to convey "the sense of swiftness and motion" (13–14). Such thoughtful description is entirely absent from Lord Henry's statements about Basil's "best work" (27). The dialogue does not cast doubt on his earlier observations (B), but it could imply that it is more important to Lord Henry to assert the painting's fitness for display at the Grosvenor.

151. (B) Lord Henry (and the reader) wonders why Basil Hallward will not send his painting anywhere: "Lord Henry elevated his eyebrows and looked at him in amazement . . . " What odd chaps you painters are!" (36–39), making (B) correct and (C) incorrect. Lord Henry continues to express his views about the painters in the final lines of the passage (E). We know the stillness in the room is due to "the rich odour of roses . . . the heavy scent of the lilacs . . . the sullen murmur of the bees . . . circling with monotonous insistence" (1–15) (A). Basil's painting is "a full-length portrait of a young man of extraordinary perfect beauty" (18–19) (D).

152. (D) While both Lord Henry and Basil share the scene and speak to each other, the focus of the passage is not on their friendship (B). The subject of their dialogue, however, is the painting, the galleries, and the artist's reputation. Lord Henry's views on the subject are evident in the counsel he offers Basil, and Basil's perspective is implied through his refusal to "send [his painting] anywhere" (34). The ornate descriptions of the setting help set a **mood** and **tone**, but are limited to the first two paragraphs only (E) and serve to communicate the purpose; they are not the purpose themselves.

Chapter 2: 20th-Century/Contemporary Prose

Passage 15. Maya Angelou, *I Know Why the Caged Bird Sings*

153. (C) The verbs describe the actions that "held a simple kind of adventure" (2) for the narrator. Serving customers in a store may not seem like a typical adventure, but the narrator uses precise verbs to portray the careful and judicious process she uses to prepare the customers' orders. The adventure is then described to be the slight risk of accidentally making an error "in the Store's favor," which would lead to her "quietly but persistently" (9) punishing herself. By listing each action she takes, the narrator presents an image of a deliberate process. Choice D is incorrect because the narrator does perceive the process as part of an adventure. Choice A is incorrect because the intention of these specific verbs is not to convince the reader that the actions are truthful, but to convey the careful and risky process of accurately preparing customers' orders.

154. (E) The process of accurately preparing a customer's order is described as "a simple kind of adventure" (2). The rest of the paragraph suggests the adventure lies in the slight risk of accidentally making an error "in the Store's favor" (7). Her careful measuring might lead to appreciation and admiration from the customers, or reprimands—which would lead to her "quietly but persistently" (9) punishing herself.

155. (A) The narrator takes such great care to accurately measure the customers' orders and earn their appreciation and admiration (see question 153). When her efforts lead to mistakes in the Store's favor, she punishes herself for her lack of judgment by denying herself her most cherished treats. She elaborates on her choice of punishment in the third paragraph by explaining exactly how "sacred" (20) the sweet pineapple treat was to her, which suggests she chose punishments that were uniquely suited to her alone. These punishments may be overly severe (D), but the intention is to describe them as appropriately chosen by the narrator to suit her purpose.

156. (C) The second paragraph focuses on the narrator's "self-imposed" (9) fines for her miscalculations in the Store. To make the fines particularly effective, she denies herself her most coveted sweets: "silver-wrapped Kisses" (10) and canned pineapples, an obsession that nearly drove her "mad" (12). The third paragraph, in this context, elaborates on her madness by describing how much she relishes the treat on Christmas and her temptation to steal a can. Choice E is wrong because she admits that she doesn't steal because she is afraid of getting caught ("I am certain . . . ") (21–23). She is being honest here, but not because she's admitting she "wouldn't allow" (20) herself to steal.

157. (E) The narrator elaborates on the pineapple-induced madness mentioned in the second paragraph by describing (in the third paragraph) how much she relishes the treat on Christmas. She would "like to think that [her] desire for pineapples was so sacred that" (19–20) she wouldn't steal a can, but she admits that it was probably the risk of getting caught that stopped her. We know from the passage that the narrator puts forth incredible effort to do right by others—like measuring customers' orders accurately to earn their praise and admiration (see question 153). Her sacred desire for pineapples is certainly complex if it tempts her to hoard and steal.

158. (B) In the second paragraph, the narrator mentions that her "obsession with pine-apples nearly drove [her] mad" (12). She explores this madness in the third paragraph, an honest discussion of how her "sacred" (20) desire for pineapples would not prevent her from stealing a can. She candidly admits that it was the risk of exposure that stopped her. Choice D is incorrect because the narrator's fear of shame is already described in a previous paragraph when she mentions her quiet punishments for inaccurately measuring customer's orders; the phrase in lines 21–23 ("but I'm certain . . . ") primarily functions to reveal the narrator's notable sense of self-awareness about this fear.

159. (B) The passage does not rely on negative word choice to describe the Store, making (B) the only incorrect option and the correct answer. The first paragraph and fourth paragraph include quotations from customers who refer to the Store's owner by name ("Sister Henderson"), which helps illustrate its atmosphere and the role it plays in the community (A). The narrator describes hearing "the slow pulse of its job half done" (31) (C). The store is compared to "an unopened present" (25) (D). The Store is given human qualities like feeling "tired" (30) and having a "slow pulse" (31)—a technique known as **personification** (E).

160. (C) The paragraph begins with an image of the store as "[a]lone and empty . . . like an unopened present from a stranger" (25–26). Then, "the light would come in softly . . . easing itself over the shelves" (27–28). Over the course of the day, the quiet, peaceful store becomes abuzz with activity, which is detailed by the list in lines 31–33. The list is capturing the activities typical of the store on any day, not one specific day (A). The list does develop the characterization of the Store's customers but not to portray them solely as demanding and particular (E). They do argue over their bills, but they also joke "about their neighbors" (33) and drop in to say hi.

161. (D) In the first paragraph, the narrator recalls customers appreciating her accuracy in measuring their items and saying, "'Sister Henderson sure got some smart grandchildrens,'" (6) which reveals that the Store's owner, Sister Henderson, is related to the narrator.

162. (D) According to the narrator, she is the only one who "could hear the slow pulse" (31) of the Store's job "half done" (31) by the afternoon. Her subtle observations of the Store's light and sounds, and even its feeling ("tired"), add credibility to this claim.

163. (D) The narrator pays such close attention to the Store that she can sense when it is "tired" (30), she hears its "slow pulse" (31) in the afternoon, and she compares the magic of its mornings to the unexpected excitement offered by an "unwrapped present" (25). Her earlier descriptions of the careful attention she paid to her work serving customers also attests to her respect for her grandmother's Store.

Passage 16. Joseph Conrad, *Heart of Darkness*

164. (B) The *Nellie*, a cruising yawl (sailboat), has "swung her anchor" (1) and comes to a rest "without a flutter of the sails" (1) because the wind was "bound down the river" and "nearly calm" (2). There is a **mood** of peaceful calmness: the wind is calm, the sails are calm, and the ship is calm. There is also a sense of anticipation because a sailboat is meant to sail: there is an imminent journey, but it must "wait for the turn of the tide" (3–4) before it journeys on. It is not eerie (C) or surprising (E) that the sails do not flutter because sails would not flutter when a boat is at rest due to a calm wind. There is no sense of threat, especially since the wind is "bound down the river" (2–3) and the "flood had made" (2) (D).

165. (B) The opening paragraph establishes a calm **mood** with the yawl's sails at rest and the wind "bound down the river" (2–3) (see question 164). The first few sentences of the second paragraph elaborate on the mythical quality of the setting: the river Thames stretches out to sea before them "like the beginning of an interminable waterway" (5–6), a reference to the unknown that lies ahead; the sails are "red clusters of canvas sharply peaked, with gleams of varnished spirits" (8–9). The sentence in lines 10–12, however, shifts to a dark and gloomy mood: the air is "dark above Gravesend . . . condensed into a mournful gloom, brooding motionless . . ." The air/sky is described throughout the paragraph ("the sea and the sky were welded together," "the luminous space"), making (A) incorrect. The descriptions are vivid throughout the paragraph, making (C) incorrect. The sense of fear is established at the end with the brooding, mournful gloom, not the beginning of the paragraph, making (D) incorrect. The **tone** is more threatening at the end, making (E) incorrect.

166. (E) (A) is a common choice if the quoted lines are not referenced—the Director's work is not actually "out there in the luminous estuary," out on the sea, as one would expect, "but behind him, within the brooding gloom," the gloom that is earlier referred to as "brooding motionless over the biggest, and the greatest, town on earth." The Director's job is back in town, focused on matters of the city (political, governmental, beauracratic), making it municipal.

167. (A) The setting is described with strong **imagery** and **figurative language**. The diction used to describe the scene establishes an eerie, foreboding **mood** and also suggests a potential **theme**. The gloom over the city appears to overpower the light, killing the "placid" (30) and pacific mood on the water. The city is associated with brooding, mourning, darkness, gloom, somberness, and potential anger; the sea, however, is calm, interminable, luminous, gleaming, still, exquisitely brilliant, benign, and unstained. The sun sets suddenly, almost as if it were "stricken to death" (39) by the gloom from the city. The clear contrasts set up between the gloomy, dark, foreboding city and the unstained, brilliant, and exquisite sea allude to potential themes and conflicts.

168. (C) The Director of Companies is described as "nautical" (15) (naval) and venerable (deserving of respect) when the speaker claims that he and the other crew members "affectionately watched his back" (13–14) and saw him as the equivalent of a pilot, who is "trustworthiness personified" (16). There are no details to suggest the Director is particularly sociable (E) or affectionate (demonstrative) (A, B). The environment is brooding, not the Director (D).

169. (D) The narrator describes the Director of Companies as "nautical" (15), "trustworthiness personified" (16). He describes the lawyer as "the best of old fellows" (21) with "many virtues" (21–22). The Accountant "was toying architecturally with the bones" (23–24). Marlow has "an ascetic aspect" (25) and resembles "an idol" (26). The descriptions are thoughtful and poetic, certainly not objective (A) or suggestive of envy (C). He doesn't compare them to each other but describes them separately (B). They are more than just tolerant of each other (E): they all "four affectionately watched" (13–14) the Director and shared "the bond of the sea" (18).

170. (A) After stating, "For some reason or other we did not begin that game of dominoes" (29), the narrator elaborates with, "We felt meditative, and fit for nothing but placid staring" (30). The context indicates that they are staring at their environment (the dynamic setting imbued with light and gloom).

171. (D) Lines 30–36 compare light and dark. The ending of the day creates "exquisite brilliance," shining water, "unstained light," and radiance. This light is contrasted with the "*gloom*" in the west, which can be interpreted as darkness because it is "angered by the approach of the sun [the light]," as if they are in battle.

172. (B) In the final sentence, the light, which is described as magnificent throughout the passage, is suddenly extinguished by the darkness—it has lost the battle and disappears as if "stricken to death by the touch of that gloom brooding over a crowd of men." This sentence creates an ominous (threatening) **mood** because something that was great and brilliant has suddenly been extinguished.

173. (C) The passage appears to use **symbolism** to **foreshadow** later events because the descriptions of the setting (the battles/conflicts between light and dark, the waterway/ horizon and land, nature and man) are likely symbolic of future conflicts that are only hinted at by the descriptions of the setting. Also, the passage opens with the boat "at rest" (2), waiting "for the turn of the tide" (3–4) to continue its journey, which anticipates later events. It is unclear who the main character—III—is from this passage. Several people are mentioned, but the narrator reveals more about the setting than any particular character. If we assume it is the narrator, the passage does not develop his character.

Passage 17. Ralph Ellison, *Invisible Man*

174. (D) After the narrator calls himself naive, he explains, "I was looking for myself and asking everyone except myself questions which I, and only I, could answer" (4–5).

175. (A) The narrator describes the answers as "often in contradiction and even self-contradictory" (3–4). The reference to his "painful boomeranging" (6) also emphasizes how perplexed he was.

176. (D) When something is "in the cards," it is predetermined, fated, meant to happen. In this context, the narrator says he was "in the cards" after clarifying that—even though he is an invisible man—he is "no freak of nature, nor of history" (9). It is not surprising or rare that he is an invisible man. It is expected, even though it took him years and "painful boomeranging" (6) of his expectations to realize it. Choice A implies that being an invisible man means his existence is doomed, but the context of the phrase "I was in the cards" indicates that the narrator means that his fate was expected and not a surprise.

177. (B) The narrator explains that his grandparents were freed from slavery eight-five years ago, "united with others of our country with everything pertaining to the common good" (13–14), which refers to their status as free citizens, "and, in everything social, separate like the fingers of the hand" (14), which refers to segregation in society (for example, separate schools, churches, and public facilities for blacks and whites).

178. (D) The narrator refers to his grandfather as "the one" (16) and later says it was "he who caused the trouble" (17–18). The narrator goes on to describe the grandfather's mysterious final message, which ends with "'Learn it to the younguns'" (27). The narrator, one of the "'younguns,'" is now remembering this moment as the beginning of "the trouble," indicating that the message has been disconcerting as he has come to understand his own identity, his invisibility. The grandfather explains that he acted like a yes-man on the surface but was actually a "traitor" (20) (C) to the whites he was supposedly pleasing; there is no evidence, however, to indicate the narrator perceives him as a meek yes-man (B) upon hearing his dying message, or a hypocrite (A). The message is unsettling to him and the others because the grandfather acted obediently with such confidence during his life and is now revealing that he was actually being treacherous. The family members, not the narrator, see him as "odd" (17) and think he has "gone out of his mind" (24) (E).

179. (E) The narrator recalls that the family members thought "the old man had gone out of his mind" (24). They rushed the children from the room and turned down the shades and the flame of the lamp to make the environment conducive to someone in the throes of death. There is no indication that they eventually come to understand his message (B). While they must feel torn and confused (ambivalent, D) about the grandfather's message contradicting the way he lived his life, they respond with surprise, shock, and bewilderment instead of ambivalence. Choice C is too extreme, and choice A would imply that they do not react at all to his behavior.

180. (C) After the grandfather tells his son to keep his head in the "lion's mouth," he elaborates by explaining he should "overcome 'em with yeses, undermine 'em with grins . . . let 'em swoller you till they vomit or burst wide open" (22–24). The " 'em" refers to whites, depicted as predatory lions. The grandfather **figuratively** describes the way he has "been a traitor" (20) and "a spy in enemy's country" (20). The country belongs to white people who still exert power over black people, who are no longer enslaved but are still separate "in everything social" (14). The grandfather resists and fights by behaving the way white people demand (obediently putting his head in the predatory lion's mouth) with the intention of overcoming and defeating them with such excessive compliance and closeness. He reveals that his meekness was actually a dangerous act, a form of protest.

181. (C) After the narrator explains that the family thought the grandfather had "gone out of his mind" (24), he adds, "He had been the meekest of men" (24–25). His dying words call for resistance, even though he appeared to live meekly, staying in his place, working hard, and raising his son "to do the same" (16). While (D) and (E) are plausible, they do not describe why the message is particularly surprising to the family who thought they knew the grandfather.

182. (D) The message is full of exhortations (urgent advice): "live with . . . overcome 'em . . . undermine 'em . . ." (21–22). The urgent advice includes **figurative** comparisons to a lion, vomiting, and exploding. The grandfather does not mean for his son to literally put his head in a lion's mouth or to overcome whites with obedience until they actually vomit and explode. These are **metaphors** used to illustrate the need to fight against the enemy.

183. (C) The grandfather's message to his son is that he should "overcome 'em with yeses, undermine 'em with grins . . . let 'em swoller you till they vomit or burst wide open" (22–24). He means that he should do as the whites say, to comply with so much obedience that it will eventually lead to overcoming them.

184. (A) The narrator states that twenty years ago, he naively sought answers from others about who he was. He then says it took him "a long time . . . to achieve a realization . . . " that he is nobody but himself. Since he has achieved a realization, he is no longer seeking answers from others. The narrator does say he is "an invisible man" (8) (E), but this is not in contrast to twenty years ago. He has been invisible always; this was "in the cards" (9) and not a shock (he is "no freak of nature, nor of history") (9). It is only later in his life that he realizes it.

Passage 18. Susan Glaspell, "Suppressed Desires"

185. (A) The comment is Henrietta's response to Steve pushing back his coffee and looking "dejected" (line 8–9). She insists that the coffee isn't the problem and suggests that the root of his dejection is a problem with him, a deeper trouble in his "subconscious mind" (line 14). Although she is bothered by Steve's lack of self-awareness, it is too extreme to say that the comment hurts her (II). Her emphasis on "*you*" and the stage direction that she speaks "*Scornfully*" in line 13 suggest that her comments are not based wholeheartedly in her concern for helping Steve (III).

186. (A) In response to Steve's dismissal, Henrietta insists that something is "wrong" (25) with him. She relentlessly lists her evidence: "You never . . . you certainly have . . . You're all . . . You're no longer . . . You won't . . ." (16–18). When Steve exasperatedly responds that he's had to listen "to volumes," she goes on, "You've ceased to . . . your work . . . You're not . . ." (20–21). This back-and-forth disagreement continues for several more lines. They are arguing, but Henrietta's speech appears even-tempered, not marked with expletives or many exclamations, making (E) too extreme.

187. (C) Henrietta assertively diagnoses Steve's irritability as an indication that he's "suffering from some suppressed desire" (30–31), likely drawing on her study of psychoanalysis. Henrietta pressures him to explore the suppressed desire in his "subconscious mind" (14) by discussing his dreams with Dr. Russell. Steve, with characteristic wit and dismissiveness, takes the phrase she uses and twists it to mock her scholarly certainty about what he needs. If he desires anything, it's "a little peace" (32).

188. (D) Steve feels it's his "duty" (65) to warn Mabel that Henrietta's inquiries are motivated by her desire to psychoanalyze her condition. He exaggerates (C) her intentions by declaring exactly what she intends to discover: "an underground desire to kill your father and marry your mother" (67), which is an **allusion** to the Greek tragedy of Oedipus (A) and has a darkly humorous effect (B). Steve's sense of "duty" stems from his own resentment at Henrietta's relentless insistence on interpreting his dreams (E). Although Steve's comment is somewhat humorous, it is too extreme to say that he is feigning interest in warning Mabel, making (D) the only incorrect choice and the correct answer.

189. (E) Henrietta might see herself as taking an interest in the well-being of her husband and sister by relentlessly inquiring about their dreams and insisting that something is deeply "wrong" (26) with Steve, but Steve's reactions reveal that she is not actually a nurturing caretaker (I). He sees her interest as primarily motivated by her own fascination with psychoanalysis, indicated by her laser-like focus on discussing others' dreams (III). With Steve, she loses patience. After many comments and assertions, she exclaims, "But, Stephen—!" (line 36) and turns "impatiently" (line 84) from him to engage with Mabel, who appears to happily cooperate with Henrietta's questions, making II correct.

190. (B) Stage directions (A) reveal that Henrietta "scrutinizes her" (53) and is "Moving closer" (64) and "Resting chin in palm and peering" (78) while talking with Mabel, showing her keen interest in getting Mabel to elaborate and reveal details about her dreams. Provided notes mark her **tone** with words like "mere surprise" (52), "startled" (56), and "sweetly" (68) (D). She repeats her questions (about breakfast, sleep, and what she dreamed) (E). Her questions are genuine (C): she is deeply curious to interpret Mabel's potential symptoms and dreams. Because she is seeking actual answers from Mabel, her questions are not **rhetorical**, making (B) the only incorrect choice and the correct answer.

191. (B) Steve boils Mabel's dream down to its key parts, emphasizing the simplicity of its meaning. His question, "What can it mean?" (83) is sarcastic: Mabel's vision of herself as a hen who is pestered closely mirrors her current interaction (and Steve's recent argument) with an insistent Henrietta. Henrietta sees Mabel's dream as "significant" (81), so Steve's remark appears mocking in response; the meaning is not hard to decipher (B). Steve does not believe in the value of psychoanalysis, so his **tone** is not meant to convey confidence in his interpretation (C, D, E). While his comment is somewhat glib, the fact that he interjects shows he is not indifferent toward Henrietta's interest in Mabel's dreams (A).

192. (C) With characteristic wit, Steve plays on others' words to reveal his own perspective. Mabel thinks psychoanalysis "might be the name of a new explosive" (89), like one used in "war" (88); Steve, having had a somewhat explosive disagreement with Henrietta about her insistence on psychoanalyzing him, claims that it *is* a new explosive, but his meaning is different from Mabel's. While Mabel is certainly naive about psychoanalysis, the intention of Steve's emphasis is to reveal that he believes Henrietta's fascination with psychoanalyzing dreams is used like a weapon and feels attacking.

Passage 19. Zora Neale Hurston and Langston Hughes, "Mule Bone: A Comedy of Negro Life"

193. (B) When others wonder what bone he is carrying, Joe asks, "Don't y'all know dat hock-bone" (11), implying that it is from such a well-known mule that they should immediately recognize it. He goes on to explain it belongs to Brazzle's "ole yaller mule" (15), who it is revealed is infamous for his evil, stubborn, and generally recalcitrant behavior. The bone is not as impressive as it is distinctive (C), and they may not have all seen the actual bone before (E), but Joe expects them to recognize it because it belongs to Brazzle's infamous mule (B).

194. (B) Brazzle exclaims, "Well, sir! . . . It 'tain't my ole mule!" (17–18) upon seeing the hock-bone—I. He reflects on his time with the mule when he shares stories of its antics throughout the passage—III. He uses physical gestures to describe a particularly contrary action of the mule (39–40) and takes the bone "in both hands and looks up and down the length of it" (17–18) while telling his story—IV. He never avoids stating a truth about the mule or intentionally provides vague and unclear details to avoid revealing information about the mule, making II incorrect.

195. (C) Brazzle shares a memory of the mule's aversion to carrying a rider: "you better not look like you wanter ride 'im!" (21). Corroborating that detail, Lindsay recalls a time when he saw Brazzle limping "down de road" (22). While the limping is surely humorous, its purpose is not to provide comic relief because the scene does not have a tragic or melancholy **tone** to break up with comedy (E).

196. (B) Throughout the scene, Brazzle recalls his mule's antics with a reminiscing and memorializing **tone**. He says, "This sho was one hell of a mule, too" (19) before he details evidence of the mule's less than favorable qualities, including his "evil" way of trying to "bite and kick when" Brazzle would "go into de stable to feed 'im" (25). The biting and kicking is not literally evil (C). In fact, it is humorously ironic that the mule would bite and kick the hand that feeds him. While frustrating for Brazzle at the time, the behavior is not brought up in this context as regrettable (A). There is not enough context in the excerpted passage to suggest the word "evil" is **metaphorical** or **symbolic** (D, E).

197. (E) Lige's memory of the mule is not at all revealed to be fallible (false). It is full of visual **imagery** (A) as we can see the mule doing an about-face to avoid "dat crooked place in de road" and hilariously going "through de handle of dat basket . . . wid de boy still up on his back" (32–34). The extent the mule would go to avoid a little challenge in his path is surprising, and the absurdity of the resulting picture does have some shock value (C). The story incites laughter, as noted in the stage direction (B, D).

198. (C) Brazzle's mule has been characterized throughout the passage as stubborn, contrary, and recalcitrant. It makes sense that Joe would be saying here that even in death (the after-life), the mule is likely causing trouble.

199. (D) All the anecdotes shared by the characters regarding Brazzle's mule share one feature: they highlight the mule's stubborn and contrary nature that they can all laugh and reminisce about years later. Brazzle tells how the mule would not carry riders, and would not cooperate in the fields (19–21) and reminds everyone of his stubbornness even in his dying moments (40–41). He also says the mule would bite and kick even when he would try to feed him (25). Lige's story shows the lengths the mule would go to in order to avoid a "crooked place in de road" (31–34).

200. (B) The characters' anecdotes about Brazzle's stubborn mule and the physicality indicated by the stage directions reveal a comic **tone** to the passage. The mule, though difficult and "evil" (24), is viewed now in death as absurdly funny in his extreme recalcitrance. Though the characters appear to be memorializing a deceased animal that was an appreciated part of their community, the tone is not dirgelike (C) because of the multiple instances of laughter and the joy they take in sharing their memories with each other.

201. (D) As Joe says, "More folks went to yo' mule's draggin' out than went to last school closing . . ." (43), which indicates that the mule's death was a significant moment for the community. The multiple anecdotes and responses to the memories of Brazzle's mule reveal that knowing that infamous mule was a shared experience in the community.

202. (C) The passage is written in the vernacular of the characters being portrayed. Their colloquial expressions, such as "die decent" (37) and "I God" (42), pepper the passage and give the dramatic scene a lively and realistic edge. The characters use **figurative language** in their observations, like Joe's claim that he "made de feathers fly" (5) when hunting and Walter's comparison of the mule's ribs to a washboard (27). The distinctive qualities of the grammar, idiomatic expressions, syntax, and style of the characters' speech, and the fact that all the characters follow those same distinctive patterns, indicate that the speech patterns are culturally specific to this community (E). The characters' speech does not appear to exaggerate the qualities of the mule. The mule's behavior and characteristics were genuinely extreme, making (C) the only incorrect choice (and the correct answer).

203. (D) Whenever a character joins in the discussion to reminisce about Brazzle's mule, they don't simply label the mule's various qualities. They elaborate on each other's descriptions with visually compelling, often humorous, stories. Brazzle begins by supporting his own assertion that he "sho was one hell of a mule" (18–19) with multiple examples made rich through **figurative language**. The mule didn't just refuse to plow, but he'd "fight every inch in front of de plow" (19). Lindsay corroborates Brazzle's claims by recalling a time when he saw Brazzle limping after attempting to ride the mule, a detail that is even more compelling because he mimics Brazzle's limp "wid one hand on his buttocks" (23). Walter doesn't just add that the mule was scrawny; he continues the thread about the mule's stubbornness by opening with "He was too mean to git fat" (26). The memory is made visual with the comparison of the mule's ribs to a washboard. Lige adds another story about how the mule refused to accompany his boy to the market, a tale full of details that compel listeners to see the whole scene: the crooked part of the road, the mule's about-face, and the funny picture of him turning around into the handle of the basket "wid de boy still up on his back" (34). Brazzle adds perhaps the most damning evidence of the mule's intractability by arguing that even the way he died was stubborn. Like the others, he develops his claim with visual details and acting out the gestures himself. Finally, Joe Clark closes out the discussion by reminding everyone that "more folks went to yo' mule's draggin' out than went to last school closing" (43–44), a poignant observation that reinforces the collective memorializing they have all participated in. The discussion is a shared experience made even more obvious with the closing stage direction that describes them all passing the bone "from hand to hand" (48), the way they passed the stories to one another, each adding to the impromptu eulogy. While the stories of the mule do seem to get more dramatic, the characters are not competing with one another (III) but adding to a shared understanding, equally participating to further develop their collective point of view.

204. (D) The mule is only present in the chapter through its bone, which serves as a relic that incites the townspeople to reminisce about its qualities. The people recall Brazzle's mule's unique characteristics with sentimentality, humor, and fondness. In their shared memories, they observe how the mule brought the community together: "more folks went to yo' mule's draggin' out than went to last school closing" (43–44). The mule and its bone are potentially **symbolic**, but there is not sufficient evidence in the passage that it is symbolic of the town's struggle or the futility of work (B, C).

Passage 20. Henry James, *The Turn of the Screw*

205. (A) The narrator recalls her experience of a day's events as "a series of flights and drops, a little seesaw of the right throbs and the wrong" (1–2): a **metaphor** for the volatile shifts in her emotions and perspectives about her environment and circumstances. The memory she describes, full of conflicting impressions and "flights and drops" (1), is certainly not simple (B), and her recollections are not all fond ("very bad days . . . doubtful again . . . made a mistake . . .) (3–4) (C) or pleasant (E). Her descriptions are contradictory, but the descriptions in lines 1–13 do not indicate the narrator's perspective is potentially unreliable. In fact, her ability to notice her conflicting perspectives in hindsight suggest she is reflecting somewhat honestly (D). (Note that in James's entire novel, the narrator's unreliability is more probable, but it is not evident in this excerpted passage).

206. (E) The state of mind is described earlier in the sentence with the phrase "found myself doubtful again" (3–4). Since the narrator "had at all events a couple very bad days" (3), she is now feeling doubtful and "indeed sure [she] had made a mistake" (4). It is *this* state of mind she is in during much of the bumpy ride in the coach.

207. (E) The narrator opens by recalling her experience of a day's events as "a series of flights and drops, a little seesaw of the right throbs and the wrong" (1–2)—a **metaphor** for the volatile shifts in her emotions and perspectives about her environment and circumstances. The flights and drops include feeling sure she "had made a mistake" and "doubtful," then having her "fortitude mounted afresh" after driving in "a commodious fly" on a "lovely June day" (8). She had previously "dreaded" (12) her arrival at her new place of employment, but then she was greeted with "a good surprise" (13). The next day, however, she experiences another "drop" (24) when she interprets Mrs. Grose's enthusiasm as suspicious, wondering "why she should wish not to show it" (41). Choice C indicates all the memories are troubling and does not describe the passage's narration as precisely as choice E.

208. (E) The narrator finds "it a great fortune to have to do with" (27) Mrs. Grose, which is a comfort after having "brooded" (37) over her relationship with her on her ride over to the house. But this relief turns to suspicion as she wonders how peculiar it was that Mrs. Grose appeared "to be positively on her guard against showing" (40) exactly how glad she was to meet her. The narrator wonders "why she should wish not to show it" (41). From the narrator's perspective, Mrs. Grose is not forthright in her expressions and reactions, which makes her feel "uneasy" (42). The narrator describes how driving to the home "on a lovely June day" (8) serves as a "reprieve" (11) from her previous "drop" (24). The "bright flowers," "golden sky," and cawing rooks (D) contribute to "a most pleasant impression" of the "greatness" of the scene upon her arrival (B). She feels treated as though she was "a distinguished visitor" (20) (A). This positive reception is even more pronounced considering her initial doubts and sense that she "had made a mistake" (C).

209. (E) The repetition of the phrase "I remember" (1) (a rhetorical device known as **anaphora**) enhances the speaker's excitement. We can picture her in a state of reverie, recalling the sensory details that left such a strong impression on her, such as the "crunch" (15) of wheels on the gravel and the cawing of the circling rooks above in the "golden sky" (17). The details are strung together with the conjunction "and" (a device known as **polysyndeton**), conveying an almost childlike sense of excitement.

210. (B) The first paragraph implies that the narrator is not upper class herself because she explains that the descriptions of this grand home "had a greatness that made it a different affair from [her] own scant home" (17–18), and she says that the curtsy given her by the civil person at the door was as decent "as if [she] had been a mistress or a distinguished visitor" (19–20), suggesting that she is neither of those (C). There are no details to suggest that she is precocious (knowledgeable beyond her years) (A), the overseer (D), or the proprietor (E).

211. (C) The "drop" echoes the drops mentioned in line 1 of the passage—the flights and drops that characterized the narrator's emotional state as she set out on her journey. The drops referred to her hesitation, so in the second paragraph she explains that she did not have any more drops, or doubts, until the next day.

212. (C) What "remained" with the narrator in line 30 is the same thing that she says "astonished [her] too." The subject, "this," which refers to her excitement, both astonished and remained with her, which adds to her sense of the "liberality" (31) with which she was treated.

213. (B) The first paragraph focuses on the setting and the narrator's impressions upon her arrival at her new place of employment. The second paragraph, however, focuses on the narrator's conflicting impressions of Mrs. Grose and the "beautiful child" (28). The child is so beautiful and impressive that the narrator wonders why her "employer had not told [her] more of her" (28–29). Mrs. Grose is "so glad" (38) to see her, but the narrator is suspicious "why she should not wish to show" (41) the enthusiasm she clearly feels. Both paragraphs mention the narrator's multiple emotions, or "flights and drops" (1) (A), superlative descriptions (paragraph 1: very bad days, most pleasant impression, a greatness, beyond his promise; paragraph 2: carried triumphantly, so charming, the most beautiful child, extraordinary charm, so glad to see me) (C), and illustrative details that allow us to picture the scenes she describes (D). The **narrative point of view** (first-person recollections) does not change in the second paragraph (E).

214. (D) The narrator explains that it is the "sense of liberality [generosity, munificence] with which [she] was treated" (30–31) that makes her so excited she cannot sleep. She goes on to list the things that she has been given: "The large, impressive room, one of the best in the house, the great state bed, as I almost felt it, the full, figured draperies, the long glasses . . . " (31–33). Mrs. Grose surprises the speaker with her friendliness (affability), but this is tempered by her suspicious "guard against showing it too much" (40–41) (A).

215. (C) The narrator recalls feeling "fear" (36) and brooding over the idea of Mrs. Grose, but she is relieved that "from the first moment [she] should get on with Mrs. Grose" (35–36). However, this relief is tempered by hesitancy when she notices "the clear circumstance of [Mrs. Grose] being so glad to see [her] . . ." (38–39). She is also confused by Mrs. Grose's "guard not to show [her gladness] too much" (40–41). This observation makes the speaker "shrink again" (38) and feel "uneasy" (42). (E) is incorrect because she only feels afraid prior to meeting Mrs. Grose.

Passage 21. James Joyce, "The Dead"

216. (C) The second sentence of the passage contains multiple clauses and conjunctions without any commas or semicolons. When it is read, we feel the frenzied and hurried state Lily must be in as she is "run off her feet" (1) preparing for the party.

217. (A) The opening paragraph alludes to the spatial layout of the house, with a "little pantry behind the office on the ground floor" (2–3), "the bare hallway" (4), "the bathroom upstairs" (6), and the stairs with a banister and a head that can be peered over to see downstairs. We also hear the "wheezy hall-door bell" (3), and the "gossiping and laughing" (7) upstairs. Several characters are mentioned, and we do feel sympathetic for Lily, who is in such a hurried state, but the **imagery** cannot be said to be partial toward her (E). There is no irony or regret in the **tone** (B), (D).

218. (A) The simple, concise statement that "Never once had it fallen flat" (13) is emphasized by its placement between two rambling statements overflowing with detail about how splendid and well-attended the affair is. It does appear to be an essential point that the dance has never "fallen flat" (13) because it helps explain the anticipation, nervousness, and frenzy permeating the scene.

219. (D) The **mood** in the house is anxious (jumpy, nervous, tense), as indicated by Lily feeling "run off her feet" (1), the two aunts feeling "dreadfully afraid that Freddy Malins might turn up screwed" (34) and "fussy" (32), and their peering over the banister "every two minutes" (38).

220. (D) Mary Jane is referred to as the "main prop of the household" right before it is mentioned that she was qualified to teach music and that her students were wealthy (19–23). The next sentence explains that the two aunts also contribute to the household as much as they can, making (A) and (B) incorrect. (C) and (E) are too rash and assuming. There are no other details to suggest that the aunts are merely using Mary Jane or that they actually see her as a prop, an object. Since they themselves contribute to the household in their own ways, it would not make sense for them to view Mary Jane as beneath them for doing the same.

221. (A) The phrases are all examples of the characters' vernacular, common expressions and linguistic idiosyncrasies of that time and place—I. The expressions are casual and informal, but do not intend to portray the characters' lack of education. They are music teachers, and Mary Jane "had been through the Academy" (21).

222. (D) The aunts may be demanding because Lily mainly gets on well with them due to her ability to carry out their orders without making mistakes, but since she does in fact get on well, it cannot be said that they are oppressive. In fact, Lily adds that they are "fussy, that was all" (30–31) (E). The aunts are discerning in that "they believed in eating well; the best of everything: diamond-bone sirloins, three-shilling tea and the best bottled stout" (28–29) (A). They both work in jobs related to music (B), indicating that they do have to earn their living (C).

223. (C) The first paragraph does set the scene; it introduces the event that is taking place by describing what the housemaid and hosts are doing. The second paragraph, however, provides background information on who these characters are, how they know each other, and what the event is. Though the second paragraph provides background on the party that explains Lily's frenzied state in the first paragraph, it isn't providing evidence of an opinion as much as it is elaborating on the characters' background (D). (E) is incorrect because the first paragraph mentions Lily and the two aunts, all of whom are also mentioned in the second paragraph. (A) is incorrect because the first paragraph does contain Lily's perspective. She (and the narrator) tells us that she is "run off her feet" (1) because she is scampering around greeting guests. No problem is set up and solved in the two paragraphs (B).

224. (D) The closing sentence clarifies the reason Kate and Julia incessantly peer over the banister. They are anticipating the arrival of Gabriel and Freddy. The sentence does justify their behavior, but it is in no way a weak justification (C). They are eager about the arrival of these guests, but they clearly do not prefer Freddy over other guests since it is mentioned that they are concerned if he will arrive "under the influence" (35–36) (A). The anxiety has not been eased by this final sentence, as Gabriel and Freddy have not yet arrived (B). A parallel is drawn between Freddy and Gabriel, but there is no evidence to suggest they have a rapport or are friends (E).

225. (B) We are only told that the aunts' eagerness for Gabriel and his wife's arrival is "what brought them every two minutes to the banisters to ask Lily had Gabriel or Freddy come" (38–39). We learn that Freddy has a history of showing up intoxicated, but Gabriel's background is not shared. The aunts are interested in parties, of course, and "the best of everything . . . " (28) (A). The aunts are Mary Jane's aunts, who they have "taken" in after her father's death (15–16), and they are Lily's "mistresses" (30) (C). Their jobs and the history of the house is mentioned in the second paragraph (D), (E).

Passage 22. Franz Kafka, "Metamorphosis"

226. (C) While the descriptions of Gregor's vermin like appearance would potentially upset a reader (B) or cast doubt on the truthfulness of the events (A), the main purpose of these descriptions is to pique the reader's interest (not convince the reader of anything [E]) by setting up a problem (C). The problem is Gregor's transformation into a vermin, which will be described in more detail in subsequent paragraphs. By emphasizing the specific details of Gregor's bewildering transformation, the opening paragraph helps readers visualize Gregor's shocking transformation and motivates them to learn more about his condition and how he might deal with this perplexing problem. While the paragraph mentions the bed, it does not focus on the setting (the room, house, weather, etc.), which is described in detail in the subsequent paragraphs (D).

227. (E) Through descriptions of the objects in his room ("a collection of textile samples" and "a picture . . . in a nice gilded frame"), we understand a little more about Gregor as a person. The textile samples reveal his line of work, and the framed picture of a woman dressed in fur evokes masochism (for readers familiar with Leopold von Sacher-Masoch's story "Venus in Furs"), or less specifically, it reveals Gregor's desires. His "proper, human room" is "a little too small," and the "dull weather" and "[d]rops of rain" (14) make him feel sad. The environment matches his mood, making (B) incorrect. The setting does not exaggerate the problem (A), and its realistic features do not confirm or reveal that the story is imagined or fantastical (C, D).

228. (A) This question asks readers to consider the **symbolic** significance of Gregor's metamorphosis into a vermin. Gregor's repeated and failed attempts to turn onto his right side evoke the sense of futility he feels at his job. The following sentence, the start of the next paragraph, supports this interpretation, as Gregor exclaims, "'what a strenuous career it is that I have chosen!'" (23). The strenuous act of turning over is parallel to the strenuous task of having to go to his demeaning job every day.

229. (E) After struggling to get comfortable in this new form, Gregor frustratedly yells out. It is notable that he does not exclaim about his transformation into a vermin, but about his "strenuous career" (23) that "can all go to Hell!" (28). It is surprising to us that even though Gregor has awoken to find himself transformed into a vermin, his thoughts are focused on his hatred of his job. We can assume that Gregor would be having the same thoughts on any morning since he does not reference his metamorphosis at all. This makes us see that Gregor's unhappiness with his daily routine and responsibilities (I) is so great that even an insurmountable and grotesque problem like being turned into a vermin does not outweigh his problem of just having to go to work for another day. It also makes us consider the **metaphorical** significance (II) of his turning into a vermin. It does not weigh heavily on him because his daily experiences in the workplace are not that different from what a vermin may experience. The difference is so slight that he barely notices it (III).

230. (B) Gregor describes his job as a travelling salesman as "strenuous." The details imply that his work life is similar to that of a vermin—scurrying around, settling for bad food.

231. (D) After Gregor says that getting up early "'makes you stupid,'" he goes on to explain that "'You've got to get enough sleep,'" implying that "stupid" in this context means foggy, in a daze from lack of sleep.

232. (E) Gregor's thoughts in lines 34–48 reveal how he is treated like a vermin in his regular human life. He describes his boss as unrelenting and demanding, demeaning "his subordinates from up there" (44). Unlike the "other traveling salesmen [who] live a life of luxury" (35–36), Gregor has to scurry around like a weak and powerless vermin. The **metaphor** of his physical transformation into a vermin (introduced in the first paragraph, making choice D incorrect) is further developed here by explaining how Gregor's emotional and working life is similar to that of a vermin.

233. (A) In the last sentence, Gregor declares that he has "got to get up [because his] train leaves at five." It is astounding to us that, despite his physical transformation into a vermin, Gregor is still determined to go to his horrible job. His decision suggests that being a vermin physically is not so shocking or noticeably terrible to Gregor because he is already like a vermin emotionally because of his work situation. Gregor's indifference to his physical transformation emphasizes how habituated he has become to being treated like a vermin in his life. We are not angry (D) at, impressed by (B), or distanced from (E) Gregor because of his decision. Also, we are not shocked (C) by his denial because Gregor appears to be aware of his transformation—he does not insist that it has not happened. In fact, he confirms, "It wasn't a dream" (7)(C).

234. (A) The narrator's **tone** is clear and straightforward. It does not express dismay at Gregor's shocking transformation; on the contrary, the tone is more objective and matter-of-fact, as if Gregor has awoken this way every morning. The passage begins with a calm, objective description of Gregor's morning. The subsequent sentence does not ask questions or reveal Gregor's own bewilderment; it merely goes on to offer a factual rendering of what Gregor does and how he looks. In contrast to the narrator's objective and straightforward tone, the tone of Gregor's thoughts is marked by frustration and annoyance toward his job. Exclamation points indicate his anger at choosing such "a strenuous career" (23). He thinks, "It can all go to Hell!" (28).

235. (E) Though he does not appear as concerned about his transformation as he is about going to work (see question 229), he is aware of what he calls "'this nonsense'" (16) and wonders aloud, "'What's happened to me?'" (7). Gregor's decision to go to work despite his condition is indicative of his dependence and desperate need to stay in his odious job to help his parents, who are in debt to his boss (C, D). He is resentful of his predicament, counting the years until he can "give . . . notice" and tell his boss just what he "thinks of him" (40–41) (B, A).

236. **(C)** Gregor's metamorphosis into a "horrible vermin" or insect is clearly the focus of the text, and a careful read of the passage reveals the metaphorical value of this transformation. The symbolic significance of the vermin **metaphor** is developed in each subsequent paragraph. First, we see how Gregor's vermin body makes him helpless. He can't even turn over: "However hard he threw himself onto his right, he always rolled back to where he was" (18–19), a clear visualization of the lack of agency he has in his human life. This sense of powerlessness is developed in subsequent paragraphs as we learn that he is bound to work in a demanding job as a traveling salesman in order to pay off his parents' debts. His boss treats him like a vermin, talking down to his subordinates "from up there" (44).

Passage 23. Sinclair Lewis, *Babbitt*

237. **(B)** Babbitt "kept himself from the bewilderment of thinking" (1–2), suggesting that he performs his job without thought or effort, in a routine, perfunctory manner. He does the same thing "[e]very evening" (2), and since "the days were blank of face and silent" (3), we can assume that he goes through his routine without much enthusiasm.

238. **(A)** This sentence is set off in its own paragraph because it contains the essential point that will be reinforced in the next few paragraphs—Babbitt's apathy toward creating his own experience outside of his monotonous routine. He is excited to be free for the evening, but "not quite sure what" (5) to do, which is reinforced later in the passage by his boredom over "having to take so much trouble to be riotous" (11), his vague (20) desire to look for entertainment that would "enable a fellow to forget his troubles" (28–29).

239. **(B)** The word "emancipated" suggests that the house has been set free. From the previous sentences, we can assume that the house is set free from the routine of work, wife and neighbors, bridge, the movies, and blank and silent days (1–3). In the previous sentence, Babbitt is described as "free to do . . . " (5), indicating that the "emancipation" is from prescribed routines. The phrase "without having to put up a husbandly front" (7–8) might lead a reader to choose choice A because it focuses on Babbitt's wife, but "unrelenting" is too extreme. There is no evidence to suggest Mrs. Babbitt is "unrelenting" in her demands on Babbitt's time. She's actually referred to as "generous" in line 2. The context of the two paragraphs suggests that it's an emancipation from nothing too burdensome other than routine "blank and silent" (3) days.

240. **(C)** The narrator adopts Babbitt's point of view when describing Verona's opinion. Because of the repetition of the word "opinion," we hear some condescension in Babbitt's view of Verona's fourth-hand knowledge of the topic she is discussing. (A), (B), and (D) are too extreme and do not recognize the humor in the repetition of the word "opinion."

241. **(E)** Babbitt only "vaguely" wants something more diverting than comic strips to read (20), which suggests he is not tenacious (B), determined, or passionately eager about making the most of his evening. He appears to be more apathetic (lazy) about finding something to do. Choice D (ambivalent) means he is genuinely torn between conflicting emotions. Babbitt is not that invested, only vaguely interested in finding something mildly amusing/distracting. Nothing that will make him think too deeply about society, politics, the church, all the "decencies" (26).

242. **(E)** Babbitt and Verona clearly do not share the same interests. It is stated that Babbitt "liked none of the books" (26) that he finds in Verona's room.

243. (E) Babbitt was "unusually kindly to Ted and Verona, hesitating but not disapproving when Verona stated her opinion . . . " (12–13). This line indicates that Babbitt would normally disapprove and potentially tease Verona about her opinions. By hesitating instead of disagreeing, he is being unusually kind, which means he does not normally respond with concordance (agreement), making (B) incorrect. (C) is too extreme and not supported by the text.

244. (A) This line is not written in quotation marks, nor is it prefaced with an indicator that it is one of Babbitt's thoughts, yet the statement is written from Babbitt's perspective, in Babbitt's voice. The narrator's voice and Babbitt's voice have commingled, making the sentence an example of the technique of **free indirect style**, where the narrator adopts the voice and point of view of character(s) in his/her own narration.

245. (E) The final paragraph follows a "restless" (19) Babbitt upstairs to Verona's room, where he browses for something "diverting" (20) to read. Settling on an "adventure story," he "clumped down-stairs and solemnly began to read, under the piano lamp" (32–33). Babbitt is not desperate to seek escape (A) since he is described as "restless" and only "vaguely" wanting something diverting to read (20), which also indicates he is hardly reveling in solitude (B). His reactions to Verona's "highly improper essays" (25) are not intended to portray him in an admiring light. The **tone** is still humorous and we get a sense that we are laughing at Babbitt and not at Verona (C). Babbitt settles on a book, so he is not perpetually unsatisfied (D).

Passage 24. Naguib Mahfouz, *Midaq Alley*

246. (D) Midaq Alley is described as "one of the gems of a time gone by . . . that once shone forth like a flashing star in the history of Cairo" (1–2), which reveals that it was *once* more appreciated and noticed than it is now (I). It is, however, still deserving of ongoing appreciation because "the alley is certainly an ancient relic and a precious one" (5) (III). Midaq Alley is not representative of the complete history of Cairo. The narrator asks, "Which Cairo do I mean? . . . Only God and the archaeologists know the answer to that . . ." (3–4), which makes II incorrect.

247. (B) The "now crumbling" (8) walls of the café known as Kirsha's "give off strong odors from the medicines of olden times, smells which have now become the spices and folk cures of today and tomorrow" (8–10). The odors stem from what used to be valuable medicine but is now simply a folk remedy or a spice to season food, a less impressive function. Just like the medicine, Midaq Alley itself is no longer the "gem" (1) it used to be—now "an ancient relic" (5) that still has "distinctive and personal" (12) value that is different from that of its past. Choice D does reference the alley's former glory (its historical value) but does not reference the current value the way that choice B does.

248. (D) The narrator describes Midaq Alley as "an ancient relic and a precious one" because "it retains a number of the secrets of a world now past" (14). But it is also worthy of ongoing attention because it "clamors with a distinctive and personal life of its own" (12) and "its roots connect with life as a whole" (13). Choice B only partially captures the narrator's perspective. The narrator is not concerned with Midaq Alley's exact place in Cairo's history (A), and present-day values are not presented as corrupting in this passage (C).

249. (C) The third paragraph is notable for its precise descriptions of Midaq Alley's features. We can see the "brown hues" (15) created by the setting sun and imagine the intensity of the darkness that is "all the greater because it was enclosed like a trap between three walls." The alley rises "unevenly" from Sanadiqiya Street and "ends abruptly . . . with two adjoining houses" (18–19). We can picture the alley with its specific shops on each side of the street and even see that the houses are three stories tall. The descriptions also have **symbolic** significance. The darkness, "veiled" (15) glow, and "abrupt end" (18–19) to the alley are literal and also symbolic of the alley's ancient glory's abrupt end.

250. (A) Midaq Alley is almost completely isolated "from all surrounding activity" (11–12)—a description that is enhanced by the image of the darkness as "enclosed like a trap between three walls" (16–17). The three walls that define Midaq Alley trap the evening darkness, which dramatizes the isolation of the place. While the alley ending abruptly (E) adds to the sense of it feeling enclosed, it does not enhance the isolation as much as the comparison to a "trap" (16). The alley could be filled with light and still "end abruptly" (18–19), making (A) a better choice than (E).

251. (A) The passage explicitly compares the alley's literal abrupt end to the end of its "ancient glory" (19). The comparison is made using the word "as," a figurative device known as a **simile**.

252. (D) The narrator does not give any indication that he lived in Midaq Alley before (A) or that the alley must be restored (C). While he does insist the alley is "one of the gems of times gone by" (1–2) and "a flashing star in the history of Cairo" (2), he is not condescending to the reader (B) or presenting facts objectively (E). His generous descriptions of Midaq Alley reveal him to be an interested observer who uses sensory **imagery** and quotes from the alley's denizens to present it as a dynamic and distinctive place.

253. (E) Reading the residents' voices through their quoted dialogue allows us to hear how the alley "clamors with a distinctive and personal life" (12) (A). We hear culturally specific references like "hookah" and "hashish" and learn about "blackouts" and "air raids" (26). Several residents are quoted, their statements following one another, allowing us to hear a variety of voices that make up the alley's community (B) and see the community coming to life in the evening as shops close and the "get-together" (23) begins (C, D). None of the residents' statements, however, indicate discord or disharmony (E). In fact, they remind one another of their evening duties and routines.

Passage 25. Rohinton Mistry, *A Fine Balance*

254. (C) Dina feels "out of place" (4) at the public libraries upon seeing "heads bent over books." She assumes that these readers are "so learned," reading dense scholarly works like Milton's *Areopagitica*. The second paragraph explains that this "impression was dispelled when she realized the reading materials . . . could range" from the Milton text to *the Illustrated Weekly of India*. The context suggests that the *Illustrated Weekly* is not seen by Dina as scholarly or intimidating, likely due to its illustrations and possibly its mass appeal. Dina's assumption is about the library patrons more than it is about the books (E).

255. (E) The context indicates that Dina's assumption about the grave scholarly library patrons is dispelled when she sees they could be reading anything from Milton's *Areopagitica* to the *Illustrated Weekly of India*, the latter text being one that is less "grave" and "learned." Of the options, the comic strip is most like the *Illustrated* periodical from Dina's perspective.

256. (B) The library is described with **sensory imagery** that evokes its smells ("musty"), its sounds ("*whoosh*," "rustling," "whispers"), and the texture of the chairs ("leather," "dusty")—I. The reference to the library as Dina's "sanctuary" (10) shows the sacred appreciation she has for the solitude and peace it provides—II. The word choice is precise and descriptive, not exaggerated, making III incorrect.

257. (A) The third paragraph does describe the harsh setting of the modern libraries (fluorescent lights, always crowded), but the function of this description is not to present them as *more* intimidating than the older libraries. And while the music may be sophisticated, Dina goes there to enjoy it and learn about it. She is no longer as intimidated as she was when she first entered the older, stately libraries. The context of the paragraph reveals that the modern libraries offer Dina an opportunity to listen to music, an activity we discover is special to her in part because of the memories it evokes about her father (D, E, C). The narrator underscores Dina's motivation to "listen to records" (21) by describing how "cold and inhospitable" (20) the modern libraries are (B). She is willing to endure those conditions for access to the music.

258. (E) At the start of the passage, the narrator describes how Dina ventured "timidly into public libraries" (3) and felt "out of place" (4) because she "hadn't even matriculated" (4–5) (graduated). By the end the narration describes how she tolerates the uncomfortable modern libraries, selecting "records at random, trying to memorize the names of the ones she enjoyed so she could play them again another day" (26–27). Even though "it was tricky" (27) and "she did not know what any of it meant" (29–30), she has the confidence to persist.

259. (A) Earlier in the passage, we learn that Dina's father would tell her that music "'makes you forget the troubles of this world" (24–25). She would "nod her head seriously" (25) in response. When she manages to identify a familiar song in the modern library, "the past was conquered for a brief while" (32), which suggests that she forgets the past, just as her father had described. Choice C states that by "conquered," Dina means that the memory of her father's loss will stop upsetting her permanently, but there is not enough evidence in the passage to indicate that the "past" (32) refers only to losing her father or that the pain is conquered permanently.

260. (C) See question 259. Dina forgets the past upon listening to a familiar song, just the way her father had. The comparison to feeling as though she had recovered a missing limb sheds light on the earlier referenced memory of her father. The comparison, in context of the passage, implies that the music brings Dina back to her father's lap, feeling complete.

261. (C) While all the lines describe Dina's impressions of the libraries or details about the libraries, her routine of "rounding off the visit by sitting for a few minutes with eyes closed in a dark corner of the old building, where time could stand still" (16–17) creates the sense that she is in a safe, comforting space that she savors.

262. (D) As readers, we wonder why Dina tolerates the crowds, the "fluorescent lights, Formica tables, air-conditioning, and brightly painted walls" (19) of the modern libraries just to listen to records. While Dina's view of the library as a "sanctuary" (10) suggests she might be escaping her current reality (C), the "ecstasy of completion" (32–33) invokes a larger influence. The reference to her childhood memory of listening to music with her father sheds light on her motivation. When he would say that music "'makes you forget the troubles of this world,'" (24–25) she would "nod her head seriously" (25) in response. The details about Dina's childhood experience with her father puts her current motivation to listen to music in a helpful context. Upon hearing a familiar song, "the past was conquered for a brief while" (32), as it was for her father, but she "felt herself ache with the ecstasy of completion, as though a missing limb had been recovered" (32–33). Given the earlier reference to her father, the music makes her feel complete, likely because it makes her feel connected to her father.

263. (E) Dina is timid about entering public libraries at first, but she learns that you don't need to have "matriculated" (5) or read Milton to feel a sense of belonging in the library. It becomes "her favorite sanctuary" (10), and she spends hours flipping through a variety of books. The passage goes on to describe Dina enjoying even the "inhospitable" (20) modern libraries, where she persists with the trying task of locating familiar songs she heard with her father as a child. The passage closes with Dina aching "with the ecstasy of completion, as though a missing limb had been recovered" (32–33), revealing the intense impact her library visits have on her.

Passage 26. R. A. Sasaki, "Driving to Colma"

264. (C) The passage opens and closes with references to the narrator's life shrinking and feeling small. At the start of the passage, the focus of her life shrinks because she is caring for her sick father, worrying about him eating and taking his medicine. At the end, the narrator connects this return to her childhood home to the urge she had when she was younger to escape it because "it had simply become too small" (30–31). Even though she wanted to escape her childhood home, the narrator does not indicate that her childhood was suffocating (D). She even explains that her desire to leave was "not because [she] hated it" (30). While (E) is true, it does not include how the phrase functions in the passage as both an opening and closing reference, one that connects the narrator's return home to care for her father with the constricting feelings from her childhood in this home.

265. (D) The focus of her life "shrinks" (1) because she is now primarily concerned with her father's health: his diet, his medicine, and his routine. She describes this new focus as entering "a new world" (7) where she "must learn the language spoken" (7–8). Her detailed list of the names of her father's medicines indicates fascination. The sounds of the medical terms are "strange" (8); she rolls them around on her tongue, appreciating how they distract her "from the question that no one can answer." She looks up the words in medical dictionaries, reading and reciting them for pleasure, for comfort, and for solace, the way one recites a prayer. While (E) is partly true, the narrator has not chosen to explore medical terms purely because of her interest. She is confronted with them because her world has shrunk, and she has become immersed in this language.

266. (A) The drugs "distract" her "from the question that no one can answer" (15–16). They keep her preoccupied so that she doesn't have to dwell on the uncertainty of her father's condition. The words do not intimidate (B), overwhelm (C), or burden (D) her. On the contrary, they intrigue her. She focuses on studying the strange vocabulary, reading medical dictionaries, and reciting the terms like she's learning a prayer. Seeing "an inexhaustible supply of allopurinol" (10) (which means they are not scarce, E) gives her "hope" because it makes her think her father will have "to live a long time to finish all of those" (11).

267. (D) The narrator explains, "I can fill my mind with recipes and names of drugs, and distract myself from the question that no one can answer" (14–16). She has returned home to care for her sick father, and she mentions that seeing "an inexhaustible supply of allopurinol" (10) gives her "hope" (10) because it makes her think her father will have "to live a long time to finish all of those" (11). These details imply that the question she avoids is about her father's survival.

268. (C) Instead of reading "horse stories or mysteries, instead of Russian novels" (18), the narrator explores "medical books, dictionaries of [her] new language" (19) now that the focus of her world has narrowed to caring for her sick father (I). Unlike her "old Japanese house" (24), which has "windows . . . opened wide to the trees outside" (25), the childhood home she has returned to now is "too small" (30–31). The wide open window is replaced with a "small square window" (28) blocked by fog (II). The list of the father's medicine is not contrasted with a detail from her past (III).

269. (D) The narrator curls up in her "favorite reading place" (17) in her childhood home to study the "strange" (8, 13) vocabulary of this "new world" (7) of caring for her sick father. Instead of enjoying mysteries and horse stories, she immerses herself in medical books and dictionaries. Earlier, she describes rolling the sounds of the pills' names around on her tongue, thinking she'll never forget them. The comparison to learning the Lord's Prayer, "or a new kind of catechism" (22), emphasizes the comfort and ritual aspect to her fascination and study. Choice C is incorrect because the medicine itself is not necessarily healing for her; it is learning about the world of her father's illness (the terms and concepts) that provides some comfort. Her study is not exactly sacred or holy (A); it is enriching and comforting to learn the sounds and subtleties of words, the way one does when memorizing a prayer. The comparison to the Lord's Prayer is a **simile** (B), but the narrator finds the strange sounds of the medical vocabulary intriguing ("roll the words around on my tongue") and her study of them comforting. There is no evidence to suggest they are frightening as compared to the words in the Lord's Prayer.

270. (A) The narrator curls up in her "favorite reading place" (17) in her childhood home to study the "strange" (8, 13) vocabulary of this "new world" (7) of caring for her sick father. She compares her study of medical books and dictionaries to learning the Lord's Prayer "or a new kind of catechism" (22). By commenting that she "was always good in school" (22–23), she suggests that this study is right up her alley, an appropriate and helpful way to find some comfort and control in this uncertain time. By mentioning she was good in school, she is clearly indicating a parallel between her childhood and current situation, but it is not likely that the narrator believes she hasn't changed much (D). Her presence at home, helping her mother take care of her father, indicates she is doing a lot more than learning a new vocabulary (B, C, E).

271. (B) The narrator has returned to her childhood home to help take care of her sick father. This house is one she spent her "life trying to escape, not because [she] hated it, but because it had simply become too small" (29–31). In her dream, she is back in her Japanese home, different from her childhood home; it is characterized by the windows that "are opened wide to the trees outside" (25), allowing the sun to shine on the tatami. When she awakes, the wide view is replaced in her current setting (her childhood room) by a fog that blocks the view from her "small square window" (28). Both homes have windows, but one, where she presumably lives as an adult, is characterized as open to the world outside. The other, from which she felt the urge to escape, is not as open. She can't even see outside the small window. The fog could signify the narrator's feelings about being home to help her parents (E), but choice B offers a more precise description of how the fog contrasts the view she sees in her dream.

272. (E) The passage is written in **first-person narration**. The narrator begins by claiming that the focus of her life "shrinks" (1). She develops this in the following paragraphs by describing the new routine of caring for her sick father, helping him eat, cataloging his pill intake, and taking up an interest in learning about medical terms and vocabulary. While the narrator does describe her childhood house as one she longed to "escape" (30), she mentions that she had not "hated it" (30) but that it had "simply become too small" (30–31), making choice C too extremely negative. The focus of the passage is not so much on how difficult and necessary her obligation is (D), or the stress (B) or guilt (A) she feels. In fact, she finds comfort in learning about the "strange vocabulary" (8) of this "new world" (7) of hers, savoring the way the medical language feels as she "rolls the words around" (13–14) on her tongue. Just as she enjoyed Russian novels as a child, she now finds some comfort in the "Russian-sounding" (13) names of her father's pills. She finds novelty and stimulation in the experience of returning home.

Passage 27. Zadie Smith, *White Teeth*

273. (E) The narrator explains that "before you know where you are, you're turning up at the weekly school council meetings . . . you're *implicated* in the school, you're *involved* in it" (17–20). The parent is not the teacher (A), and the teacher is not teaching like a parent (B). The parent is involved in the school, not overseeing the entire administration (C). While Samad may be indifferent to his role as a parent-governor, that is not a defining characteristic of the role (D).

274. (D) The narrator, adopting the **tone** and perspective of Samad, qualifies the claim that Samad sired two children willingly by adding "as willingly as a man can" (2). The suggestion is that women, not men, are the ones who are the more eager to have children and that a man is obligated to go along with the plan.

275. (E) The first paragraph refers to children, from Samad's point of view, as an infection, and parenting as a "disease" (1) he has caught. The references to a "mewling, puking underclass" (6) contributes to the image of children as germ-spreading and viral. They are "dotted along" the **metaphorical** "highway" of life, "in the crèche facilities of each service station" (5–6), which conveys Samad's perspective that they are a large part of life that he never noticed before he, too, became part of it. The phrase "this other thing" (3) captures Samad's distinct voice and perspective: we get the sense that this phrase is his, not the narrator's—II. The stress on words like "*knowing children*" (3–4), "*other people's* children" (8), and "friends of *his* children" (9) clarify exactly how exposed Samad has been to this infectious underclass.

276. (B) Even though Samad has children "willingly" (2), he feels he "caught children like a disease" (1). He did not bargain for "this other thing . . . This thing of *knowing* children" (3–4).

The passage goes on to describe how "in the early eighties, he became infected with children . . . at least 30 percent of his social and cultural circle was under the age of nine" (7–11). He had not "bargained" (2) for this, which means he was not expecting that agreeing to have children would mean such an immersion in their world. Part of this immersion is that he has become a parent-governor (A), but the "other thing" (3) broadly refers to "*knowing* children" (3–4), which includes his friends' children and his children's friends, not just the children at school (E). Willingly becoming a parent is not the "other thing" (D).

277. (B) The "strange process of symmetry" (13) refers to the parallels between how willingly becoming a parent leads to an unintended full immersion in the world of children (described in the first paragraph) and casually helping at a school fair leads to an onerous commitment as a parent-governor. The word "innocently" (14) suggests that Samad did not have the intention to become so involved in either. The "symmetry" refers to Samad's general unintentional involvement in all things related to children, not just his obligations at the school (E).

278. (D) The spring fair is mentioned in the context of how innocently and casually deciding to attend a school event leads to "turning up at the weekly school council meetings . . ." (17–18). It is too extreme to say attending this one specific fair is the point at which his life dramatically changes (E), as we have already learned in the first paragraph that he has been immersed in the world of children since the "early eighties" (7–8).

279. (C) The second paragraph's focus is to show the "symmetry" (13) between the process of becoming a parent in the first place and then becoming an involved parent-governor. The first paragraph explains how he innocently agreed to have kids, not bargaining for the other "thing that no one tells you about" (3), which is revealed to be the experience of getting "infected with children" (8) so that "30 percent" (10) of your social circle is made up of kids. This same intensity is mirrored in the second paragraph by the list of all the ways a parent-governor is "implicated" (20) in the affairs of the school: meetings, concerts, plans for a new music department, and donating funds. While other choices are partly correct, the purpose of the list is to explain the symmetry mentioned at the start of the paragraph.

280. (D) The whole passage is told by a **third-person narrator**, not Samad, but the point of view is Samad's, not the narrator's. The narration adopts Samad's own language, most obvious by the parenthetical commentary and the italicized phrases that communicate Samad's exact tonal emphasis. It is Samad who thinks the music teacher is pretty and that school raffles are fixed, not the narrator.

281. (A) The italicized phrase "*other people's* children" (8) and "friends of *his* children" (9) highlight Samad's voice (not an objective narrator's), emphasizing his point that over time, having children leads to a full immersion in the world of children (see question 280).

282. (E) The whole passage is told by a **third-person narrator** (Samad is referred to by name and as "he"), not Samad, but the point of view is Samad's, not the narrator's (see questions 280 and 281). **Free indirect discourse** describes a type of third-person narration where a third-person narrator adopts characters' thoughts, feelings, and words.

283. (A) The second paragraph describes the process of becoming fully "*involved*" (20) and "*implicated*" (20) in one's children's school. The process is introduced as mirroring the process of becoming a parent, which, for Samad, starts off casually and innocently, not having bargained for the full immersion and investment it becomes. Becoming a parent-governor is another example of how he has been consumed by "this other thing" (3) of "*knowing* children" (3–4). Instead of "dropping your children at the school gates," you "start following them in" (21). The gates are **symbolic** of a threshold between simply having children and becoming fully immersed in their world. The gates are not a literal point of no return to his previous lifestyle (B) since he certainly can exit the actual gates. While parent-governors may be over-involved, it is not the intention of the passage to comment on all parents who are parent-governors (E).

284. (D) The sarcasm is evident in phrases like "as willingly as a man can" (2), "a mewling, puking underclass" (6), the words in italics, and the parenthetical comments. These phrases lend a slightly dark comical **tone** to the descriptions of how Samad, who does want to be a parent, unanticipatedly becomes more involved in the world of children than he "bargained for" (2). Choice C does not acknowledge that the descriptions are not meant to be authentically negative, and the passage is about the process of becoming a parent, not just a parent-governor. It is also too extreme to say that Samad's experience is "humiliating" (E).

Passage 28. Upton Sinclair, *The Jungle*

285. (D) Jurgis approaches a friend to ask "what this meant" (2), which is "what Jurgis had to say" (3–4), making (B) correct. More specifically, lines 4–5, reveal that Jurgis has asked about "cases of petty graft," making (C) correct. Tamoszius elaborates on these cases by describing how "the bosses grafted off the men" (7–8) and the men "grafted off each other" (8), which refers to the stealing of money, implying that Jurgis may have asked about his low wages, making (A) plausible. Tamoszius goes on to say that the superintendent would some day "graft off the boss" (9), making (E) also correct. The word "this" in Jurgis's question does not, however, refer to "the killing beds" (3), making (D) the only incorrect choice (and the correct answer).

286. (C) The narrator says, "After Jurgis had been there awhile he would know that the plants were simply honeycombed with rottenness of that sort—the bosses grafted off the men, and they grafted off each other . . . " (6–8). Graft is definitely abundant, and the word "simply" implies that this is simply what happens on a routine basis; it is so abundant that it is common.

287. (D) Tamoszius describes the plants where he and Jurgis work as "honeycombed with rottenness of that sort" (7), referring to the commonplace incidents of graft. To elaborate, he describes the widespread nature of the graft, how it is hierarchical and interconnected (III), with the superintendent grafting off the boss, the boss grafting off the men (as a queen bee is served by all her worker bees—I, II), and the men grafting off each other. While the owner, managers, and superintendents "squeeze out . . . as much work as possible" (14–15), we cannot assume that they enjoy the corrupt system or find it sweet (IV). In fact, "every man lived in terror of losing his job, if another made a better record than he" (17).

288. (D) The comparison to men arranged in ranks and grades in the army is useful in its similarity to the hierarchical structure of Durham's that Tamoszius wants to explain to Jurgis. Durham is at the top, then the "managers, superintendents, and foremen . . ." (10–13). Discipline (A) and patriotism (B) are not mentioned in the passage. The workers are not said to be conscripted (drafted) into the plants (E), and the context of the army **simile** does not imply that these bosses are heroic as they are "trying to squeeze out . . . as much work as possible" (14–15).

289. (E) Nowhere in Packingtown (in the plants or in Durham's), is there an appreciation of a principled (conscientious, ethical) work ethic. It is noted that "old Durham in the beginning" (22) must have handed down unethical business practices to his son (A), that "the men eventually "caught the spirit of the place" because "every man lived in terror of losing his job, if another made a better record than he" (16–17) (B, C). The widespread graft among the "managers, superintendents, and foremen . . . " (10–13) indicates the ubiquitous venality (openness to bribery) that is also evident at Durham's (D). (See question 285.)

290. (E) Tamoszius explains that deception, graft, knavery, telling "tales" (31), and spying are what help a man rise in Packingtown. In other words, men who are opportunistic and seek advancement through no concern for principles or ethics are the ones who will succeed here.

291. (D) Before the phrase "'speed him up'" (33), Tamoszius is explaining what the bosses would do to a "man who minded his own business and did his work" (32–33). They would "'speed him up' till they had worn him out, and then they would throw him into the gutter" (33–34). The description of speeding up a man to the point of exhaustion implies that the command is a **euphemism** (a substitution of a mild expression for one thought to be harsh) for overworking a man—I. The quotes also indicate that this phrase is distinct from the words of the current narrative voice (Tamoszius's)—III, not that the phrase is part of an actual dialogue/conversation occurring at this point in the text—II.

292. (A) The **third-person narrative voice** is apparent in the first sentence of the third paragraph: "Jurgis went home with his head buzzing" (35). However, in the following sentence, the narrative voice moves into **free indirect style** again, and this time the narrator adopts the voice of Jurgis: "no, it could not be so" (36). This line is clearly the voice of Jurgis, not the third-person narrator. The free indirect narration from Jurgis's point of view continues for the remainder of the paragraph; the narration refers to Tamoszius from Jurgis's point of view ("a grumbler," "a puny little chap . . . that was why he was so sore"). The third-person narrator would not describe Tamoszius in these terms as he has no need to justify his own skepticism about the corruption of the plants, but Jurgis does.

293. (C) In lines 36–40, Jurgis doubts the validity of Tamoszius' claims about the company's graft and corruption. He reasons that Tamoszius is merely "sore" or making excuses because he "did not feel like work" (38–40). This response is typical of someone who is skeptical about believing new information. Jurgis cannot be said to be in complete denial (E) because he begins to notice multiple examples to support the opposing view: "And yet so many strange things kept coming to Jurgis's notice every day!" (40–41). The **free indirect style** of narration (see question 292) is evident with the exclamation point, indicating that the narrator writes this statement from Jurgis's own perspective.

Passage 29. Ngugi wa Thiong'o, *The River Between*

294. (D) The first paragraph objectively (II) describes the setting by naming two mountain ridges and a valley and stating their location using simple directional phrases and concrete diction like "side by side" (1) and "between" (2). A **simile** likens the ridges to "many sleeping lions" (4) and their **metaphorical** sleep to the "deep sleep of their Creator" (5) (III). Despite the figurative language, the description is assertive and matter-of-fact, not conditional (I).

295. (A) There is sufficient textual evidence to suggest that the lions **symbolize** the society of the region, which appears dormant, content with the sustenance offered by their environment's natural resources (river, wild beasts), but also antagonistic, "like two rivals ready to come to blows in a life and death struggle for the leadership of this isolated region" (19–21). The comparison to lions does show the valleys' potential to be dangerous, but it equally portrays the valleys as contentedly sleeping, "united by their common source of life" (18) (B). The image of the two ridges as antagonists may **foreshadow** conflict, but the battle would not be between a peaceful valley and an antagonistic one (E) as both ridges are described as facing each other "like two rivals" (19–20), making (A) the best option.

296. (E) The "many more valleys and ridges" (3) that are "lying without any discernible plan" (3) are also described as "sleeping lions which never woke" (4). These valleys appear behind Kameno and Makuyu, which frame the valley of life. The opening paragraph begins with a precise description of a setting (two named ridges border a named valley—see question 294) that is put into relief by the almost blurred background of many nameless ridges and valleys that appear asleep and without definition ("without any discernible plan" (3)). The region is described as "isolated" in the last line of the passage, but the passage as a whole does not directly support the idea that it is suffering from the isolation (D).

297. (D) The second paragraph opens with the conditional statement, "If there had been no bush and no forest trees covering the slopes, you could have seen the river when you stood on top of either Kameno or Mukuy" (6–8), which means the view of the river is obscured from atop the mountains. You "had to come down" (8)—or descend—the mountains and "[e]ven then you could not see the whole extent of the river" (8–9).

298. (D) The second paragraph explains that the meaning of the river's name, Honia, is "cure, or bring-back-to-life" (11). These characteristics coincide with the other features of the river: it "flowed through the valley of life" (6), it "never dried" (11), "scorning droughts and weather changes" (12). The river is described as not being in a hurry and possessing "a strong will to live" (12), both human-like traits, a device known as **personification** (A). The paragraph opens with a conditional statement ("If . . . you could have" (6–7)) to explain how large the river is (B). The **simile** comparing the river to a snake (C) illustrates its winding shape. The paragraph describes both what the river does (cures, scorns draughts) and what it does not do ("never dried" (11), "never hurrying, never hesitating") (13) (E).

299. (C) The third paragraph, just three sentences, stands out from the passage due to its brevity and sharp focus on the river's role in the society. It seems to summarize the more elaborately drawn out description provided in the previous paragraph, emphasizing the river's key function as "the soul of Kameno and Makuyu" (15). The entire passage is written in the past tense, so this does not make the paragraph distinct (E). The diction is not formal ("It joined them") (15) (D). The paragraph is certainly not irrelevant (A), and the idea of the river as the community's soul is not mundane(B) but poetic and profound.

300. (B) The final paragraph opens with the phrase, "When you stood in the valley" (17) and goes on to explain that, from the ground, the valleys and ridges cease to appear like sleeping lions. From the valley floor, as opposed to the view from atop Kameno and Makuyu, the two ridges "became antagonists . . . like two rivals ready to come to blows" (18–20). There is no "tangible" (19) change to the ridges, just a change in perspective.

301. (E) The **figurative language** and subjective descriptions indicate the passage is written as a story, not a historical account (D, A). There are no details to suggest the narrator has lived in the community and is remembering it fondly (C, B). The narrator tells the story in third person and spends several paragraphs establishing the setting, using both literal descriptions and figurative language to convey its significance and connection to the story's potential **themes** (for example, the valley of life's two ridges can appear as "sleeping lions" (4) or as "antagonists" (18), depending on your perspective).

302. (D) The final paragraph introduces a shift with the dependent clause "When you stood in the valley" (17), which contrasts the prior descriptions of the setting as viewed from atop the ridges. The opening sentence also alters the previous **metaphorical** comparison by explaining that the ridges and valleys "*ceased* to be sleeping lions united by their common source of life" (17–18). Instead of words like "soul" (15), "cure" (11), and "happy" (14), the setting is described with words that evoke violence, like "antagonists" (18), "rivals" (20) and "death struggle" (20). Since the view of the setting changes so dramatically just based on the location of the viewer, there is a sense of foreboding that these peaceful ridges may "come to blows" (20), that the people will "struggle for the leadership of this isolated region" (20–21). While the final paragraph is full of negative diction, the previous paragraphs are developed with poetic and descriptive language ("wound its way . . . like a snake . . . scorning droughts . . . united by this life-stream") (10–16), not vague (E) or even neutral terms (C). The shift presents the valleys as changing from passive to combative, not the other way around (A).

Passage 30. Virginia Woolf, "An Unwritten Novel"

303. (C) Line 1 explicitly refers to the expression as one of unhappiness. It is "enough by itself" (1) to pull one away from her newspaper, and the "poor woman's face" (2) would be "insignificant without that look" (2–3) and it is "almost a symbol of destiny with it" (3). The reference to "a symbol of destiny" (3) conveys the expression as overwhelming in its significant sadness. While (E) is true, the surrounding context suggests it is the actual expression itself, its weightiness and significance, that is hard to avoid. (B) is incorrect because the narrator does have a newspaper she attempts to use as a distraction, and the other passengers appear to be able to distract themselves (27–28).

304. (D) According to the passage, "Life's what you see in people's eyes; life's what they learn, and, having learnt it, never, though they seek to hide it, cease to be aware of" (lines 3–5). (B) is incorrect because "they" do not disregard what they learn in life; rather, they "never . . . cease to be aware of it" (4–5) even though "they seek to hide it" (4–5). (A) is a tempting choice, but the narrator does not ever indicate that life only consists of knowledge *reluctantly* gained. Even though there is an undertone of misery and avoidance of "life" due to its burdensome experiences and memories, the definition of life is more generally given as "life is what they learn" (4) Also, the narrator refers to the *Times* as a "great reservoir of life" (22) and she lists positive news (not solely reluctantly gained news) like births and marriages along with mundane news like court circulars among the events that make up "life."

305. (E) All five faces are "mature" (6), so the fifth person is not older than the others (B). The narrator at first says, "Marks of reticence" (7) are made by "each one of the five" (8), each one "doing something to hide or stultify his knowledge" (8) but soon reveals in line 10–11 that "the terrible thing about the fifth is that she does nothing at all." She does not have a mark of reticence, making (C), (D), and (A) incorrect. What distinguishes her from the others is that she does not play the game of concealing life with "marks of reticence": "Ah, but my poor, unfortunate woman, do play the game—do, for all our sakes, conceal it!" (11–12).

306. (E) The narrator only describes the other passengers as examples to support her assertion that "Life's what you see in people's eyes; life's what they learn, and, having learnt it, never, though they seek to hide it, cease to be aware of—what?" (3–5). The "faces opposite" (5) have the "marks of reticence" (7) that the narrator sees as customary attempts to "conceal" (12) life. The four passengers also serve as a contrast to the fifth, who "does nothing at all," who does not "play the game" and "conceal it" (11–12). The narrator's intent is not to portray the other passengers as cold, indifferent, apathetic, or secretive (B–D) because of their "marks of reticence" (7) and attempts to "conceal" life; rather, she mentions these behaviors as examples of what is expected and common and to highlight the strangeness of the woman's refusal to play along. The passengers are certainly not talkative (A).

307. (C) See question 306. The fifth person does not "play the game" (12) of concealing life (what she has learned and experienced, particularly her sadness) with "marks of reticence" like the other passengers do.

308. (A) The author does not use actual dialogue in the passage. The only phrases/sentences in quotation marks are qualified with "she <u>seemed</u> to say to me" (14) and "I answered <u>silently</u>" (15). Though they are in quotation marks, these words are not actually part of a verbal conversation. There are several instances of auditory **imagery** and visual imagery in the second paragraph, along with a **simile**: "she looked up, shifted slightly in her seat and sighed . . . she shuddered, twitched her arm . . . and shook her head. . . . Again with infinite weariness she moved her head from side to side until, <u>like</u> a top exhausted with spinning, it settled on her neck" (13–26). We can hear the woman sighing and see her moving. These observations are certainly subjective, as they are provided through **first-person narration** (E).

309. (A) The narrator observes the woman as possibly thinking, "'If only you knew!'" (14) which is in context of the woman not concealing her sadness, her life experience, like everyone else does. The narrator insists, silently, "'I do know . . . I know the whole business . . . the *Times* knows. . . . We all know'" (15–19). She goes on to cite the news coverage in the paper, such as a peace deal, a train collision, births, deaths, marriages, court cases, and more. The variety of these examples suggests that what they "know" is the various events, details, and emotions that make up life, not the specific details of the woman's experiences (B, C).

310. (D) The speaker attempts to use the *Times* as a shield (B) to protect her from the woman's unconcealed sadness, but "The *Times* was no protection against such sorrow as hers. . . . She pierced through my shield" (27–31), making the *Times* penetrable, not impenetrable. The *Times* is exhaustive in its full coverage of life events and news (see question 309); she even refers to it as a "reservoir of life" (22) (A, E). Because she relies on it "for manners' sake" (16) and to help her "play the game" (12) of not looking at life, the *Times* is also a kind of crutch (C).

311. (C) The passage is narrated in the **first-person point of view** ("me," "I"), not in **third person** (B). The passage consists of the narrator's thoughts as she rides the train and observes the behaviors of her fellow passengers, one in particular. She ponders, speculates, and makes assumptions about the significance of their actions while also revealing her own perspective on "life" and customary behaviors. There is no actual dialogue in the passage. The quoted speech is introduced as the narrator's silent expressions (E) or an assumption about what the woman *might* say (13–14).

312. (A) The narrator is most definitely *curious* about the fifth passenger, the woman, whose "expression of unhappiness was enough by itself to make one's eyes slide above the paper's edge" (1–2). She has *pity* for the fifth passenger, referring to her as "the poor woman" (2) and finding it difficult to resist "intercourse" with "such sorrow as hers" (27–28). In fact, she feels *compelled*, twice, to look over the paper's edge, the paper that is meant to be her protection from engaging with others' lives (2, 19–20). She experiences *hope* when she tries, yet again, to use her shield (the *Times*); she folds the paper "so that it made a perfect square, crisp, thick, impervious even to life" (27–29). Once armed, she "glanced up" (30), hopeful that her protection would work. It does not work, however, as the woman "pierced through [the] shield" (30–31) and dampens her courage to clay. The narrator is *resigned* as all hope is "denied" (30–33). The narrator does not experience extremely negative emotions like anger (B), disgust (C), audacity (D), or antipathy (E).

313. (B) The narrator uses a **simile** in the final lines to compare her own eyes to a body of water that the woman searches for any "sediments of courage . . . and damping it to clay" (31–32). The woman is characterized here as prowling and ultimately successful and powerful against the narrator, who is characterized as vulnerable, without any sediments of courage. (C) is a tempting choice, but the woman is portrayed more as a foe that the narrator must use a shield against, not specifically as a leader.

314. (E) The narrator opens the passage by contextualizing the woman's strangely captivating expression of sadness. She explains that we all play "a game" (12) of concealing "life" (11) with customary "marks of reticence" (7). This woman, however, does not play along. The narrator silently pleads, "Ah, but my poor, unfortunate woman, do play the game—do, for all our sakes, conceal it!" (11–12). The second paragraph details the narrator's repeated attempts at staying focused on her own "mark of reticence" (7) (reading the *Times*) and her compulsion to creep "over the paper's rim" (20) due to the woman's audible and obvious expressions of sadness. The final paragraph reveals that all hope is "denied" (32); the woman has "pierced through" (30) the newspaper shield and dampened any "sediments of courage" (31) that remained. (C) is somewhat true, but she wishes the *Times* offered better protection ("my shield") (31), not comfort, and this hope falls under the purview of (E), which is a summary of the narrator's hope as portrayed in the entire passage. Though it is implied she does not wish to interact with any passengers, her primary wish in the passage is for the woman to play the game (A).

315. (D) The narrator has made several attempts to arm herself against the woman's exposed unhappy expression. In the final lines, the narrator uses a **simile** (see question 313) to reveal what little courage she has left to fight the woman's attempts at interacting. The woman gazes into her eyes as if "damping" any "sediments of courage" (31) that remain. The woman appears to be successful: "Her twitch alone denied all hope, discounted all illusion" (32–33). The twitch, along with the other physical movements and sounds emanating from the woman (see question 308) and making it difficult for the narrator to avoid looking at her, denies all hope for the narrator. The passage ends on a note of surrender, capitulation.

Chapter 3: Pre-20th-Century Poetry

Passage 31. Anne Bradstreet, "The Author to Her Book"

316. **(E)** The poem's title clarifies the figurative comparison made in the poem. Throughout the entire poem, the speaker addresses her own book as "Thou," "thee," and "thy" in the **extended metaphor** that compares her book to her child. Her book, not an actual child, was "halting to th' press to trudge" (5).

317. **(C)** The "friends" (3) who "snatcht" (3) the book have exposed it to public view before the speaker was prepared to share it. She describes her book as "ill-form'd" (1) and "in rags" (5). The "errors" (6) are presented for the press to "judge" (6). At the book's "return" (7), her "blushing was not small" (7) because she was upset, embarrassed, ashamed, and angry that her "rambling brat . . . unfit for light" (8–9) was on display. While the book is described as having flaws ("errors"), the flaws do not cause the blushing as much as the speaker's lack of confidence in the work she wrote with her "feeble brain" (1).

318. **(C)** The speaker confesses, "I washed thy face, but more defects I saw,/And rubbing off a spot, still made a flaw./ I stretcht thy joints to make thee even feet,/ Yet still thou run'st more hobbling than is meet" (13–16). It is ironic that in her attempts to amend the book, she actually makes it worse. (A) is true but does not express the irony of her attempts to improve the book actually having the opposite effect.

319. **(D)** The speaker tells her book, "In better dress to trim thee was my mind,/ But nought save home-spun cloth, i' th' house I find" (17–18). She would have trimmed the book in better clothes (edited, improved it), but all she had in the house was mediocre home-made cloth, which would not be acceptable to her or worthy of her book. In this comparison, the speaker expresses her belief that she lacks the proper tools and skills to create the book she expects from herself.

320. **(E)** The speaker implies that her book is unfinished/unedited (A) when she describes it as "snatcht" from her side when it was only dressed in "rags" (5). She eventually sends it "out of door" (24) after giving up on amending it, indicating it was unfinished. The book was disseminated prematurely (B) because it was "snatcht . . . by friends, less wise than true,/ Who abroad exposed [the book] to public view" (3–4). She goes on to describe the numerous "errors" (6) in the book that make it fallible (C) and how she tried and tried to "amend" (12) its "blemishes" (12) by rubbing, washing, and stretching it. Regardless of all these attempts, though, "more defects [she] saw" (13), making the book irreparable (D). There are no details that imply the content of the book is polemical (controversially argumentative) (E).

321. **(C)** The speaker's **tone** is self-deprecating (undervaluing oneself) because she has little confidence in her writing. She is mortified that her book would be "exposed to public view . . . in rags" (4–5). She is concerned that "all may judge" (6) her for a piece of writing she does not have confidence in. She admits that even with revision (rubbing, washing, and stretching), the "more defects [she] saw" (13) and the revision itself "still made a flaw" (14). Even though she does compare the book to her offspring, her tone is not nurturing (B) because she speaks about the book/child with harsh diction like "rambling brat" (8), "unfit for light" (9), and "irksome" (10). She is also more con-cerned about what others will think of her because of her sloppy book/child; she is not as concerned for the actual book/child. The subject of the poem is the author and her relationship with and attitude toward her book, and she is not vengeful (D) or acerbic (bitter) (E) toward it because she tries to improve it. The poem is composed of **heroic couplets** (rhyming pairs of lines in iambic pentameter), making the tone less severe and harsh, certainly not academic (A).

322. (C) The speaker laments that the book was prematurely "snatcht" and "exposed to public view" and taken "to th' press to trudge" (3–5). She then tells her book, "In critics' hands, beware thou dost not come,/ And take thy way where yet thou are not known" (20–21). The speaker is deeply concerned about how critics view her work, and this worry is so intense as to make her actually unproductive, making (A) and (B) incorrect. Though perhaps unhealthy, this relationship may not be unconventional. Regardless, the poem does not suggest that it is normal or abnormal (D). (E) is too extremely negative.

323. (C) The poem's primary device is the **extended metaphor** that compares the speaker's unfinished, "ill form'd" (1) work to a child dressed "in rags" (5) With this comparison, the speaker communicates both her shame and lack of pride in her work and her "affection" (11) for it, which makes her want to protect it from those (the press, critics) who "may judge" (6) its flaws. The industry may be seen as harsh in its judgment, but this is not the main focus of the speaker's address (B). The **heroic couplets** and rhythmic beat certainly create a playful **tone**, but the poem is not about the trials of parenting (D). The comparison of her book to a child might be morbid considering she casts it "out of door" (24), but the comparison is a metaphor, not a **simile** (E).

324. (D) Like a fastidious (careful, picky) artist would view her painting with a critical eye (D), the speaker also views her book as not good enough to be published and read. She rubs, washes, and stretches (13–15) the book in an attempt to lessen the errors, but only creates more. She is embarrassed that her book has been "snatcht" from her prematurely and "exposed to public view . . . in rags" (3–5). Though she does use the **extended, implied metaphor** (see question 323) of a child to talk about her relationship with her book, the relationship cannot be described as nurturing (B) because she speaks about the book/child with harsh diction like "rambling brat" (8), "unfit for light" (9), and "irksome" (10). Teach-ers (A), bosses (C), and directors (E) serve in supervisory roles, but the speaker implies, through the metaphor, that she is not merely disappointed in her pupil or subordinate; rather, she sees the flaws in her book as flaws in herself. She takes the criticism more person-ally than a teacher, boss, or director would. The book, like a child, is a part of her.

325. (A) Though she is disappointed in her unrevised writing, the poem conveys a lot more emotion than mere dislike (B). Through the **metaphor**, the speaker shows how a writer views her work as part of herself, that she has "affection" (11) for it and an innate drive to improve and take care of it. Though the poem does suggest a work can always undergo more and more revision and still not be perfect, this is not the overall purpose of the poem (C). The harsh critics are referred to, but they are not the focus of the poem (D). The hardships of motherhood (E) are implied only tangentially through the discussion of the poem's main topic, the artist's relationship with her work.

326. **(C)** The speaker is fine with her work leaving so long as it does not fall into "critics' hands" (20) and only roams "'mongst vulgars" (19) who would not be as discerning as the critics and so won't notice its flaws (A). The speaker has already attempted to improve the work ("I washed thy face, but more defects I saw") but lacks the "home-spun cloth" (18) to "trim" (17) the book in "better dress" (17), so she resorts to casting it "out of door" (B, D). She instructs the book to only "take thy way where yet thou are not known" (21), so that its flaws cannot be attributed to her, not because she hopes the "vulgars" (19) will be more generous with their critiques. The speaker tells the book to say its mother cast it out because she was poor, suggesting that she sends it out (publishes it) possibly because she needs the income (E).

Passage 32. Emily Dickinson, "Success is counted sweetest . . ."

327. **(E)** The speaker says lines 3–4 ("To comprehend a nectar/ Requires sorest need") to provide an image that supports the claim in the first sentence: "Success is counted sweetest/ By those who ne'er succeed" (1–2). In this context, "comprehend" means to truly know something. People who do not attain success *truly know* what success is, just as one must be in need of a nectar to truly know what it is. (B), (C), and (D) are all definitions of the word "comprehend," but in the context of the poem (E) makes the most sense.

328. **(C)** The phrase "purple host" (5) refers to those who are victorious, "Who took the flag to-day" (6). The speaker says "Not one" (5) of the victorious "Can tell the definition,/ So clear, of victory,/ As he defeated, dying" (7–9)—making I incorrect. The defeated hear "The distant strains of triumph/ Break agonized and clear" (11–12)—III. "The subject of the poem is that "Success is counted sweetest/ By those who ne'er succeed" (1–2)—II.

329. **(D)** Lines 5–6 say, "Not one of all the purple host/ Who took the flag today," indicating that the purple host are those who won, who were victorious, who "took the flag" (6). In this context, purple is associated with victory.

330. **(C)** The sounds of victory are "distant strains" (11) and "agonized" (12) because the defeated are far (figuratively and literally) from the sounds of triumph that surround the victorious. When one is defeated and dying, the sounds of victory are agonizing because they are in such stark contrast to their own experience of defeat, and they are a painful reminder of the loss. The other answer choices make assumptions that are not directly supported by the text.

331. **(A)** The poem primarily contrasts the victorious ("purple host" (5)) to "those who ne'er succeed" (2). The comparison (a **simile**) is made clear with the word "As" (9). To paraphrase, the speaker says not one of the victorious can tell the definition of victory as clearly <u>as</u> those who are defeated and dying. There is no evidence to suggest that the victory was not earned (B). Collaboration is not mentioned in the poem (C). Soreness and sweetness (D) do appear to be contrasting concepts; however, in the poem, those who are sore due to their defeat are also those for whom "Success is counted sweetest" (1).

332. **(C)** The first sentence (1–2) of the poem is an example of a **maxim**, a self-evident truth, a proverb or wise saying. The other two sentences of the poem provide images (the nectar and the winning army) that illustrate the maxim. The opening statement is not stated as a hypothesis (A) or a theory (D) that the speaker is proposing (B) for consideration or research; on the contrary, she is posing the statement as a known truth, which she elucidates with images.

333. (D) The speaker opens the poem with a **maxim**, (a wise saying or proverb), which can also be described as an adage. The **tone** of the poem is similar to the tone of an adage—which offers a piece of thought-provoking wisdom. (B) and (C) assume that the speaker is lecturing to the reader when she is actually providing her own insightful observation about life. She is not envious of those who have achieved success (E). (A) is a tempting choice, as the defeated do experience sorrow; however, the poem as a whole includes this sorrow to share the larger maxim, making (D) the better answer.

334. (D) The poem's main point **(theme)** is communicated in the first two lines, "Success is counted sweetest/ By those who ne'er succeed" (1–2). The other two sentences offer more images to elucidate the same idea—the nectar is understood only by those who are in *need* of it, and the sounds of triumph are clearest to the defeated.

Passage 33. Jayadeva, Excerpt from *Gita Govinda*

335. (A) The first verse serves as the poem's **overture**, the introductory part or prologue. An introductory speaker (who is not the speaker for the remaining verses) sets up the scene by introducing Radha, her love-interest Krishna, and the maiden who will sing the remaining verses.

336. (A) The **appositives** in lines 1–5 provide epithets for Radha and Krishna. An appositive is a noun or noun phrase that further describes a noun nearby. For example, the appositive after "Beautiful Radha" is "jasmine-bosomed Radha" (1), which is also an **epithet**, any word or phrase applied to a person or thing to describe an actual or attributed quality.

337. (E) The **simile** in line 25 serves to highlight the commanding powers of spring when the speaker compares the dazzles from the blossoms to "Kama's sceptre, whom all the world obeys" (25). Since everyone obeys Kama's sceptre, the simile makes us see how commanding spring's influence and bounty is, which almost justifies Krishna's infidelity—he has succumbed to spring's influence. The flowers are not compared to a person (D) but to a sceptre.

338. (A) The poem is rife with sensory **imagery** that portray the setting as ripe for amorous behavior, presenting Krishna's attention to dancers (and not Radha) as understandable. The wind "brings fragrance on its wing" (7), the "bees hum and the Koil flutes her love" (9), "every branch . . . Droops downward with a hundred blooms" (14–15), and even the "spears on all the boughs . . . Seem ready darts to pierce the hearts of wandering youths and maids" (20–21). The descriptions allow us to smell, hear, and see the setting as one that would compel Krishna to spend time with "damsels many a one" (40).

339. (A) One can understand the meaning of the phrase based on both its vocabulary and the context. Throughout the poem, the maiden sings of the feelings of love that arise with the arrival of spring. A "goblet" (27) is a drinking vessel; "nectar" (27) means both the sweet secretions of flowers and, classically, the life-giving drink of the gods. This particular nectar "steeps" (27) human souls in "languor" (27), languor being a feeling of laziness or tenderness. Therefore, the best answer is (A), the drunken feeling of love.

340. (B) The **repetition** of "alone" (41) as the closing word of many verses emphasizes the contrast between what Krishna is doing (cavorting with other "damsels" (40)) and what he is avoiding (being alone during such an amorous season). The repetition of "alone" (41) also explains and justifies Krishna's behavior by reminding Radha that "'tis sad to be alone" (11), "'tis hard to be alone" (17). In the third repetition of alone, the speaker asks, "who can live alone" (23), revealing her own understanding of Krishna's many romances. In the fourth and fifth mentions of "alone" (41), the speaker insists, "none will live alone" (29) and "he will not live alone" (41), removing any judgment toward those who seek the romantic company of multiple damsels. This is a state Radha must accept, according to the maiden. The poem does not specify that Radha is Krishna's wife or that the other damsels are additional wives (D). The speaker of most of the poem is Radha's maiden, and the word "alone" (41) does not contrast the maiden to Radha (E).

341. (B) The poem's **refrain** serves to reinforce the speaker's empathy for Krishna by repeating the idea that "'tis sad to be alone" (11) at the end of each verse (11, 17, 23, 29, 35, and 41), which serves as a type of justification for Krishna's flirting and cavorting with many women. The maiden who sings the song seems to have understanding and empathy for Krishna, given the difficulty of being alone during sensual springtime. While this refrain may make Radha feel lonelier (C) since she is, in fact, alone while Krishna is enjoying himself with other women, the refrain first and foremost shows the maiden's understanding of Krishna's actions, which she is describing throughout the song.

342. (B) Although "fair" (3), Krishna is "all-forgetful" (3) and consumed with "earthly love's false fire" (3–4). As Radha "waited by the wood" (2), Krishna indulges his desires with "the dancers." This would suggest that Krishna's attitude toward Radha is best described as (B), oblivious and unaware. There is no evidence to suggest Krishna is ambivalent (torn between conflicting emotions) toward Radha. He is not avoiding her intentionally or preferring the dancers, because of his complicated relationship with Radha.

343. (A) In line 34, "thine other self, thine Own" refers to Krishna. The maiden sings this song to Radha. "Thine" is an archaic form of "your" and signifies familiarity. Therefore, the "you" here is Radha. Her "other self" then refers to her beloved Krishna, who dances with "those dancers" (34).

344. (E) While the maiden may be incriminating (D) Krishna by singing of his trysts with other women besides Radha, the best answer is (E), apologetic. In celebrating the fertility and bounty of springtime, she would seem to be justifying Krishna's behavior. He, too, is following the natural order of things. Furthermore, the repetition (**refrain**) at the end of each verse that such an environment makes it impossible to be alone would seem to further excuse Krishna's transgressions (see question 341).

345. (D) We can infer that all these names are the names of types of foliage. "Kroona" (18) is paired with the word "flowers" (18), indicating that it is a type of flower (18). "Ketuk" (20) is paired with the word "glades" (20), indicating that it is perhaps a type of grass or plant (20). "Keshra" (24) is described as yellow and with blossoms (24), "Pâtal" (26) is paired with the word "buds" and feeds sleepy bees (26), and "Mogras" (31) are "silken" and exude a "perfume fine and faint" (31–32).

346. (A) The song does not imply that Krishna is at all faithful. He is certainly promiscuous (B); he flirts, dances, and cavorts with many others besides Radha. He must be dexterous (agile, skillful) in that he dances, presumably well, with the dancers in the jungle (C). He also must have some charm (D) to captivate these other lovers. He indulges (E) in his desires by cavorting with other damsels.

347. (B) The overall **mood** is exultant. As the first verse reveals, Radha waits with her maidens while her lover Krishna is elsewhere, cavorting with other women. Radha may very well be jealous (A), but it is one of her maidens who sings the song that follows. Rather than being admonishing (scolding) (D), the maiden may be attempting to make excuses for Krishna's unfaithfulness through the song when she repeats at the end of each verse that it is "sad" or "hard" to be "alone" (11, 17). But this is hardly conciliatory (appeasing, soothing) for Radha (E). The maiden describes at great length the fertility and bounty of nature in springtime; the mood is celebratory, even ecstatic. Therefore, the best answer is (B), exultant.

Passage 34. Andrew Marvell, "To His Coy Mistress"

348. (D) The first stanza contains verbs like "had," "would," and "should" to indicate conditional and hypothetical situations and actions. The speaker says that he *would* be more than willing to be patient and wait centuries for his addressee to "show her heart" (18) if they actually had that much time (1). The specific actions are not regrettable (undesirable, unwelcome) because he would welcome them if time permitted (A).

349. (E) Throughout the first stanza, the speaker is making the point to his addressee that if there were plenty of time, it would be fine to delay their physical expressions of love. Since they do not, however, actually have a "hundred years" (13), he implies that the addressee's modesty ("coyness" (2) hesitance, prudery, shyness) is a crime.

350. (C) The speaker's references help illustrate what more time would allow them to do. They create a vivid impression that he hopes will persuade his addressee that he would happily delay their physical love if circumstances were different. Citing examples like finding rubies by the Ganges, relaxing by the Huber, and enjoying each other until the conversion of the Jews dramatizes how long, in fact, he would wait. The point of this stanza is to compliment her and make her think she would be worth waiting an eternity for if they had an eternity.

351. (E) The speaker compares his love to vegetables, which slowly grow to be strong over time. He uses this **metaphor** to emphasize how strong and long-lasting his love is for his addressee.

352. (B) Throughout the first stanza, the speaker attempts to convince his addressee that he would be happy for them to slowly express their love and passion over centuries if they had that amount of time. Beginning in line 12, he details how much time he would spend adoring her specific features (eyes, forehead, each breast) and then apportions "thirty thousand to the rest;/ An age at least to every part" (16–17), which we can take to mean her remaining physical characteristics and other qualities.

353. (B) The **imagery** in the first stanza is lustful because the speaker wants his addressee to be convinced of his enduring passion for her—I. He conjures up images of endless infatuation and amorousness. He will adore her forehead, eyes, and breasts for hundreds and thousands of years. The second stanza, however, contains much darker imagery—I—as the speaker now tries to emphasize the fact that they do not have thousands of years to wait; rather, they will soon face death ("marble vault") and faded beauty (25, 26). Their love will turn to "dust" (29) and "ashes" (30)—I. The **tone** does change from the first to the second stanza, but it is not quite a change from arrogance to desperation because the tone of the second stanza is not quite desperate— II; rather, the speaker here seems more grave (serious, intense) than in the first stanza because the imagery is of death and decay. The compliments are noticeably missing from the second stanza, especially in contrast to the incessant flattery provided in the first—III.

354. (C) The phrase essentially means "time flies" (22). In fact, the speaker characterizes time as actually flying in his "winged" (22) chariot. The phrase is also in the context of emphasizing how little time we have on earth, how we must "seize the day" and indulge in our desires.

355. (E) The focus of the second stanza is on the bleak reality of time passing, the inevitability of death, and the temporal nature of youth and beauty. In this context, the speaker qualifies his addressee's "honour" (29) with the word "quaint" (29) (old-fashioned) to emphasize the inappropriateness of her "coyness" (2) and choice to delay physical expressions of passion, given the circumstances (time is flying). According to the speaker, her modesty and prudence are not admirable; rather, this "honour" is merely charming and ultimately out of place, unsuited to the reality of their situation. Since the speaker describes chastity as appropriate if time were not an issue, it is too extreme to say he disdains it (B).

356. (B) By comparing his addressee's youth to "morning dew" (34) on her skin, the speaker is emphasizing the ephemeral (short-lived) nature of her youth and beauty. Morning dew exists only in the morning; it does not even last more than a few hours. Dew also connotes freshness, virginity, and purity, which also describe the youthful and modest addressee. The speaker is trying to make the point that, as dew lasts only a short time, so will the addressee's youth.

357. (C) Time is not easily defeated because its winged chariot is "hurrying near" (22), and they must strive to act like "am'rous birds of prey" (38) to avoid languishing in Time's "slow-chapp'd power" (40). They will need "to roll all [their] strength" (41) to simply make Time "run," since they "cannot make our sun/ Stand still" (45–46).

358. (A) The speaker concludes his argument with a proposition in the final stanza. The repetition of "Now" (37) creates a sense of urgency to act, as does the **figurative comparison** to "am'rous birds of prey" (38) who must "devour" (39) time. The **tone** is confident ("Let us roll our strength") (41), not desperate (E). There are references to the present time in other stanzas (19, 21), so those references do not make the final stanza distinct (D). All the stanzas include significant figurative language, not just the final stanza (C).

359. (D) The speaker's argument follows the structure of a syllogism, which is a logical argument consisting of a major premise ("Had we" (1) enough time, he would happily love her slowly and strongly—stanza one), minor premise ("But . . ." (21) that is not the case as Time is "hurrying near" (22)—stanza two) and conclusion ("Now therefore . . ." (33)

they must "at once our time devour" (39)—stanza three). The speaker's argument does not culminate in a logical, airtight conclusion, but he mimics the syllogism's style, perhaps to create the appearance and sound of a foolproof argument.

Passage 35. Christina Rossetti, "Winter: My Secret"

360. (C) The question "I tell my secret?" (1) and the subsequent response "No indeed, not I" (1) imply that someone has just asked the speaker if she will tell her secret or stated that she would. The question "You would not peck?" (21) and the subsequent response "I thank you . . . " (21) also imply that someone has just told the speaker they would not "peck." Both these questions are written as restatements and responses to another's comment or question. (A), (B), and (D) describe common reasons for asking questions, but overlook the context and **tone** of the quoted questions from the poem. (E) is incorrect because the speaker is not at all communicating hope when she asks, "I tell my secret?" (1).

361. (A) In line 6, the speaker responds to the addressee's plea to hear her secret with, " . . . well/ Only, my secret's mine, and I won't tell" (5–6). The **tone** here is certainly juvenile. The reader can imagine a child responding this way, and the rhyme helps to communicate that sing-song, teasing tone. (B–E) are too extreme for the lighthearted, coy teasing and playful rhyme evident in the poem.

362. (A) The first stanza introduces a dilemma, a predicament, that the poem will continue to develop. The quandary is that the implied addressee would like to know the speaker's secret, but she is purposely withholding it while also suggesting she may reveal it under certain circumstances. The specific setting is never actually developed in the poem, though seasons are alluded to. The references to the seasons and environment are **symbolic** and not descriptions of the actual setting (B). While a reader may view the speaker's teasing about her secret as indicative of her enjoying the power she wields over her addressee, that characterization would develop over the course of the poem (not in the first stanza alone) (D). While the first stanza does introduce the relationship between the speaker and her addressee (he wants something she is not readily supplying), it does not *develop* the relationship (E). The first stanza does have a regular **rhyme scheme**, but its particular rhyme scheme is not carried into the remaining stanzas. Also, the rhyme scheme is a device and stylistic choice that helps to communicate the purpose; the rhyme would not be the purpose itself (B).

363. (D) The wraps and clothing are **symbolic** of the speaker's protection from those who incessantly inquire after her secret (symbolically). The word "wraps" (12) does rhyme with "taps" in line 13 (A), but the question asks about the main purpose of the word.

364. (C) As described in question 363, the weather (draughts, winds) is **symbolic** of overzealous people who are interested in the speaker's secret. The **figurative language** in these lines serves to dramatize the winds/people as threatening. The speaker has to wear "wraps" (12) to protect herself (her secret), but the winds would still manage to nip and clip through them if she were to open her door.

365. (D) Capricious means fickle and unpredictable. The speaker does not "trust/ March . . . Nor April with its rainbow-crowned brief showers,/ Nor even May, whose flowers" (23–26) may wither with just one frost. The weather in spring is too inconstant to be trustworthy. Winter, however, is consistently overbearing with its biting, nipping, clipping, and whistling. Summer is consistently warm, languid, and still. (A), (B), and (E) more closely describe winter and summer. There are no details to support that spring is never-ending (C).

366. (D) The winter winds are **symbolic** of the meddlers who intrude and pester the speaker about her secret. She wears "wraps" (12) and shuts her door because this burdensome meddling makes her want to protect her secret even more. She even asserts to her addressee in the first stanza that he's "too curious" (4), which is keeping her from revealing her secret to him. In spring, however, she considers it more, but there are still instances of rain and frost, so there are still those who pry into her private matters and pester her. Summer, however, may be ideal, since the "warm wind is neither still nor loud" (32). The meddlers have retreated and quieted down. Under these conditions, when people stop harassing her or expressing incessant interest, "Perhaps [her] secret [she] may say,/ Or [he] may guess" (33–34).

367. (D) The speaker mentions her addressee is "Too curious" (4) (too eager, overzealous) as part of her response to his implied request to hear her secret, making (A) correct. She also teases the addressee by suggesting that "perhaps there's none" (7), making (B) correct. The **figurative descriptions** of the nipping and clipping and whistling winter draughts make the speaker depend on her "wraps" (12) to protect her from the pecking of "every wind that blows" (20). The descriptions of the wind serve as believable descriptions of intrusive secret-seekers, and she wears her "wraps" (12) and does not "ope to everyone that taps" (13) to impede their intrusion. All of these details provide sufficient support to interpret the speaker wants to protect her privacy and so does not reveal her secret, making (C) correct. The playful **tone** and word choice indicate the speaker enjoys the exclusivity of her secret and the power she wields over her addressee who has asked to know it. This reveling is most evident in lines 7–9: "Or, after all, perhaps there's none:/ Suppose there is no secret after all,/ But only just my fun," making (E) correct. The poem does not, however, include details that imply the speaker is worried specifically that the secret will hurt others, making (D) the only incorrect reason (and the correct answer).

368. (A) The juvenile **tone** of line 6 (see question 361), the playful rhyming, teasing, and coyness all reveal the speaker's attitude toward her addressee is one of mild amusement. She is enjoying dangling her secret just out of reach, of leading her addressee to think she will reveal it and then suddenly switching to suggesting there might actually not be a secret at all. She is playing a game and literally says that perhaps this is "just my fun" (9). While (D) is true—the speaker does appear willing to engage with the addressee—this is not as specific as (A) in describing her *main* attitude.

369. (E) The weather **symbolizes** those who are intrusive and overzealously interested in the speaker's secret. Like wind, they bite and nip, they whistle and bound and astound her. They are relentless, so she must stay indoors and not "ope" (13) her house's door "to everyone who taps" (13). Here, the speaker reveals the parallel between the nipping wind that comes "whistling through [her] halls" (14) and the people who knock on her door. The winds are symbolic of prying people, making the house and her clothing ("wraps and all") (17) symbolic of her refuge and protection. Since the clothing is her protection from the weather/ those who pry, then her nose, in line 19, is symbolic of her secret, which must not be shown (18) to the "Russian snows" (19) (i.e., the intrusive meddlers).

370. (E) The speaker's playful **tone** (see questions 361 and 368) and **figurative descriptions** of her reasoning for not revealing her secret (see questions 365 and 369) do not attack or anger her addressee (A, C). She even acknowledges his kindness in asserting that he would not "peck" (20) like the bothersome winds (other prying people) when she says, "I thank you for good will,/ Believe" (21–22). Once she has gone through the seasons, articulating why winter and spring preclude her from wanting to share her secret, she arrives at summer, with its calm and warm stillness, and the addressee (if he is indeed paying attention) would recognize that this season (or the time when the overzealous meddlers quiet down) may lead to her disclosure. Her words, "Perhaps my secret I may say,/ Or you may guess" (33–34) would lead the speaker to feel hopeful. The words "Perhaps" and "may" make (D) not likely.

371. (D) The final stanza consists of one **periodic sentence**, a sentence in which the independent clause appears only after a series of dependent clauses. The speaker continues the sense of anticipation that has built up in the first two stanzas by further delaying the declaration ("my secret I may say") (33) when she places it after a series of dependent clauses. There are **end rhymes**, but the beat is not exactly steady, and the poem does not end with an actual revelation, just a suggestion of one to come ("perhaps") (33), making (A) incorrect. The word "perhaps" (33) is repeated, but the speaker does not communicate antipathy (dislike, aversion) (see questions 361 and 368), making (B) incorrect. The adjectives "warm," "still," "loud" (32), and "drowsy" (29) are hardly uncommon (C), and the independent clause ("I may say" (33)) is not in passive voice. The subject performs the verb, which makes it active voice, so (E) is incorrect.

Passage 36. Phyllis Wheatley, "An Hymn to the Evening"

372. (E) The verbs in lines 1–6 are "forsook," "shook," "Exhales, "purl," "renew," and "floats." All these verbs evoke our senses. We hear the thunder shake the plains, we smell the incense that is exhaled, and we see and hear the music float and the notes renewed. These verbs are not literal (D) because the spring does not actually breathe. They are not repetitive (C); each one is unique. They are not mundane or ordinary (B); the thunder is not commonly referred to as *forsaking* the eastern main and birds are not ordinarily described as *renewing* their notes when spring arrives. The verbs are not passive (A), as "sun" (1) precedes the verb "forsook" (1), so the subject performs the action, making the construction active.

373. (B) The speaker describes her environment with exclamations like "Majestic grandeur!" (3) and "what beauteous dies are spread!" (7). The exclamations reveal that her awe is not restrained (held back), making (A) incorrect. Her respect for the environment's grandeur is shown through her detailed descriptions and **figurative language**. She respects the power of the thunder, as it "shook the heav'nly plain" (2). She alludes to the wind as "zephyr's wing" (3) and notes that the "blooming spring" (4) carries not merely a scent but "incense" (3–4). The speaker's enthusiasm is not meant to reveal fear of her environment (C); rather, her amazement is generated from appreciating its power and grandeur. Her enthusiasm is not exactly whimsical (D) because her word choice clearly indicates reverence.

374. (B) Lines 1–8 focus on describing the environment with unrestrained awe, **figurative language** (see question 373), and sensory **imagery** (see question 372), but line 9 introduces people ("our") into the poem. Lines 10–18 continue to focus on people ("our" and "my"), those who "wake more heav'nly," and whose "drowsy eyes" are sealed. Lines 9–18 do not contain consternation (worry, dismay), making (C) incorrect. The entire poem is subjective, not just lines 9–18, making (A) incorrect. The sun is setting in the west, creating a deep red in the sky, in line 8, so line 9 does not signal a change from daybreak to nightfall (D). Also, the entire poem contains dramatic description and not tempered praise (E).

375. (A) If read as prose, the sentence in lines 8–10 says, "But the west glories in the deepest red: so may our breasts with ev'ry virtue glow, the living temples of our God below!" The speaker says that the glorious beauty and grandeur in "all the heav'ns" (7) that glows deep red may also live inside "our breasts" (9), in our hearts and souls, when we are virtuous. The virtue is what would make our breasts glow because it would mean we are living temples of God here on earth; that is, we follow in his footsteps and develop his virtue within ourselves. The temples in this case are **metaphorical**, not actual churches erected in honor of God (B). "Secular" describes something having no religious or spiritual basis, and the "living temples" (10) are certainly a religious reference (D).

376. (E) The slumbers will be placid (calm, peaceful, restorative) only if we are virtuous and live by God's example. (See question 375.) We are "living temples" (10) when "our breasts" (9) glow with virtue. Our "weary mind" (13) will be soothed because we are living virtuously, which will allow us to "wake more heav'nly, more refin'd" (14), and "guarded from the snares of sin" (16). The drawn curtains do not *cause* the slumbers to be placid; they signal that night has arrived (B). The scepter does seal the speaker's eyes, but the scepter does not *cause* the slumbers to be placid (D). The slumbers are likely quiet (A), but the question asks *why* the slumbers are placid/quiet.

377. (C) The placid slumbers "sooth each weary mind" (13), which means that sleep can mollify (B). Placid slumbers allow us to "wake more heav'nly, more refin'd . . . More pure, more guarded" (14–16), making (A), (D), and (E) correct. Sleep will seal our eyes and our song will cease; we will be soothed and placid, not stimulated and awake, making (C) the only incorrect choice (and the correct answer).

378. (E) She is grateful for the restorative powers of night and sleep and views the scepter with respect (see question 379).

379. (B) The speaker portrays God as regulating day and night, since he "draws the sable curtains of the night" (12), which signals nightfall—I. God inspires his devotees to live virtuously, to glow with the deepest red of the heavenly skies (7–10)—II. The speaker's reverential **tone** and word choice indicate respect, appreciation, and awe for God; she does not feel intimidated, forced, or coerced. A reader may be tempted to choose III if misreading the reference to "Night's leaden sceptre" (17) (see questions 378 and 382).

380. (C) A **couplet** is two lines of verse, usually in the same meter and joined by rhyme, that form a unit or complete thought. The final couplet is in lines 17–18. The **alliteration** is evident in the words "scepter," "seals," "cease," and "song." The lines describe the soporific power of night, and the repeated "s" sound complements this description with its smooth and sleepy sound.

381. (E) "Night's leaden scepter seals [the speaker's] drowsy eyes" (17) which makes her song cease until the morning. The context reveals that Aurora must be a reference (in this case, an **allusion** to a Roman goddess) to the morning.

382. (E) The **alliteration** (see question 380) and **personification** of Night in the final two lines contribute to their soothing and sleepy tone. The speaker seeks to evoke a feeling of slumber here. Repose means lying down and resting. Readers focusing on the "leaden sceptre" (17) may be tempted to pick (A), (B), or (D), but the scepter is not threatening or intimidating; rather, the speaker is grateful for the restorative and protective powers of night and sleep, which are **symbolized** by the scepter.

383. (A) Considering the reliance on exclamations and the reverential **tone**, the poem does not make repeated use of understatement to convey its message. There are three instances of exclamation, which show the speaker's unabashed reverence for her environment (see questions 372–373). The poem consists of multiple **couplets** (see question 380) that contain essential ideas. There are numerous instances of **metaphor**: living temples, sable curtains, leaden scepter. Sensory **imagery** permeates the entire poem (see question 372).

Passage 37. Walt Whitman, "O Captain! My Captain!"

384. (A) Line 4 is part of the independent clause that begins in line 3: "The port is near, the bells I hear, the people all exulting,/ While follow eyes the steady keel, the vessel grim and daring." The clause "While follow eyes the steady keel" (4) refers to the noun in the preceding clause, which is "the people" (3) who are exulting. They are exulting (rejoicing, triumphant) because "the prize . . . is won" (2), and they are not yet aware of the captain's demise. "Formidable" describes a noun that inspires awe or intimidation due to its grandeur, size, strength, power. The observers are exulting while in awe of the ship's formidable features that helped assure victory. It has been victorious, and the people are exulting, not lamenting the damage done to the vessel (E) or worrying about it pulling into the port (C). The boat is returning, not departing (B). The speaker is not looking at the vessel; he is looking at "the people all exulting" (3) and describing their eyes (D).

385. (A) The speaker tells his heart to not leave "the little spot" (6) where the Captain lies "cold and dead" (8). In other words, he is telling himself (his heart) never to forget the moment and place of his captain's death. (E) is a close answer, but the command to his heart ("O heart! heart! heart!") (5) indicates that he is telling himself not to forget, hoping and pleading with his heart to always remember, while (E) indicates that he is certain he will not forget.

386. (C) The "bells," "flag," "bugle," "wreaths" (9–11), and crowds in the third stanza serve dual purposes in that they describe the celebration the crowd planned to have upon the captain and the ship's victorious return and also happen to describe a funeral, which is appropriate since the victory parade must turn into a funeral upon receipt of the news that the captain has died.

387. (D) The captain has not arrived home safely; he has died on the ship. Both the captain and the ship achieved their goals ("the victor ship") (20) (B), ended their heroic journeys ("its voyage closed and done") (19) (A), and are being celebrated (E). They are both **metaphorical**; the captain is actually Abraham Lincoln, and the ship is the United States of America, but without this background knowledge, a reader can interpret the metaphorical potential of the "captain" and his "ship" (see question 392) (C).

388. (A) In the fifth stanza, the speaker no longer refers to the captain in exclamatory sentences like "O Captain!" (13). Instead, his references are calm statements like "My Captain does not answer . . . " (17). The change in **tone** mirrors the speaker's acceptance of the captain's state. In the third segment of the poem (stanza 5), the speaker is no longer in denial but now acknowledges that the captain "does not answer . . . does not feel my arm . . . has no pulse or will" (17–18). The speaker no longer begs the captain to "rise up" (9) because he knows the captain has "[f]allen cold and dead" (24).

389. (B) The first segment (stanza 1) shows the speaker discovering his captain has died (. . . on the deck my Captain lies,/ Fallen cold and dead") (7–8). The second segment (stanza 3) shows the speaker is in a state of denial about the death ("It is some dream . . .") (15). The third segment (stanza 5) shows the speaker accepting the reality of his captain's death (" . . . he has no pulse nor will") (18) (see question 388).

390. (B) The **tone** of the poem is not uplifting (A); rather, it is elegiac, which means it has the tone of an **elegy** (a funeral song, a mournful poem). The word "captain" is not part of a rhyme at any point in the poem (D), the message is not that mourning can be musical (C), and the speaker is not exulting (rejoicing) in their victory (E); rather, he is clearly mourning.

391. (C) In the final stanza, the speaker exhorts the shores to "Exult" (21) and the bells to "ring" (21). This noisy celebration is in contrast to the speaker's "silent tread" (22) due to his mourning the loss of the captain.

392. (A) In the poem, the captain and the ship are **metaphors** for a political leader and his citizens who have just achieved an important victory. The actual leader is Abraham Lincoln, the victory is the Civil War, and the country is the United States of America. Though this would be difficult to determine with just the poem at hand, the references to the captain and the ship are likely metaphors for some kind of leader and group since the diction in the poem carries multiple levels of meaning. The speaker refers to the captain as his "father" (13) in the final stanza, which also provides a clue to the metaphorical value ascribed to the captain. (B) is the literal interpretation of the captain, not symbolic. There is no evidence to suggest the captain was controversial (C); rather, the poem portrays him as victorious, loved by the speaker and the people, who are exulting in the victory he was instrumental in achieving. (D) is incorrect because the captain is a person and would symbolize another person as opposed to an entire industry. The references to the captain more logically apply to a person than the naval industry.

393. (E) See question 390. The poem is most similar to an **elegy**, a mournful poem or funeral song.

394. (E) The speaker has moved from denial in the third stanza ("It is some dream") (15) to acceptance of the captain's death in the final stanza. He acknowledges that the captain "does not answer" and "has no pulse or will" (17–18). Once he realizes this, he is in a mournful state as he decides to remain on "the spot [his] Captain lies" (23) while the shores and bells ring and "Exult" (21).

Passage 38. William Wordsworth, "The world is too much with us"

395. (E) By "Getting and spending" (2) and not preserving or appreciating the natural world, "we lay waste our powers" (2) and "have given our hearts away" (4)—our powers have been forsaken, squandered on material pleasures instead of the sea and wind. While (D) is accurate—the speaker suggests we should have used our powers differently—choice E captures the speaker's **tone** of remorse and regret. While our powers do appear minimal compared with the impressive powers of nature, the poem as a whole does not see human potential to observe and appreciate nature as a grossly exaggerated power. The poem's message about these powers is that we had them and regrettably wasted them, making (A) not as accurate as (E).

396. (B) The phrase "Getting and spending" (2) is modifying the subject that appears immediately following the modifier, which is "we." The context of the poem helps clarify that the speaker would be referring to "we" as the subject of "getting and spending" (2) because he goes on to assert that "we" also "give our hearts away" (4) and "are out of tune" (8) with the beauty and powerful sounds of nature.

397. (D) The phrase "sordid boon" (4) is an **oxymoron** because two opposite words are placed together for effect. "Sordid" (4) describes something that is disgusting and distasteful, and a "boon" (4) is a benefit, a gift, an advantage. The surrounding context explains that the speaker disapproves of people's negligence of the natural world and preference for modern technological and industrial advancement. He claims, "we lay waste our powers:/ Little we see in nature that is ours" (2–3). He is saying that people do not bother to appreciate what they can see in nature because they prefer material pleasures. They ignore the "Sea that bares her bosom to the moon;/ The Winds that will be howling at all hours" (5–6). We have lost the "tune" (8), the ability to harmonize with nature and to hear the winds howling.

398. (C) Line 5 contains **personification** of the sea, who "bares her bosom to the moon," and lines 6–7 contain a **simile** that describes the winds as "howling at all hours/ And are up-gathered now *like* sleeping flowers." Both devices reveal the majestic beauty and power of nature. The next line clarifies the speaker's intention with these descriptions. He bemoans, "For this, for everything, we are out of tune;/ It moves us not" (8–9). Clearly, the speaker laments that the sea and winds' actions and qualities are going unappreciated by "us" (9) (E) may be a tempting choice considering the winds "will be howling at all hours" (6), but the context reveals that this howling is currently "up-turned now like sleeping flowers" (7), which is hardly intimidating.

399. (E) Lines 5–6 contain **figurative language** that emphasizes the majestic beauty and power of nature, specifically the sea and winds. Lines 13–14 return to this motif by using figurative language (in the form of **allusions** to Greek gods Proteus and Triton) to illustrate that same inspiring beauty that would make the speaker "less forlorn" (12).

400. (D) The first eight lines follow an *abbaabba* **rhyme scheme** and the next six lines follow a *cdcdcd* rhyme scheme,—dividing the poem into an **octave** and a **sestet**—creating a **Petrarchan sonnet** where the octave generally presents a problem or dilemma that is explored (sometimes solved) in the sestet. The structure helps illustrate that the speaker sees our squandering our powers on material pleasures as a lamentable problem. The sestet does not provide a solution, but it does describe a hypothetical alternative had we not wasted our powers, if we were Pagans simply experiencing "Proteus coming from the sea" (13) or hearing "Triton blow his wreathed horn" (14). The poem does have a consistent rhyme scheme that expresses a sense of loss and regret, but the closing **couplet** does not alleviate this loss (E), because the speaker is describing what he wishes he could have done. The problem is not exacerbated (worsened) in the sestet (C), because the speaker is pondering the benefits of having been a Pagan so that he would not be in this current predicament. A Pagan who worships non-Christian gods would be enjoying Triton's horn and seeing a mighty Proteus "coming from the sea" (13).

401. (C) The title and first line of the poem contain its **theme**: "The world is too much with us." Here, "world" does not necessarily mean the environment of the earth and sky because we know that the speaker appreciates the "Sea" (5) and the "Winds" (6). He capitalizes them to emphasize their importance. So, if the "world" is "too much with us" in a negative way, then "world" must refer to the industrialized, modernized, technologically advanced world in which we are "Getting and spending . . . lay[ing] waste our powers" (2). The speaker characterizes this advancement as negative and destructive; it is a "sordid boon!" (4), a benefit/advantage that is dirty, grubby, foul.

402. (A) Paganism is a religion other than one of the main world religions, specifically a non-Christian or pre-Christian religion. The **metaphor** compares Paganism ("a creed outworn" (10)) to a mother's breast and a Pagan to a baby being "suckled" (10) by that creed/breast. The Pagan, with his belief in other gods, would be enjoying the "sight of Proteus coming from the sea" (13). The comparison implies that the outworn creed of Paganism provides comfort and nourishment to a Pagan, the way a mother's breast offers the same to a baby. Essentially, the speaker compares himself to a baby who is in dire need of such consolation. He would even go so far as to be a Pagan to get it.

403. (C) When the speaker says he would "rather" (9) be a Pagan so that he might glimpse Greek gods like Proteus and Triton, which would make him "less forlorn [sad]" (12), he is expressing his desire. This is not an actual solution (E). He says only that he would rather be a Pagan, not that he will actually convert to this "creed outworn" (10). While his references to the Greek gods do demonstrate his knowledge (D), that is not the primary intention of the **allusions**. (B) is also a vague and incomplete answer. He does not express optimism (A) through these **allusions** because he is not actually going to become a Pagan and escape his forlorn state.

404. (D) The **theme** of the poem as a whole is best described by (D) because the speaker first laments that people ("we") have allowed the "world" to be "too much with us" (1), meaning we are consumed by "Getting and spending" (2) and we "lay waste our powers . . ." (2). The "world" that is "too much with us" (1) is the material world that we have created with our technological and industrial "powers" (2), which the speaker describes as a "waste" (2) because these powers only encourage "Getting and spending" (2) and distract us from noticing Nature's "Sea" and "Winds" (5–6). This is tragic because "we have given our hearts away" (4). The "boon" (4) (benefit) of progress is "sordid" (4) (dirty, grimy) because we have paid a big price for such advancement. (A), while expressed in the poem, is an incomplete description of the overall theme. (B) is a slightly crude and extreme way to describe the theme. Choice B is not wrong but is general and somewhat vague compared to (D). (C) and (E) are expressed in the second stanza but do not describe the poem as a whole.

Passage 39. Countee Cullen, "I Have a Rendezvous with Life"

405. (B) If a reader is not familiar with the word "Ere" (3), the context establishes that it must mean "before." In lines 1–4, for example, it makes sense that the speaker hopes his rendezvous will come *before* his "youth has sped" (3) and *before* "voices sweet grow dumb" (4) due to the loss of hearing in old age.

406. (E) Lines 1–4 contain references to time and create anticipation ("In days I hope will come,/ Ere youth has sped . . .") (2–3)—I, II. Lines 5–6 contain a reference to time with the word "When" (6) and a sense of anticipation for spring's arrival—I, II. Lines 1–4 express the poem's **theme** that the speaker is eager to seize the day before he is too old to appreciate life's joy, a theme that is reinforced in lines 5–6—III.

407. (D) Lines 5–6 say, "I have a rendezvous with Life,/ When Spring's first herald hums." The word "herald" means the "first sign, signal, or indication." The signs of spring that would hum are insects and birds buzzing and singing, signaling spring's arrival. (C) is incorrect because vexing means annoying and bothersome. The speaker anticipates spring and its pleasures; he is not bothered by them.

408. (C) "Some would cry" (7) that it is better to sleep through life in order to avoid its obstacles ("the road, the wind and rain" (9)) than to "heed the calling deep" (10), the calling to seize the day and experience life. The speaker indicates that it is the challenges in life that inhibit "some" (7), not their introversion (E) or their obliviousness to what life has to offer (A). They may be aware of life's positive experiences, but they are too fearful of its challenges to experience them.

409. (B) The "some" (7) who "cry it's better" (7) to avoid "the road, the wind and rain" (9) by sleeping are fearful of life's challenges. In line 12, the speaker admits, "Yet fear I deeply, too, . . ." (12), drawing a parallel between the fear of "some" (7) and his own fear that he may miss out on life's pleasures. "Fearsome" means "causing fear" not feeling fear, so (A) is incorrect.

410. (E) In line 9, the speaker describes "some" as fearful of "the road, the wind and rain." In lines 11–14, the speaker compares and contrasts that fear to his own. He says, "Though wet nor blow nor space I fear," and the "wet," "blow," and "space" are parallel to the fears attributed to "some." The word "wet" corresponds to the "rain," the word "blow" corresponds to "wind," and "space" must correspond to "the road." The speaker says he does not fear the same things as "some," but he does share the emotion of fear because he fears that "Death should meet and claim me ere/ I keep Life's rendezvous" (13–14). The speaker does fear an untimely death, but the reference to "space" precedes mention of this fear so it cannot be *in response* to this fear (C). The "wet" and "blow" refer to potential stormy obstacles, but "space" does not (A).

411. (D) The speaker does say that he is motivated to seize life before his "youth has sped" (3), before his mind and hearing weaken, but he does not intend to convey "Life" (1) as consisting strictly of youthful pleasures (E). In lines 9–11, he recognizes the harsher aspects and experiences in life ("the road, wind and rain") but decides that they are not to be feared but to be braved in order to benefit from the more positive experiences. He keeps life's rendezvous, which means he fully engages with all that life has to offer so as not to miss out on the pleasures that can be fully enjoyed in youth.

412. (E) The context of the poem as a whole indicates that the "rendezvous" (1) the speaker keeps and has is a meeting. He encounters the experiences of life, whenever and however they come, which also implies that the "rendezvous" (1) does not have to be planned ahead, making (A) correct. He engages (C) with life's positive and negative experiences. He does not interview (E) life, which would imply a sort of power structure with the speaker assessing life's merits.

413. (B) The speaker is greatly influenced by the concept of "Life" (1) and all that it embodies, the good and bad. The possibility of an untimely death also greatly motivates the speaker to "keep Life's rendezvous" (14). While they are formidable (inspire respect, impressively powerful), the speaker doesn't aim to decrease their strength (C). While the capitalization does indicate **personification**, the speaker does not *fear* life, and he views Death as inevitable and unpredictable, *not* as calculating and threatening (C). The word "intimidating" indicates that Life and Death make the speaker do something unpalatable, against his will, but enjoying the pleasures of spring is not intended to appear unpalatable (A). Life and Death are not Greek gods (D).

414. (E) The speaker's main concern is the need to make the most of life before his "youth has sped, and strength of mind,/ Ere voices sweet grow dumb" (3–4). The speaker does allude to youth's temporality, but he does not intend to say that dying young is guaranteed (A). He wants to seize the day ("keep Life's rendezvous") (14) "Lest Death should meet and claim" (13) him before he has had a chance to fully experience life. The drawbacks of aging are mentioned, as is the crippling fear of "some" (7), but neither is the main concern (B, D).

Passage 40. Kahlil Gibran, "Defeat"

415. (E) The poem as a whole is written as an **apostrophe**; the speaker addresses defeat, which is an experience and feeling, as if it were a person who can answer back ("Defeat" is also capitalized as if it were the name of a person), even though it cannot. The speaker does not include details or develop a story about his own defeat (A, B), and the poem is not explicitly written as a letter (C) or speech.

416. (D) In the second stanza, the speaker refers to "Defeat" as "my self-knowledge" (4) because it is through "Defeat" that the speaker *knows* he is "young and swift of foot" (5). He has found joy in "being shunned and scorned" (8). "Defeat" is valuable in that it helps the speaker avoid feeling "trapped by withering laurels" (6). Laurels, or awards and recognition from others, would preclude the speaker from appreciating "the joy of being shunned and scorned" (8).

417. (C) In the third stanza, the speaker lists the messages he has "read" (10) in Defeat's "eyes" (10). The messages are listed using **parallel structures**: "to be . . . is to" is repeated in lines 11–13, emphasizing the cohesion of the messages. Ordinarily desired qualities, like being "enthroned," "understood," and "grasped" (11–13), are viewed by Defeat as associated with negative qualities, like being "enslaved," "leveled down," and "consumed" (11–14). The speaker does not appear overwhelmed (B) by these messages since he opens the stanza by addressing Defeat as "my shining sword and shield" (9). He clearly uses Defeat's wisdom as guidance (A). The parallel structures create a predictable and steady sound, not a discordant one (D). The parallel structures do contribute to a steadier beat and rhythm (E), but the primary purpose is best described by (C).

418. (A) The **metaphor** of the "sword and shield" (9) is meant to emphasize "Defeat's" (9) emboldening powers. The speaker calls defeat his sword and shield and then explains what he has learned from "Defeat" (9)—namely, that success enslaves people and keeps them "leveled down" (12). The context does not indicate that "Defeat" (9) is a sword and shield because it is brave or valiant (E), but rather that the knowledge "Defeat" (9) has given the speaker has emboldened him the way a sword and shield would. It has made him feel strong, powerful, and protected.

419. (C) In the third stanza, the speaker describes different types of success ("enthroning," being "understood," and "grasped") (11–13) and how they result not in happiness but in enslavement. In other words, success is overrated.

420. (D) Lines 13–14 say, "And to be grasped is but to reach one's fullness/ and <u>like</u> a ripe fruit to fall and be consumed." In this **simile**, the speaker compares "one," or a person who is "understood" (12) and "grasped" (13), to a ripe fruit that falls and gets consumed.

421. (A) The speaker characterizes "Defeat" as distinct (B) ("none but you") (17), useful (C) ("You are dearer to me than a thousand triumphs . . ." (2), "In your eyes I have read . . ." (10)), brave (D) ("my deathless courage") (21), and bold (E) ("my bold companion") (15). He does not, however, think "Defeat" is enviable (A), which would indicate that he is jealous of Defeat when he actually sees Defeat as his guide and mentor.

422. (D) The poem's **refrain** is found in lines 1, 4, 9, 15, and 21 and enhances the poem's ode-like quality because, through the repetition of the same phrase, a lyrical, chorus-like sound is created, which coincides with the style of the **ode**. The poem is also ode-like because the speaker addresses and praises "Defeat."

423. (E) The speaker's address to "Defeat" as his "deathless courage" (21) shows that with "Defeat" comes the ability to face obstacles and danger. He can "laugh . . . with the storm" (22) and bury what "dies within us" (23) (like failures). Even though "Defeat's" courage is "deathless" (21), meaning it is without death, the speaker does not use the phrase to mean that "Defeat" is immortal (D) but rather that "Defeat" provides him with an almost invincible courage, "with a will" (24) that allows him to "be dangerous" (25). Though the reference to graves and death might be dark, the message is hardly dark (A).

424. (B) The speaker sees "Defeat" primarily as his valued companion in that "Defeat" teaches him ("Through you I know that I am . . ." (5)) about himself and the world. Though "Defeat" is also his "companion" (15), their relationship is not primarily one of friendship (A), which implies an equal balance of give and take. The poem indicates that the speaker learns from and receives guidance from "Defeat" and does not necessarily offer the same in return.

425. (A) The **mood** that is established by the end of the poem is one of confidence: the speaker and "Defeat" will "laugh together" (22) in a storm, "dig graves for all that die within" (23) them, and "stand in the sun with a will" (24). These lines indicate that the speaker, with "Defeat" next to him, can face anything with confidence.

Chapter 4: 20th-Century/Contemporary Poetry

Passage 41. Pamela Hart, "Kevlar Poem"

426. (C) The poem introduces "[t]he woman who invented Kevlar" (1) by naming what she liked to do with her father (I)—go on walks in the woods, walks that clearly had an influence on her scientific curiosity and experimentation. On those walks, she named trees and plants, "collected leaves to press and save" (4–5), and "sketched the sky and fern beds" (6). These actions, along with her later "spinning" (18), concocting, and weaving, indicate a lifelong sense of curiosity (II). The poem does not suggest or indicate that the "woman who invented Kevlar" (1) was motivated to change the world through her inventions (III). She is portrayed more as someone who was curious as a child and continued to experiment with materials, contemplating chemicals, due to a love for "the messy/ astonishing world" (15–16).

427. (A) The woman who invented Kevlar is described with almost supernatural descriptions as she experiments, *spinning* strands of a polymer *brew* to *concoct* something synthetic and strong. She appears almost magical and extraordinary as she alters materials for new purposes. Although this image evokes witchcraft, it is too extreme to say that it explicitly compares her experimentation to witchcraft (B). These lines do contain an abundance of **alliteration** (*c*ontemplated *ch*emicals, *s*pinning *s*trands, *s*ynthetic and *s*trong), but choice D does not address the significance of the **figurative language** that portrays the woman as almost magical in her power to create.

428. (B) Lines 11–13 treat Kevlar **symbolically** by suggesting that this incredibly protective material could not figuratively protect against "heart disease/ or her sadness" (12–13). There are no details to suggest that inventing Kevlar is the woman's only significant accomplishment (E), although it is a defining one.

429. (D) The poem introduces "[t]he woman who invented Kevlar" (1) by naming what she liked to do with her father: go on walks in the woods, walks that clearly had an influence on her scientific curiosity and experimentation. (See question 426.) Her father's death is suggested to be influential since it is mentioned, along with her sadness, in lines 11–13, which precedes the description of her experimenting with the "messy/ astonishing world" (15–16). The woman "loves" (15) this world and is portrayed as in her element when she's "spinning strands" (18) and "contemplating chemicals" (17), immersed in the environment like she was when, as a child, she explored with her father. Her invention is portrayed as resulting from her love for experimenting and her scientific curiosity, not from a motivation to change the world, making III incorrect.

430. (A) It is certainly ironic that the woman who invented Kevlar, an indestructible material that, when woven into "the panel of a bulletproof vest" (24), saves lives, cannot use the material to protect her father from his death or herself from the pain of losing him. While the line literally says that Kevlar couldn't save her father, its purpose is not to present the invention as unsatisfying (E): she does not invent Kevlar as a way to save her father, who died "when she was ten" (11). Even though "there was no Kevlar for heart disease/ or her sadness" (12–13), the woman does not set out to invent a strong material because her father died of heart disease (C). While the father's death has potentially influenced the woman to continue experimenting with materials from the "messy/ astonishing world" (15–16), it is unclear whether his death motivates her to intentionally invent Kevlar specifically.

431. (C) The poem begins with a description of the woman on walks with her father during her childhood. We see her name, press, collect, and sketch the natural world with the same curiosity and astonishment we see later in the poem when, as an adult, she "contemplates chemicals" (17) and brews and concocts. The father is mentioned again when it is explained that he dies. This detail comes midway through the poem, separating the woman's childhood from her adult experiences. Clearly his death has had an influence on her continued passion for experimenting. While the woman and her father shared a bond, the poem is not about fathers and daughters bonding in general (E). Kevlar is treated **metaphorically** when it is suggested that it did not protect the woman from the pain of losing her father, but the poem as a whole does not engage with this metaphor (D). We do learn about the woman who invented Kevlar, but the poem's style is not purely biographical since it does not detail many events in her life, and the details shared are poetic, not simply informative (B). The only invention mentioned is Kevlar, so this poem is not about important inventions in general (A).

432. (E) While the father plays an influential role in the woman's life, it is not clear that he served as her scientific mentor. Her childhood walks with him were a time for her to observe the natural world (name, collect, press, save, and sketch what she finds), but there is no evidence to suggest that her father guided her scientific curiosity. The text suggests he served as a loving companion, not a scientific mentor.

433. (C) Before line 12, the woman who invented Kevlar is described in almost repertorial fashion: the speaker lists her actions on walks with her father as a child ("naming . . . collected . . . press and save . . . sketched" (3–6)). She also "liked to sew" (9). At line 11, when we learn that her father died when she was ten, the **tone** shifts. The remaining lines present the woman, now an adult, using almost mystical language. She "contemplated chemicals/ whole *spinning* strands/ of a polymer *brew*/ to *concoct*/ something synthetic and strong . . ." (17–21). She takes materials and transforms them through experimentation. We see her in her element, loving the "messy/ astonishing world" (15–16). Although it is sad that the woman lost her father, whom she loved, the focus is not on mourning his loss (A, B), and the speaker does not pity the woman (E). On the contrary, the speaker's use of mystical descriptive language shows a reverential attitude toward the woman. Choice D is incorrect because the speaker's reverence is expressed in the mystical/spiritual descriptions of the woman experimenting. The poem does not shift *from* a reverential tone *to* a spiritual one.

Passage 42. David Hernandez, "I Made a Door"

434. (C) The first ten lines describe the speaker as actively constructing a door (took, sawed, painted, nailed, drove, forbade) to impede raccoons and possums from intruding. Line 11, however, introduces a shift from confidence to self-doubt. The rest of the poem describes how "Failure enters the mind" (20) and destroys his confidence. While the other choices describe how the poem develops, they are not describing significant shifts. Line 15 does not transition to a solution (D). Line 9 does introduce the reason why the speaker has created a door, but this is not as notable a shift as choice C. Line 6 simply adds detail to the speaker's process of making the door and does not create a shift in the speaker's perspective, **tone**, or emotions (A).

435. (E) Lines 12–14 describe the sounds that first indicate to the speaker that his "homespun" (7) door has not worked. Through the sensory **imagery** (the "paws on wood, the tapping claws, slow rasp of fur scraping") (13–14), we can hear and visualize the intruders' actions just as the speaker does (I). The intruders' actions are revealed through a list in a sentence fragment. Like the speaker, we hear separate sounds, each one another clue that something is not right with the door (II). Now that we hear and visualize the intruding visitors, we have the context to understand the speaker's sense of failure, which "burrows into [his] marrow" (21) the way the rodents burrow through his "homespun contraption" (7) (III).

436. (D) The questions help demonstrate the shift in the speaker's confidence (A) about the door he has made. In the first ten lines, he uses an **active voice** to describe his building process (took, sawed, painted, nailed, drove, forbade), emphasizing his control over the situation and ability to solve the problem. The questions develop his sense of self-doubt (B), contrasting his earlier confidence (C), and also demonstrating how "[f]ailure enters [his] mind . . . burrows into" (20–21) him (E).

437. (E) Serotonin is a neurotransmitter most commonly associated with happiness. The speaker's serotonin is amended when he discovers that his "homespun contraption" (7) has not worked. The rodents do not cause happiness the way serotonin does; in fact, their trespassing through the door decreases the speaker's serotonin, making (E) the only incorrect option (and the correct answer). The speaker makes the door, but by the end, he discovers the door has made him. Both the speaker and the door take on the role of shaping and creating something/one else (D). The sounds of the rodents' trespassing (tapping, clawing, scraping) parallel the intruding thoughts of self-doubt ("One thought./ Two. How did he slip in?") (17–18). The speaker attributes his success with the rodents' actions (C). The speaker interprets the rodents' trespassing through his "homespun" (7) door as an indication that he has failed, which he sees as an indication that he is "flawed from head to heels" (22), like his door (A, B).

438. (C) See question 437. Serotonin is a neurotransmitter most commonly associated with happiness. The speaker describes failure as entering his mind, burrowing into his marrow, calling him "flawed from head to heels . . . mistakes down to [his] cells" (22–23), which "amends" (24) his serotonin, or changes his happy, confident mood.

439. (D) Speaking, entering, and burrowing are animate actions attributed to failure (a device known as **personification**), which endows failure with power over the speaker (I) This power is also emphasized through **active voice**: "Failure . . . Says I am flawed from head to heels" (20–22). Failure is the subject that labels the speaker, which emphasizes the command the speaker feels his failure has on his sense of self-worth (III). While the actions of burrowing and entering evoke the intruders from lines 12–14, the parallel descriptions do not serve to show that the speaker is not at fault. The speaker blames himself for the failure of his "homespun contraption" (7), allowing his mistakes to "alter [his] serotonin" (24) (II).

440. (A) The poem's title, "I Made a Door," is twisted in the last line of the poem in which the door is now the subject and the speaker is the object (a passive construction, not active [E] or a fragment [D]). The poem's stanzas develop the speaker's humbling experience of discovering that his creation was unsuccessful, which leads to a dramatic change in his self-perception.

His failure to make a functioning door "amends" (24) his serotonin, convinces him he's "all mistakes down to [his] cells" (23). By the close of the poem, he realizes that the experience he is recounting is not about what he has made, but about how his efforts and failure have exerted a control over his sense of self-worth, a more significant outcome than losing control over the project (C). While the speaker does play on the word "made" (26) in the final line, the effect is more significant than lightening a mood (B).

441. (C) The speaker describes his experience making a door that does not work to block raccoons and possums, and his significant feeling of failure that results. In describing the experience, the speaker uses **personification** to give the door power to make him ("The door made me.") (26), to define him as a failure ("all mistakes") (23). Failure, too, is given **metaphorical** treatment as it "finds a fissure" (20) and "burrows" (21) into his marrow. The final line, "The door made me" (26), is certainly not literal. The door is a metaphor for the speaker's investment in allowing himself to be defined by his accomplishments and mistakes. The poem does not contain **heroic couplets** (A). While there are a number of simple action verbs (painted, made, took, says), there are more precise and figurative ones as well (forbade, tapping, scraping, burrows) (B). The speaker's struggle is not only with the natural world (raccoons and possums) but more with his own sense of his self-worth (D). The poem includes sensory **imagery** that allows us to picture the "homespun contraption" (7), to hear the animals scraping and tapping, and to imagine failure burrowing into the speaker's marrow, making (E) a likely answer. However, the sensory imagery develops the metaphorical treatment of the door and failure, making (C) the best choice.

Passage 43. David Tomas Martinez, "To the Young"

442. (A) The title of the poem clearly indicates it is addressed "To the Young," and the poem itself reveals that these specific young people (the black male, Chicano rockers, and white boys) are "split/ down the middle . . . a new,/ mixed breed" (6–18). The young people described in the poem have affinities for music and fashion that are stereotypically associated with ethnic and racial groups different from their own, defying the stereotypes of how black, Chicano, or white males dress.

443. (E) The black male mentioned in line 1 is "dressed like a punk rock/ hipster club kid" (1–3) (A). He is "like [his] mother" (8) in that he tries to "make a new,/ mixed breed" (17–18)—adopting the fashion and musical tastes stereotypically associated with a different racial group; his mother tries, by actually sewing together different styles, to make a new one (B, C). Like the teddy bears that the black male ties to his sneakers to achieve the desired look, the blond cornrows help the "white boys" (23) adopt their desired look (D). The speaker addresses the young but does not give any indication that he is similar to or different from them (E); rather, he acknowledges and respects their experiences.

444. (E) The poem implies that a black male generally does not dress like a "punk rock/ hipster club kid" (2–3). By doing so, the black male addressed in line 1 makes "a new,/ mixed breed" (17–18), a **metaphor** for mixing one look with another to represent a distinct sense of identity (I). The mixed breed refers to both his identity and the reinvented clothes that the mother reimagines by sewing them at the crotch (III). The joining of two separate looks/identities/sensibilities is enhanced by the intentional line breaks in "split/ down the middle" (6–7) and "new,/ mixed breed" (17–18). In both examples, a connected phrase is separated by splitting it down the middle so it is on two separate lines (II).

445. (E) Chicano rockers moshing and wearing leather jackets and skinhead pins are like the black male who invents "a new,/ mixed breed" (17–18) by adopting the style and tastes of a different group. Chicanos are not commonly expected to wear skinhead pins; the ones mentioned here also create "a new,/ mixed breed" (17–18) by adopting the look commonly associated with another group. The "white boys" (23) attempting to create the look of "corn/ rows" (25–26) using gel are another example that develops the image of the specific "young people" the poem addresses.

446. (B) The poem opens with a direct address to a "black male (1)." When the speaker says, "Only Chicano rockers . . . and white boys" (19–23) can "know/ your pain" (27–28), he is still addressing the black male from the first line. Chicano rockers and white boys, like the black male who "dressed/ like a punk rock/ hipster club kid" (1–3), are also "split/ down the middle . . ." (6–7). The pain refers to the splitting and forging of a new identity, a "mixed breed" (18). The poem implies that a black male is not ordinarily dressed like a punk rock club kid and that a Chicano does not normally mosh wearing a skinhead pin. Adopting the look and tastes of a different social group, in which you are a minority, involves some emotional pain as the members struggle to both stand out and fit in and get their look just right. The pain goes beyond the physical discomfort felt by the mother (A) and getting their clothes and accessories just right (C), making (B) the best choice.

447. (D) The speaker addresses a black male who is "dressed/ like a punk rock/ hipster club kid" (1–3), who is "split/ down the middle . . ." (6–7)—"Only Chicano rockers . . . and white boys" (19–23) who are similarly split "can know/ [his] pain . . . And their mothers,/ too" (27–30). While the speaker acknowledges the pain the young people experience, he does not exactly pity them (A), which would be condescending. The poem does not dwell on their pain or describe it as some big sacrifice or elaborate on the negative consequences of their chosen style. Instead, the speaker uses concrete details (such as teddy bears on shoes, pink acid-washed jeans, skinhead pins, dark-blond cornrows) to describe their choice of style, honoring it. He notices them, acknowledges their pain, respects their experience enough to capture it through insightful comparisons (mother and son, black male and white males) and apt **metaphor** ("mixed breed" (18)). The speaker doesn't praise (E) these young people so much as he recognizes their situation as unique, difficult, and worthy of attention.

448. (E) See question 447. The poem is not meant to be amusing (A), most evident with the acknowledgment that there is an element of pain involved in being "split/ down the middle" (6–7) and "making a new,/ mixed breed" (17–18) not only with clothes but also with one's identity and sense of self. While the poem does acknowledge how mothers share their sons' pain—and one mother even supports their desires to achieve a certain look—the poem's focus is not to celebrate mothers and sons in general (C). The poem does philosophi-cally consider the experience of identity representation, but it is more specific to describe it as a recognition of a plight experienced by specific young people since the poem is addressed to them and only addresses identity in terms of how they attempt to create theirs, making choice E better than (D).

449. (C) The black male is "split/ down the middle,/ Like [his] mother" (6–8) who helps him "make a new,/ mixed breed" (17–18) by spending three hours reinventing his jeans. She is clearly supportive of his efforts to adopt a very distinct look. Only Chicanos and white boys who similarly desire the looks of groups they are typically not associated with can know his pain, "[a]nd their mothers,/ too" (29–30). The mothers' pain could involve concern or hesitation about their children's choices, but the reference to the mother sewing her son's desired outfit strongly suggests the relationship is supportive.

Passage 44. Dorothy Parker, "Men I Am Not Married To"

450. (D) The speaker repeats the phrase "No matter" (1–3) and references streets (lanes, byways, alley, path, avenue, for example) to emphasize that these men she is not married to appear everywhere, no matter where she goes. Just as she sees the men again and again, we see the same phrases or words again and again.

451. (E) The men she is not married to "seem to spring up everywhere" (7)—the **figurative expression** "spring up" (7) conjures an image of men appearing suddenly and spontaneously wherever the speaker looks. In the context of the poem, the speaker is repeating that she is not available to men. Their springing up everywhere reminds her again and again that these are all the men she will never be married to. The men do seem to "spring up" (7) everywhere without warning, making their appearances unpredictable (D), but the reference does not comment on the nature of men and how unpredictable they are in general.

452. (D) After nine lines of repeating that everywhere there are men she is not married to, the speaker offers her perspective. She stares at them "in wonderment" (10), declaring that she would likely be married to one of these men were it not "for heaven's grace' (11)." Since she thanks heaven that she is not married to any of these men, it follows that she does not want to marry them (B, C).

453. (E) The phrase set off by dashes ("but only fair") (15) emphasizes that the speaker thinks these men are *only fair*—just ordinary, nothing special, "no species rare" (13). There is not enough evidence to suggest she is seeking to marry someone exceptional, since she could be currently married (D, C). It is too extreme to say she dislikes the men because they are homely (B), and we do not know whether any of them are actually single (A).

454. (C) After stating that she will not marry these men who are "only fair" (15), the speaker adds that "worry silvers not their hair" (21). The men she is not married to do not feel worried that she is not interested in them, so worry will not cause their hair to gray. It is too extreme to say that the men do not care about women in general (A). Choice B is incorrect because the men do not actually stay young because of lack of worry; they will still age. The reference to silver hair is a **figurative** way to say that they are not troubled by the speaker's unavailability.

455. (D) The speaker observes that the men are not worried that she is not married to them, but lines 23–24 are distinct because the speaker reveals how she feels about their indifference. She notices it and finds it "curious" (23), or strange. This is a subtle change from the confident, emphatic declarations in the previous lines, which hints at her possible disappointment that her disinterest is matched by theirs. Her conviction to not marry them is not undermined (E)—she simply finds it "curious" (23) that the men do not seem concerned.

456. (E) In lines 21–24, the speaker mentions that the men are not worried that she is not married to them and that she finds this a little curious. In the poem's conclusion, she makes sure to address their disinterest by asserting that if the men had "the chance" (26) to share their life with her, they would "doubtlessly tender [her] the air" (28) or take the chance, offer their hand in marriage, give her their attention.

457. (E) The consistent **rhyming pattern** and **repetition** create a playful, light, singsong **tone**. The reference to the men's mothers and their impressions that their sons are magnificent like bears and "ace-high" (19) conjures a funny image. The poem has a playful tone, but it is not exactly silly (B) or jolly (D) since the poem coherently expresses the speaker's point of view.

Passage 45. Tracy K. Smith, "The Good Life"

458. (C) The speaker characterizes "some people" (1) as wistful when she compares their **tone** to those recalling "a mysterious lover/ Who went out to buy milk and never/ Came back" (2–4). For "some people" (1), money, like a mysterious lover, is desirable but hard to retain. They enjoy it while they have it and then wonder about it when it's gone. The word "mysterious" (2) suggests they don't understand what happens to their money, perhaps they aren't too careful with how they spend it. There is no evidence to indicate they are desperate (E) or suffering (D). Since they speak about it as if it were a lover, they are not indifferent (A). The lover is also part of a **simile**, so the poem does not suggest they are actually looking for love (B).

459. (D) The comparison helps communicate "some people['s]" (1) experience with money. For "some people" (1), money, like a mysterious lover, is desirable but hard to retain. They enjoy it while they have it, and then wonder about it when it's gone. The connection is valid, not ridiculous (A). Also, the poem does not have a comic **tone**, so it is not likely the comparison was *meant* to be comical. While some may think losing money is worse than losing a lover (E), the context of the comparison shows that "some people" (1) do not feel this way. While poverty is unjust (B), the poem's **figurative language** does not create a dark **mood**; the comparison in line 2 alone does not directly highlight the unjust nature of the wealth gap.

460. (B) The speaker is nostalgic (thinking fondly of the past) about the years when she lived only on "coffee and bread" (5) and was "[h]ungry all the time" (6). This deprivation made her desire and relish "the good life" she temporarily enjoyed on payday, when she could indulge in a satisfying meal of "chicken and red wine" (10). While living on coffee and bread does suggest she was poor (A), she still had a job and earned enough to enjoy "the good life" for at least a night or two. Living on coffee and bread as opposed to dining on chicken and red wine does allude to income inequality (D), but the question asks about the intention behind the phrase given the context of the poem. The "nostalgic" (4) and whimsical **tone** suggests the poem is not meant primarily as a comment on economic conditions (see question 459).

461. (B) In this comparison, the speaker is leaving a home where she survives on "coffee and bread . . . Hungry all the time" (5–6) and "walking to work on payday" (6) with the same urgency and need as "a woman journeying for water/ From a village without a well" (7–8). The village doesn't have a well for water, and the speaker's home did not have enough food to satisfy her hunger. There are no details to suggest she lives in a slum (A).

462. (E) "[S]ome people" (1) speak about money as if they do not fully understand it— how to hold on to it, where it goes, and why it's gone. They certainly would not be accustomed to having chicken and red wine every evening. In comparison, "everyone else" (9) who does indulge in such a way would appear fortunate. There is not enough detail about "everyone else" (9) to suggest they are showing off (C, D) or rude (A), or even particularly deserving of their satisfying meal (B). The way that "some people" (1) talk about money they have lost sparks "nostalgia" (4) for the speaker, so they do not seem resentful. They wouldn't see "everyone else" (9) in a negative light; they would be more likely to wonder at the "good life" others get to consistently enjoy.

463. (D) When the speaker hears "some people" (1) talk about money they no longer have, she observes a wistful **tone** (see question 460), which makes her "nostalgic" (4) for the years when she also lacked money. The reference to nostalgia indicates that she is currently not in this situation. Only in her past was money coveted (A) and scarce (E). The poem indicates the speaker worked for money, but the evidence does not indicate her money is necessarily well-earned (C).

464. (C) The speaker explicitly compares her younger self to a woman who lives in a village without a well and must journey for water. She is not directly comparing herself now to her younger self (E). She mentions "some people" (1) to indicate what sparks her nostalgia, not to serve as a direct comparison to herself (B).

465. (D) The speaker opens the poem by describing what sparks her nostalgia for a time when she was struggling financially. Listening to the way "some people" (1) wistfully talk about money that they once enjoyed but now have lost makes her reminisce. She reflects on the times when money seemed to disappear shortly after payday, leaving her with daily meals of coffee and bread after having splurged for a night or two on chicken and red wine. The poem is titled "The Good Life," likely a reference to the rare pleasure of indulging in the finer things on payday, which was maybe all the more special because it was so infrequent. While the poem describes spending and enjoying money when you have it, even though that means it will disappear like a mysterious lover, it is not written as an **ode** to luxurious pleasures (E). It is better characterized as a reminiscence.

466. (C) The poem is full of common, everyday words that combine to reveal subtle connections and help readers visualize a memory. Simple verbs like "lived," "hungry," and "walking" (5–6) help illustrate a time the speaker fondly recalls. The poem makes effective use of several comparisons (direct and indirect), not just a single extended one (D). The poem consists of one sentence broken into 10 lines, but the purpose of the lines is not to highlight the complexity of the speaker's desire for the finer things (E). The poem focuses more on her fond memory of the time when she fully indulged in the finer things for a night or two, even though it meant living simply on coffee and bread until the next payday.

Passage 46. Rabindranath Tagore, "The Home"

467. (B) The **simile** in line 2 compares the sun to a miser (scrupulous saver) to convey the disappearance of sunlight. The sun's light is compared to gold, and the sun holds on to its light (gold) as scrupulously as a miser (cheapskate) holds on to his money. (C) and (D) both say the simile contrasts two things when the purpose of a simile is to show similarities between two things, to compare them. While the simile does emphasize how dark it has become, (E) does not describe the simile's effect as well as (B).

468. (E) Line 3 contains an abundance of **alliteration**. Four words in this line start with the same letter/sound: "*d*aylight . . . *d*eeper . . . *d*eeper . . . *d*arkness" (3), which creates emphasis on the encroaching darkness.

469. (D) In context, the phrases "widowed land" (4) and "her arms" (13) are examples of **personification**. The land is given the human characteristic of being a widow, and the "darkened earth" (13) is given human characteristics with the phrase "surrounding with her arms" (13). In the first instance, the land is widowed because it has been harvested, presumably to nourish those who live there. In the second instance, the earth's "arms" (13) surround the homes, which reinforces the idea of the land as nourishing and nurturing.

470. (D) The second sentence of the poem differs from the first in that the description of the setting is further developed through auditory **imagery**—the silence coming from the "widowed land" (4) enhances the depletion the speaker sees in this scene. The sun is setting, so light is disappearing; the land has been reaped, so it too is vacant and silent. While the second stanza introduces silence into the poem, it still evokes movement by describing the daylight as sinking "deeper and deeper into the darkness" (3) (A). Both stanzas allude to the setting sun and approaching darkness (C, D). The first stanza, not the second, mentions the speaker's action of pacing (E). **Figurative comparisons** (B) help establish mood in both stanzas ("like a miser" (2) and "widowed land" (4)).

471. (D) The third stanza contains a contrast between sound and silence, describing the boy's voice as "shrill" (5) and the "track of his song" (6) as noticeable against the "hush of the evening" (6–7). There are no references to light (E) or day (A), only the "dark" (3, 6, 10, 13) and the "evening" (7). The boy's boyhood is not compared to manhood (C), and even though the boy and the sky are mentioned (B), it is the boy's noise that contrasts with the sky's hush.

472. (E) The fourth stanza describes the location of the boy's village home; it is "at the end of the waste land" (8), the "widowed" (4) and harvested land described earlier in the poem. His home, however, is not widowed or "wasted" (8) at all. On the contrary, it is "hidden among" (9) an abundance of life: "the banana and/ the slender areca palm, the cocoa-nut and the dark green/ jack-fruit trees" (9–11). All these specifics serve to emphasize the richness, fecundity, life, and comfort evoked by the boy's home and community, which is even more pronounced when contrasted with the desolate and depleted "waste land" (8).

473. (D) The fourth stanza provides rich visual **imagery** of the boy's village home. We can imagine its geographical location ("beyond the sugar-cane field, hidden among the shadows of . . .") (8–9), we can see the tall and slender trees loom over the home, we can feel the coolness of the shade created by the slender trees, and we even see the precise colors of those trees and smell their fruit. The preponderance of fruit trees and mentions of color provide a noticeable contrast to the "waste land" (8) beyond, the "widowed land" (4) nearby. While the home is remote (E), the amount of specific visual details emphasizing the contrast between the depletion of the "waste land" (8) and the rich life growing near the boy's home makes (D) the best choice.

474. (A) The speaker notices that the families are happy ("glad") (15) and their happiness does not know its own "value for the world" (16); in other words, happy families are unaware of how valuable their bliss is to the world (A). The earth is described as "darkened" (13), but there are no clear details that suggest the families light it up (B). The final sentence can be interpreted to mean that the speaker wishes he were a part of these families (C), but this is an inference and the question asks for a paraphrase. The earth opens "her arms" (13) around the glad families, but there are no details that suggest the earth's role is to protect them from a harsh environment (E). In fact, the families appear quite content with their "mothers' hearts" (14) and comforts of home.

475. (E) The speaker feels reassured upon seeing that there is life, joy, love, and comfort for others, beyond the waste land, among the shadows and darkened earth. The gladness of those "young lives" (15), blessed by "mothers' hearts" (14), has value for the world, according to the speaker, who characterizes himself as "lonely" (12). Ascribing value to the scene he observes means that he does not feel envious (B) or only mildly satisfied (C). The common comforts of the homes and love from mothers are not luxuries and do not create a sense of indulgence (D). The speaker is separate from those in the homes because he is a passerby, not because the homes are exclusive and excluding him (A).

476. (E) The poem is written in **free verse** (prose), not in rhyme. The speaker thoughtfully observes a scene and poetically describes his interpretation of what he sees: the way the sun hides its gold, how the darkness silences a reaped ("widowed" (4)) land, and how a boy's voice sounds like a song. The poem does not focus on the speaker himself (A, B), and while the stanzas do increase in length, they do not identify a dilemma or present it as increasingly complex (C). The poem is not formally divided into an **octave** (stanza with eight lines that typically presents a problem) and a **sestet** (six-line stanza that offers a solution) (D).

Passage 47. Sara Teasdale, "From the Woolworth Tower"

477. (D) The poem opens with the speaker and her companion entering the "brilliant and warm" (3) corridor of Woolworth Tower, "eager for greater beauty" (1). The descriptions of them as "[v]ivid with love" (1), seeking beauty, and exiting the dark night to enter a cozy and bright corridor convey a sense of promise for a positive experience. This sense changes to one of dread as they ride up the tower, overwhelmed by "angry/ Howls" (8–9) and "a terrible whirring" (14). The speaker's companion is referenced at the start and end ("I cling to you") (12) of the stanza (A), sensory adjectives are used throughout ("brilliant," "warm" (3), "swirling" (8), "whirring" (14)) (B), and the speaker anticipates the journey as the stanza opens ("eager for greater beauty") (1), and then anticipates its end as the stanza closes.

478. (B) The **simile** in lines 8–9 compares the air to "a hundred devils" (9) to communicate the intensity of its "swirling" (8) and "angry/ Howls" (8–9). The air is **personified** as angry, but "violent attacker" is too extreme of an interpretation that is not supported by the lines (A). The adjectives are not obscure (C), the comparison to "a hundred devils" (9) is not ironic (D), and the description of the air does not soften the threatening **tone** (E)—it contributes to it.

479. (B) The "terrible whirring" (14) that "deafens" (14) the speaker's ears refers to the loud mechanical sounds made by the elevator car as it shoots upward. Whirring refers to mechanical sounds or the sounds of a bird's wings steadily moving.

480. (D) Line 15, distinct from all others in that it makes up its own stanza, does not shift tense from the previous stanza, which is also written in the present ("we come . . . slides open . . . receives us . . . ") (2–5). The short elevator ride up the tower does not feel short to the speaker: she notices every sound, clings to her companion, and uses dark adjectives and **figurative comparisons** to describe the ascent (see question 478). The length of the first stanza reflects the dread she feels. The second stanza, however, needs just one line and four simple words to convey that the flight is over (B, C)—there are no harrowing sounds to describe, no clinging, and no sharp shooting upward. The separation of the line from the previous stanza (A) and its isolation in its own stanza (E) emphasize the difference between the relief and calm the speaker feels once the ride ends—especially in comparison to the anxiety she feels in the first and third stanzas and the reflective **mood** of the fourth stanza.

481. (C) The speaker's questions recall the opening of the poem, where she and her companion have eagerly entered the "brilliant and warm" (3) corridor seeking "greater beauty" (1) atop the tower. Now she wonders, "Why have we sought you?" (19), indicating that the "angry/ Howls" (8–9) and "terrible whirring" (14) from the previous stanza have caused her to question her choice. There is no indication that these questions are spoken aloud; they are more likely her thoughts, as is much of the poem (A, B). Choice E is too extreme and not supported by the text. Choice D belittles the speaker's fear of heights and the sensory overload she experiences.

482. (D) Eternity does not literally have an edge, so this phrase is meant **figuratively** to illustrate the feeling the speaker has atop the Woolworth Tower, looking down and beyond. The speaker's intention is not to exaggerate (A); rather, she uses **imagery** to communicate a feeling. Describing the precipice as the edge of an eternity portrays the speaker's sense of the vastness in front of her and the precariousness of her current state. While she may earnestly feel that she is on the edge of eternity, she likely knows that she is not (C).

483. (E) Lines 26–34 include a variety of descriptions of the light as the speaker sees it from atop the Woolworth Tower. The lights are "a thousand times more numerous than the stars" (27), they loop and mark, they cluster and splash, and they change from gold to "bluish steel" (32). The comparison to dew highlights the light's fragility, making (C) incorrect. The descriptions of the lights do not solely create a sense of fear and doom as the "clusters and splashes of living gold" (31) suggest the speaker is in awe of the light she observes, making (A) incorrect.

484. (E) Upon reaching the top of the Woolworth Tower and observing the lights, the speaker notices the "strident noises of the city" (35) are now "hallowed into whispers" (37), and the ferry whistles are mere "shadows of sound" (40). This is a noticeable contrast to the angry howls of the first stanza.

485. (D) The speaker describes the "warm millions" (42) beneath them as "consumed by their own desires" (43). She lists several actions, such as preparing food, sobbing, bending over a needle, laying out the dead, and bringing a child to birth. The speaker feels their "sorrow . . . torpor bitterness . . . frail joy . . . Like a cold fog wrapping" (50–53) her round. She is reminded, as she looks down from atop the tower, that these "blood-warm bodies" (55) will be "worthless as clay" (56) and their desires and emotions will have passed to "other millions" (55–59). The people below are unaware of the temporality of their existences. The

simile comparing the feeling to a "cold fog" (53) suggests that this realization is chilling to the speaker.

486. (D) The emotions from the millions below rise up to the speaker and her companion "like a cold fog wrapping us round" (53). In the next sentence, the speaker looks one hundred years ahead, when all the "anguish, the torpor, and the toil/ Will have passed to other millions/ Consumed by the same desires" (57–59). Being on the top of the tower, looking at humanity and civilization below, the speaker gains some perspective on the temporal nature of human life. The reminder is chilling, like a cold fog.

487. (D) Like the "warm millions" (42) below, the "other millions" (58) one hundred years from now will carry on the same actions and feel the same emotions. The speaker goes on to state that "[ages] will come and go" (60) while the sea will remain "[b]lack and unchanging" (64). While the life cycle is wondrous (E), the speaker intentionally repeats the word "millions" (41, 42, 58) to highlight the parallel between the people living today and those who will live one day, "[c]onsumed by the same desires" (59). The phrase itself does not highlight the wonder of the life cycle.

488. (A) In the first stanza, the man-made tower is described with strong action verbs ("A metal door slides open" (4) and "The car shoots upwards" (7)), as are the lights ("mark" (29) and "change" (32)). But from her vantage point atop the tower, the speaker reflects on the temporality of human civilization and acknowledges the permanence of the natural world. In lines 60–62, she states what will inevitably happen: the ages of man will "come and go" (60), our lights will be extinguished by the darkness, and our man-made tower will crumble back into the earth. This idea is suggested earlier in the poem, but lines 60–62 do not present evidence (B). The speaker is not exactly worried about this idea earlier in the poem; she is more frightened by the sensory overload she experiences journeying up the tower (C). The speaker is not showing earth's weakness; rather, she emphasizes its permanence (D). While the tower comes to an end, it is "laid on the earth" (62), which can be described as an expected and final rest as opposed to an inexorable doom (E).

489. (D) The **figurative** reference to eternity ("the abyss of eternity") (71) is similar to the figurative reference in line 25 ("the edge of eternity") (25). In both references, eternity is presented as a defined space to emphasize the speaker's sense of how high up she is, how far she has traveled, and how far she can see from the top of the Woolworth Tower. Since this reference occurs twice in the poem, it does not make the final stanza distinct from the others. The other choices all describe unique qualities of the final stanza: the **tone** changes from anxious, fearful, observant, and ominous in previous stanzas to uplifting ("Love has crowned us/ Victors") (72–74) in the final stanza (B). The speaker feels like a victor, which is a strong contrast to the insecurity and fear she feels in previous stanzas (C). She directly addresses her companion as "Beloved" (67) (E). The final stanza articulates the theme that "sorrow, futility, defeat . . . cannot bear us down" (68–70) (A). Themes are developed in earlier stanzas but not articulated in full until the final stanza reveals the speaker's discovery that "Here on the abyss of eternity/ Love has crowned us/ For a moment/ Victors" (71–73).

Passage 48. William Butler Yeats, "That the Night Come"

490. (A) The poem as a whole describes the woman as desiring death, not being able to endure the "common good of life" (5), and behaving as if the events of life are to be tolerated and "bundled away" (11) until her anticipated death arrives. (B), (C), (D), and (E) are supported by the poem, whereas (A) indicates that the woman, though she herself does not appreciate the "common good of life" (5) thinks that this common good is in general unappreciated. There is no evidence to suggest she has this view.

491. (B) The subject of the poem is "She" (1) who "lived in storm and strife" (1). Lines 2–12 directly refer to "her soul" (2), which is still considered to be part of "She"/her. While "a king" (6) is mentioned in the poem, this reference is part of a **simile** comparing "her soul" (2) to a king who bundles time away in anticipation of his wedding night. He is not a subject of the poem, making (E) incorrect.

492. (D) The word "storm" in line 1 is a **figurative description** meant to emphasize the "strife" (1) experienced by the subject of the poem. While it could be an exaggeration, it is unclear from the poem what the woman's life is actually like, making (A) a weak choice. Line 1 introduces "She" (1) as the subject of the poem and lines 2–12 continue describing the subject by focusing on "her soul" (2), making (B) incorrect. The phrase "storm and strife" (1) provides a figurative description of the woman's hardships, not objective, making (E) incorrect. The figurative language continues throughout the poem, with a **simile** in line 6, among other examples, making (C) incorrect. The one distinguishing feature of line 1 is that it contains a complete thought, an independent clause.

493. (C) The subject to which "it" (4) refers is the word "soul" (2). When written as prose, the sentence reads, "Her soul had such desire for what proud death may bring that it could not endure the common good of life" (2–5). The subject of the sentence is "soul" (2), not "death" (3) (A). It is the soul that cannot endure the common good of life, not the desire (D). While the soul can be conflated with "Her," the word "soul" (2) is the subject that has desire and cannot endure the common good of life, making (B) and (E) incorrect.

494. (C) The king is mentioned in a **simile** that compares the woman's behavior to that of a king who cannot wait for his wedding night so he can consummate his marriage with his queen. The purpose of such a comparison is to further illustrate the emotional state of the woman, who is the main subject of the poem (line 1). The simile shows that the woman is anticipating her death as eagerly as the king anticipates his wedding night. While their emotion of eagerness is similar, the actual things they each desire are different: death and marriage. They are different in gender (A) and possibly class status since he is a king (E), but these differences are not emphasized in the poem. Their way of living (B) is the same (she lives like a king who . . .), as are their attitudes (D) toward life (they do not live for the moment but for the future).

495. (E) The speaker appears to be intimately familiar with the inner state of the poem's subject ("She") (1). The speaker is able to describe the manner in which the woman copes with life and what her soul desires. This knowledge indicates the speaker is **omniscient** in his point of view. Because the speaker conveys the woman's predicament, desire, and inner state with **imagery** and **figurative language** (see questions 492 and 494), it cannot be said that he is indifferent, making (B) incorrect. His description is more sympathetic and understanding than harsh, making (A) incorrect. There are no details to indicate the speaker is providing guidance like a mentor would (D) or indulging the woman (C).

496. (A) Lines 2–12 comprise one complex sentence with several clauses leading up to the mention of the woman/king's much anticipated goal: the arrival of death/night. Because of the many dependent clauses preceding the final line ("That the night come") (12), we feel the woman's anticipation and longing. This does not contradict the idea in line 1 (E); it develops it. The sentence is long and complex, but not a run-on (B). There is some **end rhyme** (C) in the poem (strife/life, kettledrum/come, day/away), but it does not serve to lighten the **mood** around the woman's desire for "proud death" (3). The comparison in lines 2–12 is between a woman's soul's longing for death and a king's anticipating his wedding night, not between love and death (D).

497. (E) The **simile** compares the woman's anticipation for "what proud death may bring" (3) to a king who is so excited for his wedding night that he needs to fill his day with loud and exciting distractions to "bundle time away" (11). The comparison makes the woman's excitement for death more vivid by providing an image of an eager and impatient king.

498. (C) Her soul "could not endure/ The common good of life" (4–5) because of its desire for death. Instead, she lives with dramatic, explosive, loud distractions as a way to "bundle Time away" (11) until death arrives. The "trumpet" (9), "kettledrum," (9) and "the outrageous cannon" (10) represent the uncommon, spectacular ways the king and—through comparison—she endures life.

499. (A) Both the woman and the king are impatient for something (death and the wedding night, respectively). The king covets night because at night the king will be able to consummate his marriage, which is compared to the woman reaching "proud death" (3). Night is not characterized as foreboding (II) because the king and woman eagerly anticipate night—it is positively associated with what each of them desires (wedding night/proud death). Night is also not interminable (never-ending)—III; it is only the day that is presented as interminable because the king (and woman, through comparison) must "bundle Time away" (11) to pass time until night comes.

500. (A) The poem is about a woman who "had such desire/ For what proud death may bring" (2–3) that she lived like a king who filled his day with fanfare and distractions to pass time until his wedding night came. The woman's anticipation for "proud death" (3) is equated with the king's impatience for his wedding night. Enjoying time (C) implies that they relish and savor the distractions they occupy themselves with while they wait for what they really want, which is not what the king is doing when he packs his day with "[t]rumpet and kettledrum" (9). They definitely do not ignore time (E) because they see it as something that needs to be "bundle[d]" (11) and spent; they see it as an obstacle in the way of attaining their desired goals.

NOTES

NOTES